BRITAIN AND THE COMMONWEALTH ALLIANCE
1918–1939

CAMBRIDGE COMMONWEALTH SERIES

Published in association with the Managers of the Cambridge University Smuts Memorial Fund for the Advancement of Commonwealth Studies

General Editor: E. T. Stokes, Smuts Professor of the History of the British Commonwealth, University of Cambridge

Further titles in preparation

BRITAIN AND THE COMMONWEALTH ALLIANCE 1918–1939

R. F. Holland

First published 1981 by
THE MACMILLAN PRESS LTD
London and Basingstoke
Companies and representatives
throughout the world

Printed in Hong kong

British Library Cataloguing in Publication Data

Holland, R. F.
  Britain and the Commonwealth Alliance, 1918–39–
  (Cambridge Commonwealth Series)
  1. Commonwealth of Nations – History
  I. Title II. Series
  909′.09′712410822   DA 18

  ISBN 0–333–27295–1

To my parents

Contents

Acknowledgements

This book arose out of a doctoral dissertation completed at St Antony's College, Oxford. Particular gratitude is owed to Dr A. F. Madden, for his friendship and advice; to D. K. Fieldhouse, for a term's supervision which pointed me in new directions; to Lord Garner of Chiddinghurst, for passing a critical eye over the original text; and to Hillia Thomas, of the University of Amsterdam, for her encouragement. The University of Birmingham, the Bodleian Library in Oxford, the Confederation of British Industries and Lord Ponsonby of Shulbrede have all kindly allowed me to use materials in their possession. Above all, the staff of the Public Record Office must be thanked for their constant endeavours. Finally, I am grateful to the Institute of Commonwealth Studies in London University for providing me with the facilities to complete this volume.

1 The Commonwealth Problem: Origins and Formation 1900–1925

This study is concerned with what the Commonwealth relationship meant to British policy-makers, how perceptions of it changed and how it was 'managed'. The first problem is to define at what point the diaspora of British overseas settlement solidified into a coherent political entity. Certainly in 1900 the Commonwealth did not exist. The Australian colonies were only about to be federated into a union; Ireland was subject to recurrent instability; whilst Britain was actually at war in South Africa. The mass phenomena of Empire – the Empire Shopping Weeks, the Empire Exhibitions and Empire Day celebrations – really date from the mid-1920s, and the current work is based on the assumption that it was only at this point, when the scale of Britain's post-1918 problems became clear, that a Commonwealth 'system' came to exist: it was a response to weakness, not an expression of strength. It is necessary, however, to begin by briefly outlining just how the main lines of that relationship were delineated between 1900 and 1925.

From Vereeniging to Versailles

The roots of Commonwealth lay in broad political changes taking shape in the early 1900s. These changes were the mature expression of what later became a fundamental characteristic of the twentieth-century situation: an accelerating competition among states to mobilise technical and economic resources to extend their power. This preoccupation with the mobilisation of power was central to the thinking of Joseph Chamberlain and Lord Milner, the two arch-exponents of the imperial tradition. Both recognised that international rivalry, state growth and economic transformation had shattered the nineteenth-century securities surrounding British society. To counter this new insecurity they believed that the state had to manage its resources more effectively than in the past. Both were convinced that the liberal democracy which had emerged after 1867 had proved inadequate to this task; the political

1

elites in Westminster, immersed in the petty selfishness of the factional struggle, had consistently ignored vital British interests. This is not to say that Chamberlain or Milner were anti-democrats but rather that, in their view, the democratic process had to be made to work more effectively in the national interest.[1] Imperial reorganisation was their means to this end. It was in the Empire that stable markets could be located, which held out assurances of continued supplies of raw materials and food, and which provided some hope of insulation from the untidy rhythms of boom and slump in the international economy.

Chamberlain and Milner never managed to control the Conservative party, whilst the Liberal party after re-election in 1906 remained loyal to its internationalist ideology. But the theme of efficient national reform nonetheless crystallised into a consensus which spread across the political spectrum. This consensus was related to the debacle of the South African war, which had finally ended at Vareeniging in May 1902, but it was reinforced by the parallel challenge of German economic and naval power. The Liberals themselves had to develop a policy to meet this situation, and they found it in the concept of social improvement – a healthy social organism and therefore an enhanced quality of human resources available to the state would provide national security. But was this enough? Was not some quantitative expansion of resources (an expansion possible through constructive imperialism) critical to Britain's future? Important elements in the military leadership thought so. The Committee of Imperial Defence was established in 1902 to effect liaison between the Army and Navy staffs, but it was also hoped to incorporate the self-governing Dominions into a system of military planning.[2] The Committee's purely consultative role was designed to convince the colonial premiers that they could participate in its discussions without infringing autonomy. They did so, if sporadically, beginning with the attendance of the Canadian Minister of Munitions in 1903. The 1907 Imperial Conference regularised the position whereby a Dominion had the right to attend the Committee whenever an issue arose which touched its interests. As the international crisis deepened, however, defence and foreign policy issues reacted increasingly upon each other. At the 1911 Imperial Conference, therefore, a radical departure was taken when the British Prime Minister, in a closed session of the Committee of Imperial Defence, put before the Dominion leaders the facts of Britain's international position. W. K. Hancock comments that in so doing Asquith was ushering colonial leaders into the *arcana imperii* of Empire,[3] for just like any sustained relationship in power politics, it was ultimately based on guns. By 1914 the outlines of an imperial military machine were in being.

How did the Dominions react to these developments? Emphasis has usually been given to the growth of Dominion nationalism between 1900 and 1914. Both Australia and Canada refused, for example, to order their naval activities within a British Admiralty framework, and in 1909 they opted for separate 'fleet units'. Laurier's statements at the 1911 Imperial Conference on the constitutionality of secession is often seen as the point at which Dominion nationalism assumed a distinct political form.[4] But this is only one half of the story. Viewed as a whole, the striking thing is that economic and political developments after 1900 were forcing Dominion interests to seek closer connections with the imperial polity. Thus Dominion military personnel pushed strongly to establish liaison with their British counterparts who could give them information and equipment, and who could (through secondment and cooperation) broaden the horizon of their own careers. Much more important than this, however, was the economic dimension. From the late 1890s agricultural productivity in the Dominions was creating vast surpluses, and the only market for these commodities was Great Britain. In 1897 Canada first introduced Imperial Preference into its tariff and began its campaign for reciprocal benefits; other Dominions soon followed; and from then on Dominion demands for near-monopoly access to the British consumer never diminished. Important political effects flowed from this. Dominion politicians could now have their careers directly affected by decisions taken in the UK, and they therefore sought to duplicate their means of access to the British establishment. In short, British interests were intersecting with, and sometimes rebounding off, those of the Dominions with increasing frequency. This process of intersection can be seen in two main ways. First, it was part of that tightening of commercial links taking place in the international economy. Second, it was part of a preoccupation with military security which, as crisis followed crisis, intensified patron and client relationships in world politics. It was because the Dominion societies were conscious of forces pushing them towards extended collaboration with Britain just when anti-imperialism was becoming a political fashion that they acted out such intense contradiction within themselves. For example Laurier at the 1911 Conference declared the right of secession whilst simultaneously closeting himself with other Empire leaders to discuss military and diplomatic strategy.

When war finally came in 1914 none of the Dominions hesitated to declare their co-belligerency with Britain. This, and the Commonwealth military effort which followed, gave ample scope for the war propaganda machine in the UK to make the picture of an Empire finally and irreversibly united one of its major themes. Certainly Dominion losses on the Western Front, at Gallipoli, and even in Allenby's campaigns in the Middle East, were heavy, and their soldier stereotypes (the Australian 'Digger', for example) became part of the peculiar culture of the veterans. It was the realistic assessment that Dominion manpower had become by 1916 critical to Allied operations which prompted Lloyd

George to incorporate other Empire leaders in the higher management of the war, and his attempts in this direction were part of broader institutional reforms at home.[5] Thus the old departmental Cabinet was replaced by a smaller and more autocratic war Cabinet, and it was this body which was periodically widened into an Imperial War Cabinet with the Dominion leaders included. The latter body possessed an executive authority which made it very different from earlier Imperial Conferences. To some extent these changes were cosmetic because Lloyd George only let fragments of authority fall into the hands of his new creation, but none the less it presented a highly visible image of an imperial council and it allowed Dominion leaders to believe that they could influence British policy. Indeed, the war had made such access to imperial decision-making vital for them. Thus Borden of Canada had soon found that he could not run his manpower and production programmes from Ottawa. He moved to London, leaving his Cabinet behind, and found that his position was one of some strength for he controlled the flow of Canadian supplies and had his own troops and sources of information in Flanders. But if this gave him prestige with the British, it was potentially disruptive in Canadian politics: if the Allied effort were to falter, Borden would be tarred with the British brush. This was what happened when the 1917 offensive collapsed and the conscription issue erupted in Quebec. Borden had to seek a way of distancing himself from British institutions whilst remaining part of them. The same sort of pressures were working on other Dominion leaders. It was in this tactical milieu that the famous resolution IX of the 1917 Imperial War Conference emerged. This plainly stated that the Dominions were not part of a centralised polity but were 'autonomous nations of an Imperial Commonwealth' and that common action was based on mutual consultation. With this declaration of constitutional separateness the British leaders convinced Dominion Prime Ministers, and the Dominion Prime Ministers convinced their political supporters, to tolerate a final period of combined military effort. But if resolution IX had lubricated Anglo–Dominion cooperation in the last stages of war, it had enormous consequences on the Commonwealth relationship in the peace to be ushered in by the Versailles Settlement.

The Paris Peace Conference

After the Armistice, the immediate imperial problem was what part the Dominions should play at the Paris Conference. The Prime Ministers were determined to participate in the settlement because only then could they claim to have advanced the position of their respective countries. The Dominions also had concrete interests at stake. The most conspicuous of these concerned the redistribution of Germany's former colonies. Australia, New Zealand and South Africa were all intent on retaining the territories they had occupied in the early phases of war.[6] At first Lloyd George, with the pressures of war lifted, showed few signs of being concerned with Dominion representation, tending to equate them with other small powers (such as Serbia) who had suffered heavy losses and yet who could expect to have little impact on the settlement terms.[7] In the end a compromise emerged in the form of dual representation: the Dominions were represented by their own delegates, but their Prime Ministers also formed a collective panel from which one was always selected to serve as a member of the 'British Empire Delegation' led by Lloyd George. Once in Paris, however, this scheme faced much tougher opposition from President Wilson, who regarded it as a piece of imperial trickery to multiply 'British votes'. Only when Lloyd George indicated that dual representation for Dominions was a position he could not give up did Wilson accept it. This was not the last time that the international status of the Dominions was acquired less by Dominion pressure on Britain than by British persistence in the face of strong foreign opposition.

At first 'dual representation' worked well at Paris. Hankey, the Cabinet Secretary who headed the Empire Delegation secretariat, was able to convince himself that he was operating a radical mechanism for the making of imperial policy. He wrote home to his wife:

> My mind is chock full of a great scheme of Imperial development which I have actually carried out: that is to say, I have got approval that I shall have an assistant secretary from each Dominion for the work of the British Empire Delegation. . . . In short – I have actually started a great Imperial Office. It is at this moment in existence.[8]

Dominion Prime Ministers, acting in their capacity as Empire delegates, were installed as chairmen of important committees; Borden, for example, became chairman of the committee on Macedonia. Inter-imperial differences did, it is true, occasionally break surface. Hughes clashed with Smuts and Lloyd George when he called for crushing reparations to be levied on Germany, and he annoyed the Canadians by describing the Americans as unwanted intruders into the Pacific.[9] Meanwhile British officials were sceptical of the Australians' and New Zealanders' capacity to administer the tropical possessions they now demanded.[10] All this was part of a regional differentiation in the interests of the various Empire nations. Broadly, however, there were no fundamental policy divergences during the Paris Conference. But, if the Dominions were successfully integrated within the conference machinery, it rapidly became clear that they had only a minimal part in its operational decisions. Indeed, decision-making at Paris did not flow through the committee structures but rather seeped out through the walls behind which the Great Powers were huddled in very private caucus.

As the 'Council of Ten' was reduced down to the 'Big Four' (Wilson, Lloyd George, Clemenceau, Orlando), the other powers could only look on helplessly. On the issue that counted most for the Dominions, that of colonial annexations, they were completely dependent on Lloyd George overcoming Wilson's commitment to territorial self-determination. Even then they had to be satisfied with the attenuated form of a 'mandate' whereby the question of sovereignty was left undetermined and the new League of Nations could claim rights of supervision. The result of thus being deprived of real political power led the Dominion Prime Ministers to prize more highly their status as separate delegates. P. Wigley phrases this process well:

> dual representation, when tested against the realities of international diplomacy, offered the dominion delegates two quite distinct roles. Their role as status-seekers had nothing to do with influencing policy; while the little influence they did enjoy was not based upon their separate representation. Thus it came about that, as the hopes of influencing imperial policy continued to fade, the more limited victory of separate dominion representation assumed an increasing importance in its own right.[11]

Separate representation allowed the Prime Ministers to present their electorates with some evidence of having obtained a new influence in world affairs. The politics of international status, which preoccupied the Dominions for much of the 1920s, can thus be traced back to the Paris experience; it was rooted in frustration, not success; and only the crises of the 1930s were to reveal its essential hollowness. Although a united imperial front had therefore been obtained at the Paris Peace Conference through a series of expedients, it remained questionable whether Anglo–Dominion interests could be coordinated in the confused post-war world ahead.

The Commonwealth Problem 1919–24

Although, as we shall see, the first half of the 1920s saw important changes within Anglo–Dominion relations, the idea of Commonwealth was initially pushed into the political background. The immediate post-war years were a time of introspection for all countries. Public opinion everywhere shrank from external associations as the scale of the 1914–18 tragedy took focus. Moreover, as the successive European conferences at Cannes, Hythe and Rapallo indicated, the political crisis in Europe continued, and this militated against the hopes of those in

Britain who wished to see a disengagement from continental affairs and the construction of an imperial system. Finally, the chief problems for all political leaderships after 1918 were internal ones of economic stabilisation. For all these reasons the early 1920s witnessed little emphasis on the Commonwealth as a political entity.

It followed from this that constitutional change in the Empire ceased to have the significance of 1917. At the Imperial Conference of that year it had been firmly agreed that when peace came a full-scale constitutional conference would be convened to regularise and amplify the new status of Dominions. Smuts argued vigorously at the 1921 Imperial Conference for this plan to be implemented[12] because it connected intimately with his party political strategy in South Africa: by projecting himself as a statesman who had solved the vital problem of the balance between interdependence and liberty within the Empire he hoped to prolong his personal role as the stabilising pivot within the Union. But Smuts quickly learnt that all the other Commonwealth delegates, led by Hughes, were against any renewed movement. This preference for immobility in other Dominions also arose from domestic political considerations. Thus Hughes and Borden feared that further constitutional debate would only confirm a pattern of confrontation in their societies (conscriptionists against anti-conscriptionists, imperialists against anti-imperialists, English against French) which as centre-politicians they were eager to see broken up. Meanwhile in the UK the restoration of the old pre-1914 bureaucratic procedures reduced the momentum for change. In particular the permanent officials of the Colonial Office regained a good deal of their influence in imperial affairs and were able to frustrate Milner's desire to restructure Commonwealth relations and make it a Cabinet priority.[13] British officials even came to question the extent of the Empire's transformation brought about in the war period. Thus by 1921 the Dominions Department was arguing that separate Dominion representation at the League did not carry with it any automatic measure of constitutional change.[14]

But if constitutional matters did not amount to a live 'question', certain Dominions were still led at points to demand specific 'rights', and this in turn kept a legal debate in motion. The Canadians' insistence on concluding a formal agreement with the USA on the usage of halibut fisheries without a corroborating UK signature resulted in an extension of the Dominions' treaty-making powers as a whole. The Canadian motive here, however, was not to lay any ideological claim to autonomy, but simply to give themselves more negotiating flexibility with their powerful southern neighbour. The British reaction to this shows how differentiated UK departmental responses were becoming. The Foreign Office came to support the extension of Dominion Governments' powers to enter into unilateral local engagements. This was because, without such an extension, those Governments would become increasingly unable to control political and economic groups within their own jurisdiction, groups whose scale and radius of operation had been extended by the War and were soon causing regional, not merely national, complications; and the Foreign Office was determined that the Dominion Governments should look after their own problems, instead of dumping them on Whitehall's lap. In the context of American Prohibition and the widespread involvement of Canadians in 'bootlegging' along the border, the Foreign Office was sensibly aware of the advantages in leaving the Dominions to their own risk-laden devices. The Office was, of course, careful not to say this too plainly because it conflicted with the new rhetoric of a cooperating Empire, but it was implicit in its memorandum for the 1923 Imperial Conference on the Canadian–US halibut treaty. 'Both the rights and liabilities [of such a separate agreement] will be confined to that Dominion, and the Government of the Dominion concerned', the memorandum ran, 'will be responsible for seeing that the Treaty is observed.'[15] The Foreign Office acceptance of the Dominions' treaty-making capacity did not mean that it was now disinteresting itself in 'Empire foreign policy'. The reverse was to be true as international conditions worsened. But it did reflect the Foreign Office's determination that the Dominions should not complicate Britain's already difficult task of maintaining good relations with the other major Powers, and especially with the USA. Meanwhile the Dominions Department of the Colonial Office took a different view of matters. E. J. Harding, who in 1923 was appointed Permanent Under-Secretary, sought to undermine the Foreign Office position by describing it as secessionist. The rival submission by the Colonial Office to the Imperial Conference emphasised that foreign Governments should be constantly reminded that in their dealings with His Brittanic Majesty they were dealing with an Empire-state and never with a mere part of it. After quoting from some legislation of 1882, the submission continued

> It would appear that the Treaty relations of His Majesty in respect of any part of the Empire cannot be considered without an interest – actual or contingent – to the remaining parts, and that the main desideratum is to maintain the principle that no important Treaty relations should be entered into without due consideration of their possible effect . . . on the Empire as a whole.[16]

The most significant aspect of this formula is that, despite the reference to past legislation, it was wholly new. Harding and his colleagues saw their chief task to be the preservation of the UK's Empire-image in world politics, and after 1918 they felt intensely uneasy about the Dominions' commitment to the Empire's international solidarity. Their response to this was the hasty improvisation of a legal rationale for such solidarity, suitably attired in the rich costume of an ancient (or at least a late nineteenth-century) constitution. In the same way the famous *inter se* doctrine of Empire relations (i.e. that the nature of the relationship between Commonwealth members was qualitatively different from the relations subsisting between a Commonwealth member and a foreign country) was a product of the moment designed to frustrate the Irish Free State's claim to an independent diplomatic personality;[17] this doctrine allowed the Colonial Office to contend that equality among Commonwealth members did not mean that each part had the legal right to establish a separate dialogue with other nations. It is therefore clear that much of the unravelling of Empire relations which went on after the Balfour Declaration on political autonomy of 1926 was really the discarding of ideas and rhetoric of a recent and essentially tactical provenance.

The legal politics of Commonwealth, then, span off from the Dominions' extra-national involvements. This is usually described in bland terms of the Dominions coming to 'maturity', and the chief expression of this pubescence is found in the Dominion participation at the League. This participation did mark a critical broadening of experience. The Canadians' sustained campaign against the obligatory sanctions embedded in Article X of the League Charter showed that at least one Dominion Government was prepared to define a point of view and pursue it with determination; finally in September 1923 they managed to obtain virtually unanimous agreement that sanctions were only feasible on a discretionary basis. But in fact the really important processes by which the Dominions were entering international politics took place at less rarefied and usually more regional levels. A few examples of these developments must suffice.

Economic and social change on the Pacific slope of North America was overwhelming the legal fact of the Canadian–US border, so that the Governments of California and British Columbia were having to coordinate their policies on irrigation, forestry, transport and even police methods, a sequence of pressures with as much scope for friction as for agreement.[18] Meanwhile in southern Africa the growth of the Union's political and economic sway within the region brought it into contact and occasionally conflict with European powers other than the British. In particular the South African rivalry with the Portuguese was pushing that Dominion into manoeuvres at the international level to deny Mozambique financial support.[19] In certain restricted fields a Dominion government found (not always with pleasure) that its nationals or institutions were breaking beyond even this enhanced regional role. Thus, in one interesting episode, the accumulating resources of Canadian banks led them into the heady world of international financial politics. When the British, American and French banks formed a consortium to curb China's excessive borrowing policies, the Chinese tried to look outside the consortium limits for easier money, and they found it in the form of Canadian financiers eager to locate opportunities for overseas investment; the consortium organisers were soon in a state of near panic as they sought ways to exert leverage against these new competitors in the loans market.[20] All this amounts not to a steady, ordered advance into political adulthood, but a complex, disjointed and largely uncontrolled penetration by Dominion interests into the outside world. Thus, although in the later 1920s the Dominions were still only partly meshed into regional and global patterns of negotiation and confrontation, their interaction with these larger systems was expanding fast.

Whilst this integration of Dominions into regional and international politics was taking place, however, considerable shifts occurred in the strategic balances of the major powers. From an imperial perspective the nature of this change is perhaps best characterised as the replacement of the Atlantic by the Pacific as the centre of world strategic gravity. The destruction of the German High Fleet at Scapa Flow had dramatically reduced the scale of naval competition in Europe, even though the Italians and French continued to build in their race for Mediterranean dominance. Meanwhile Japan had skilfully exploited her Allied status in war and her role during the anti-Bolshevik intervention to further her claim to be the pre-eminent Pacific nation. Finally, the United States emerged in 1918 as the leading economic and military power in the world. These factors had the effect of dragging the focus of international power and competition westwards from Europe. Thus, before 1914, the industrial capacity to wage major wars was essentially confined to Europe; non-European military operations in the nineteenth century were either acts of colonial adjustment or localised wars (however bloody) which had limited effects on world politics. After 1918 such capacity had ceased to be a European monopoly. This had fundamental implications for the British Empire. In the pre-1914 situation the various Dominions had only been connected to military–strategic problems through the umbilical link with Britain, for it was only Britain which was directly threatened by a European conflict. But nearly all the Dominions were immediately affected by movements in the Pacific, which now became a probable source of unrest. This meant that the members of the Commonwealth were now more directly involved in strategic issues. In the early post-war years this led to the optimistic assessment that it would be commensurately easier to graft the Dominions into Empire defence policies. The Admiralty especially intended to exploit the fact that war-time naval organisation had obliterated the separate Dominion forces and introduced a plan whereby Empire navies would be centralised through a series of interlocking Local Boards. Lord Jellicoe was sent off on an Empire tour in 1919 to explore how much scope there was for integrated planning.[21] He found that the answer was very little, not least because financial policies throughout the Commonwealth were geared to retrenchment and deflation. Still, the optimism persisted, and underlying it was recognition that the pattern of world competition was radically new. In early 1923 the question arose whether the Joint Overseas and Home Defence Committee could cover Dominion questions, such as ports, without triggering complaints that Dominion autonomy was being infringed. A Colonial Office official concluded

> I see no risk of misunderstanding. The Australians understand perfectly that their defence is bound up with the protection of ports outside their borders, and I do not doubt that other Dominions are equally well informed. They are too aware that the critical dangers are not in the same areas as in 1913.[22]

But in fact there were already signs in the early 1920s that a more generalised 'Commonwealth involvement' in strategic issues might generate differences of perspective between imperial partners. This became apparent over the question of Anglo–Japanese treaty renewal. This treaty had been made in 1902, renewed in 1911 and extended during the war. It had become a central element in Pacific stability. As long as it lasted the precise level of British naval armaments in the Far East did not matter because no other possible combination could match Anglo–Japanese resources in the area. For the Japanese the Treaty was a means of access to international politics and a crucial symbol of psychological and racial acceptance. For British possessions in those waters, and above all for Australia and New Zealand, the stabilising logic of this agreement was of obvious benefit. But the logic of Anglo–Japanese relations did not fit with the imperatives of Anglo–American cooperation, and it was the latter which was emerging as the main priority in British foreign policy. The financial viability of the British Government hinged on a settlement of her War Debt owed to the US at a low interest rate, and in a context of severe economic crisis, questions of solvency overrode those of strategy. But in return the US soon began to demand two main concessions: the first was 'parity' with the UK in naval strength and the second was the abandonment of the Anglo–Japanese Treaty when it came up for renewal in late 1921. These desiderata on the part of the Americans reflected the strength of the US Navy Board within the lobby politics of Washington. By establishing a nationalist rhetoric of 'parity' with the British, the American navalists provided themselves with an ideological and strategic justification for bureaucratic expansion. The dislodgement of the UK from her Japanese relationship was a means to this end because it would make the British dependent on American help to provide new mechanisms of stability in the Pacific. The makers of British foreign policy were therefore confronted with a large and awkward choice.

Sir Auckland Geddes, the British Ambassador in the United States, was one of several influential British officials who felt that a critical moment had arrived in the transformation of the UK's interests. In a long memorandum forwarded to Curzon, the Foreign Secretary, Geddes stressed the fact that the Harding Administration had taken a fundamental decision to concentrate American resources on Pacific, not Atlantic, development.[23] This meant that for the first time in modern history the European economies would not be the prime factor in world growth. The United States might ensure that the British stake in the extra-European world was protected as economic and social pressures built up in those areas. But Geddes continued

> On the other hand, the new policy means that Great Britain must acknowledge, in its turn, the naval superiority of the U.S. in the Pacific. Australia, New Zealand and Canada must recognise the ground of common interest with the U.S. and look to this country for protection rather than Great Britain. In short, one of the principal bi-products of the tentative Harding naval policy is the formal announcement to the world of a great union of English-speaking peoples of the world.[24]

Geddes's recommendations for British policy, however, meant giving up any unilateral capacity to act outside the limits of an English-speaking consensus, a consensus shaped in the American image. It was this issue of unilateralism which went to the heart of the British foreign policy debate between the two world wars, and the question of the Anglo–Japanese treaty renewal indicated how divided were reactions within the establishment. Curzon and Lloyd George took the view that the grant of an American veto over British decisions was an abdication of world responsibilities, whilst Winston Churchill argued that the slightest appearance of maintaining an Anglo–Japanese front against the United States was a suicidal course of action.[25] This volatile situation was made even more complicated once it became clear that the same lines of division existed among different Dominions. The Australian view was that, until such time as the Americans were prepared to give firm guarantees to their white allies elsewhere in the world, good relations with Japan were essential. In contrast, the Canadians were determined that nothing should get in the way of Anglo–American friendship, and they saw the Treaty as a major obstacle to their vision of Anglo–Saxon hegemony. Searching for some leverage on this situation, the Canadian Government threatened to establish separate talks with the Americans on the topic unless the UK moved immediately in this direction.[26] The British reaction was simply to put off any decision until the Imperial Conference could meet and discuss the problem.

When the Conference convened it proved to be the first occasion when Commonwealth partners indulged in a rough-and-tumble debate on a central issue of foreign policy. A bland consensus emerged that a new Pacific Pact should be attempted which included Britain, Japan and the United States. But it was difficult to see what this could mean because the old Treaty had not least been designed to restrict American influence in the first place, and the new formula certainly represented a major departure. In fact no final decision had to be made because during the Imperial Conference President Harding issued invitations to a naval disarmament conference in Washington, so that the related problems of Pacific diplomacy and naval ratios were transferred to a new and more comprehensive agenda determined by the United States.

The British were constrained by financial considerations into accepting this *fait accompli*: Foreign policy formulation in the UK was thus becoming increasingly subject to new sources of pressure and polarisation. As such, the Whitehall bureaucracy could not control decision-making as grandly as they had done in the past. In this fragmenting situation it was possible for other interested parties, such as Dominion Governments, to make their voices heard, especially if they could find allies from within UK departments. When it is understood how strategic change was transforming the balance of power and exerting strains within alliance systems such as the Commonwealth, the recurring emphasis on 'Empire Foreign Policy' from the mid-1920s onwards can be seen, not as an atavistic response, but as a way of retaining some capacity for unilateral action and incorporating new elements in the policy process.

There is no doubt that it was in Britain's interest that relative naval power be regulated by international conference. In the economic and political conditions of 1921/22 it would have been totally impossible for her to participate in a new building race; unlike Alice, she would be unable to stay in the same position even by running twice as fast in terms of expenditure. Thus anything that prevented the escalation of competitive construction was desirable. But, by the same token, the UK bargaining position was decidedly weak when the Washington Conference opened in November 1921, because all the other negotiators knew that the UK could not stand the consequences of a breakdown. It was inevitable that one task of the Conference would be to write off some of the capital of Britain's world position, capital which had been degraded by the war into a paper commodity. The British–American–Japanese capital ship ratio of 5:5:3 secured this objective because it effectively meant American naval supremacy in the West and Japanese naval supremacy in the East; this new strategic arithmetic made the One Power Standard, which had long formed the basis of imperial defence assumptions, a mockery.[27] The other provisions of the Washington Treaties also tended clearly in this direction. The Four-Power Agreement (Britain, Japan, the US and France) which emerged from the talks on Pacific affairs was an insufficiently specific document to ensure that the status quo would be successfully policed; whilst the non-fortification clauses, which prevented Britain from improving the defences of Hong Kong and the Americans those of Guam and Wake, improved Japan's strategic position by pushing back British and American effective operational limits to Singapore and Hawaii respectively. Most significant, however, was the Conference decision to declare a ten-year veto on new naval construction in the capital ship category. Because it was probable that expenditures would simply be shifted to naval research over that period, at the end of it the existing margins of superiority for the UK would be swamped by rapid construction of 'new model' fleets. This anticipatory factor was a major source of uncertainty. More broadly, however, the 'naval holiday' ushered in an era of disarmament, and it was Britain, the greatest Empire-nation of them all, who proved to be the most enthusiastic disarmer. This made sense in the context of Britain's priorities of financial retrenchment and the avoidance of future wars. But it was this process of disarmament relative to other Powers which was to erode Commonwealth associations, because the rationale of that association was mutual protection. The Washington Conference marked the point at which the balance between military and political strategies in the preservation of the British Empire shifted in the direction of the latter. This made the mobilisation of diplomatic support, however, all the more necessary, and the subsequent emphasis on 'Empire Foreign Policy' was clearly shaped by this situation too.

At the Washington Conference the Dominions had been represented through the medium of the British Empire Delegation and had not had the Paris advantage of separate representation. Whereas certain Dominions had been major sources of manpower during the Great War, none of them had significant enough navies to merit full participation at the 1921 meeting. For Canada, nonetheless, the outcome was satisfying: British policy had been shifted along an American axis. But for Australia and New Zealand, who were dependent on British naval power, it meant that their security was poised on a fine knife-edge: behind the numbers game of the Washington ratios lurked questions of mastery and survival. The Antipodean suspicion of British reliability, and the proclivity to look elsewhere for emergency assistance, began at this point. The significance of the Singapore base in the story of inter-war strategy, and in particular in the course of Anglo–Australian relations, is therefore easily understood. Before Washington, the idea of an Empire naval base at Singapore was barely formulated. Afterwards it became an index of Britain's intent to ensure that the 1921 decisions marked the limits of the Empire's retreat from strategic dominance. By the time of the 1923 Imperial Conference the main lines of the debate had been drawn on this issue, and they did not change much over the next sixteen years. From the Australian viewpoint there were two sets of questions. The first concerned whether the British really intended to expend the resources required to make Singapore into a first-class base. The second was whether, once built, that base (so far away towards the Malaysian mainland) really constituted an effective defence for the Antipodes against Japanese aggression. The variables built into these questions were complex. The Australians learned quite early on that much depended on British party politics when the Labour Party, having formed its first government in January 1924 and committed to disarmament, froze all new construction at Singapore. But whoever ruled in Britain, financial constraints made any major defence effort unlikely. Moreover, whatever the state of the base, it was doubtful that the Royal Navy had a sufficient fleet to provide the necessary capital ships for eastern operations in a crisis. Much would clearly depend on the time it would take for emergency units to steam from Atlantic and Mediterranean waters to the Pacific. Frantic calculations as to cruiser speeds, the distribution of coaling stations and oil stocks sprang from this situation. The answer, which all the technical experts came to, was plain: Britain's navy no longer provided her Pacific possessions with reliable physical guarantees. The politicians, in Britain and the Antipodes, could not admit this to their publics, because the alternatives were either the admission of changed circumstances or increased taxation. This explains the sparring of Amery and Bruce at the 1923 Imperial Conference, with both of them avoiding the really awkward questions, and settling on an uneasy consensus that the Singapore plan would be the key to Empire strategy in the future.[28] Australian diplomatic historians subsequently emphasised how the British authorities deceived their Antipodean counterparts on matters of strategy, and there is some truth in this; but more interesting are the political forces which made the British and Australian establishments party to a collective deception of public opinion. What is clear is that by the mid-1920s a gap had opened up between the resources and liabilities of imperial defence, and this put the Commonwealth under important new strains.

The extent to which doubts and suspicions were entering Commonwealth exchanges was exemplified by the Chanak episode which immediately preceded the 1923 Conference.[29] This followed the failure of the British and French to negotiate a stable peace with the Turkish sultanate; a failure compounded when the nationalist Turkish forces of Kemal Ataturk advanced from the Anatolian interior, succeeded in literally pushing the Greek troops, who had been encouraged by Lloyd George to invade Turkey, back into the sea at Smyrna, and then swept north to confront the Anglo–French positions at the Straits. It was obvious, also, that the French would not resist Ataturk if he sought to control the Constantinople peninsula. The British Foreign Office was equally opposed to any confrontation with Turkish nationalism, because it feared reverberations throughout the Moslem-colonial world.

But Lloyd George and Winston Churchill were both determined to stem Ataturk's advance, the former because of his relationship with Venizelos, the Greek leader, and his romantic ideas of a new Greek hegemony in the eastern Mediterranean, and the latter because of his determination to prove that the Gallipoli campaign of 1915 had not been entirely in vain. But how could Britain act alone without incurring the castigation of world opinion as a whole, for it would appear to be a blatant piece of opposition to political self-determination by the Turks? Characteristically Lloyd George and Churchill came up with an exotic formula: a great imperial military expedition to defeat the rebellious Turk at Europe's gateway and protect the graves of Gallipoli. This was designed to touch the nerves of Christians, xenophobes and the 1915 class of the bereaved, so many of the latter being Australians and New Zealanders.

There were two barriers to this plan. The first was cautious Whitehall officials. The second was Dominion governments who would certainly do everything to stifle the scheme at birth before their chauvinist publics could become excited by it. The two British leaders evaded these problems by sending official telegrams to the Dominion governments requesting military support outside Whitehall office hours, so that Dominions Department personnel arrived at work the following morning to find the process already in motion, and by arranging a leak of their plans to Beaverbrook's *Evening Standard*, so that the Dominion press were already alerted when their Prime Ministers took the crucial decisions. From this point, however, the scheme fizzled out.

General Harington, the local British Commander at the Straits, and Ataturk preferred to compromise than to fight. But the Dominion leaders played a part in negating the chances of a 1914-style response by the Empire. The New Zealand Government did immediately agree to participate, but the Australians hesitated a number of days before doing so, by which time the critical moment had passed. Mackenzie King, the new Prime Minister in Canada, claimed that war was a matter for Parliament and, as Parliament was in recess, no prompt decision was possible. Smuts was conveniently absent on a hunting expedition when the British telegram arrived in Pretoria, and was equivocal on his return.

The lesson of this experience was that, if the Dominions could no longer be fully reliant on the UK for protection, neither could the UK always be certain that the Dominions would identify with an imperial struggle. Chanak, indeed, passed into Dominions' legend as an example of the ruthless intrigue the British were prepared to exercise so that

Commonwealth military resources could be put at their disposal. The Imperial Conference of 1923 met with these events still fresh in the mind.

Underlying all the themes that have so far been outlined, however, was a deep economic crisis. This crisis produced a politics of dissent in Britain and the Dominions which gained much of their expression through both socialism and anti-imperialism. It is a matter of irony, then, that the early post-war period saw ideas of an 'Empire economy' taking more explicit shape than ever before. Initially the focus of British commentators was on Empire migration. As it was by no means clear between 1918 and 1920 whether the UK would face a shortage or a surplus of labour once the peacetime economy stabilised, the official interest in migration was not so much to expand it as to make sure that it was carefully regulated.[30] But once it became clear that the problem of industrial unemployment was long-term, the migration lobby (above all, the Overseas Settlement Committee) gathered the support of influential bodies such as the Ministries of Health and Labour. It was the UK's need for some alleviation of unemployment, combined with Australia's pressure for British capital aid in its development programmes, which finally produced the Empire Settlement Act of 1922. For the first time the UK was committed to the subsidisation of British migrants to Empire destinations. But by 1922 the economic problems facing all Commonwealth countries had reached a point where the marginal redistribution of populations could have little corrective effect. The tremendous intensification of world competition in manufactures from 1920–1 onwards shattered prices, employment levels and finally demand to an extent which in many cases exceeded the later dislocations of the early 1930s. It was in this context that the emphasis shifted from migration to the concept of expanding, or at least protecting, Empire trade; in other words, the creation of an Empire trade bloc which could provide some insulation from the fierce price competition in international markets. In 1923, therefore, an Imperial Economic Conference met which completely overshadowed the Imperial Conference proper and articulated a coherent programme of Empire development: Men, Money and Markets.

How did the Whitehall bureaucracy view these economic departures? The answer is at best sceptically, at worst contemptuously. The Colonial Office in particular disliked inflated ideas of imperial development. They knew very well that neither Canada nor South Africa were willing to take substantial numbers of British migrants. But they also suspected what development enthusiasts indignantly refuted: that the Australian government was only using the migration idea as a means of easing capital aid out of the British taxpayers' pockets and manoeuvring the British government into giving preferential treatment to Australian produce. The Australians were indeed persistent in using monies given under the terms of the Empire Settlement Act in ways not previously agreed with the British authorities.[31] Even worse, this migrant finance would, it was felt, simply be used by Australian politicians to bribe their constituencies. Thus the Western Australian government used theirs to benefit the mercantile interests of Perth, not the northern and relatively voteless tracts of the state where the development challenge really lay.[32] One Colonial Office official summed up the departmental attitude. 'The development of Western Australia is not for us', he minuted, 'but for the Australians.'[33]

These attitudes applied with even greater force when the prospects of Empire development widened to take in trade and finance as well as migration. Harding stressed that the volume of export trade to the Dominions was not large enough to improve radically the British economy's performance, even if (as was unlikely) they proved willing to increase the UK proportion of their imports; the Crown Colonies already sent the great preponderance of their produce to Britain, so that the margin for expansion in British–colonial trade was very limited. At the same time it was very difficult to see how fostering trade between Nigeria and any other part of the Empire would help the situation in England.[34] The other Whitehall departments broadly shared this perspective. Thus the Treasury had consistently tried to restrain migration expenditures even after 1922, and it was stringently critical of any ideas of Empire currency cooperation because it suspected these of being a front for an attempt to shift the burden of the Dominions' top-heavy public indebtedness onto the UK.[35] The Board of Trade feared that Empire development might not only affect the overall volume of British exports by disrupting foreign trade, but would in the end disorganise Empire trade itself; thus the Board opposed the application made by the South African Iron and Steel Corporation for assistance under the Trade Facilities Act, for it would in the long term reduce UK steel sales to South Africa.[36] Finally, the Ministry of Agriculture (although it was not yet as explicitly antagonistic to the Dominions as it later became) attacked the suggestion that the UK government should give marketing guarantees to Dominion producers, pointing out that such a departure would enrage UK agriculturalists who had themselves never received sustained Government help.[37] The bulk of bureaucratic opinion, then, was, as it always remained, suspicious and ultimately antagonistic towards 'Empire development'.

It was the politicians who were drawn towards this concept because it provided them with at least the appearances of a policy. It allowed them to speak assertively of 'bold policies of productive development', and for the Conservatives it was particularly important because an imperial strategy as a means to economic survival validated a central part of their traditional ideology. It was this political use of Empire regardless of economic facts which appalled the Dominions Department of the Colonial Office. They were naturally reticent about putting their criticisms into plain print, but when Leopold Amery began to press for a comprehensive plan of Imperial Preference to be prepared for the Economic Conference their reaction was obvious. Harding commented that Amery's suggestion required political action because the Government remained at least superficially pledged to Free Trade, and he went on

> As the authority of the Imperial Conference would almost certainly have to be invoked in support of the scheme at a general Election, the effect would thus be to import into the Imperial Conference an atmosphere of local party politics, and I should have thought an undesirable one, as it has always been held to be one of the strong points of the Imperial Conference system that party politics are best left on one side.[38]

This was essentially what happened when the Economic Conference met.[39] Its proceedings were divided into two parts. The first and more open part consisted of a series of preferential deals within the limits of the British government's commitment not to tax major food items without a specific electoral mandate to do so; so Baldwin restricted himself to guaranteeing Dominion producers a market for fruit, currants, canned salmon, hay and a few other minor commodities. The second and much more secretive part consisted of talks on the comprehensive agreement covering staples such as wheat and meat that could be made if the Conservatives were to win the next election on a protectionist platform.

After the Conference, Baldwin dissolved Parliament and fought an election with cry of 'Empire trade development'. This was a considerable miscalculation, because on the trade issue the British electorate still reacted as consumers who wanted to maintain their access to cheap foreign food rather than to the expensive Dominion commodities. The Labour party thus entered office for the first time not, in reality, as a force for socialism, but as a means of keeping living costs down. Ramsay MacDonald, sensitive to this fact, quickly scrapped all the arrangements concluded at the previous Conference. Dominion agriculturalists and their Governments were not pleased to have the cup of British food preferences dashed so suddenly from their lips, and economic misunderstandings soon multiplied. But it can be concluded that for the present the Commonwealth relationship had been irreversibly affected by the deflationary crisis. It had become politicised in the sense that Governments had begun to seek solutions to their problems within its framework. This was, perhaps, unavoidable because after 1900 the various Commonwealth economies had become so closely connected that action taken by one Government was reverberating upon the others; none of them, however anti-imperial a governing party might be in its rhetoric, could afford to ignore the benefits of dialogue. But how much coordination did the interlocking pattern of the constituent economies actually permit? Was there not as much potential for confrontation as for agreement within the economic structure of Commonwealth? Only the Depression of the 1930s would answer these questions. But nonetheless by the mid-1920s the idea of a Commonwealth trade strategy had become, for the first time, integral to British politics.

Whilst economic conditions had thus deteriorated after 1920 the presiding Governments of the Commonwealth had all come under increasing pressure. A majority of the Dominions during and immediately after the war had been governed by distinctly conservative administrations whose prime constituency lay among the old British settler elites now struggling to maintain their dominance against incoming groups. These administrations therefore emphasised the imperial link as part of their sectional appeal at home. The conservative monopoly of office, however, was swept away by post-war slump, and the equilibrium moved in favour of political parties whose programmes were filled with the slogans of national independence, or which at least showed signs of a disturbing equivocation where Empire cooperation was involved. Australia enjoyed a mild form of this transition with Hughes's intense conservatism being replaced, in February 1923, by Bruce's pragmatism. In Canada Arthur Meighen, Borden's Conservative successor, had already been replaced by the Liberal Mackenzie King in the elections of December 1921.

Mackenzie King's attitude to Empire was shaped by two early experiences in office. The first was Chanak, which had a lasting effect on him because it showed the British would not shrink from appealing to a Dominion public behind the back of its political leadership. The second was his dispute with Lord Byng, the Canadian Governor-General, who in a confused parliamentary situation in October 1925 first refused the Liberal leader a dissolution and then granted one to Meighen. In fact Byng acted according to all the constitutional rules, but the circumstances presented Mackenzie King with an appealing claim for the voters' affection – the British favoured Meighen because the Conservatives were the lapdogs of the imperialists.[40] Mackenzie King realised that there were limits to the effectiveness of an anti-imperial strategy, but that whilst kept within bounds there were votes to be had and the UK could be firmly put in its place too. Henceforth he was to be obsessed with the petty tactics of Commonwealth relations and with the need to preserve an area of discretion for Canada within Empire policy; and because Canada was always poised between Australian conservatism and South African radicalism, these new emphases had a significant effect on the overall balance of Dominion views.

More important than the course of change in Australia and Canada, however, were events in South Africa and Ireland. The latter had always been the laboratories in which the political objectives of the Empire-state were developed; the issue of British control was, after all, much more explicitly drawn in these relatively turbulent societies than in the more homogeneous and less polarised worlds of Australasia and British North America. In South Africa Smuts had gradually had his power-base undermined after 1918.[41] His position depended on maintaining a virtual monopoly of English votes which, when combined with his personal fiefdom of 'moderate' Afrikaners, gave a solid majority within the Union legislature. But his increasing collaboration with large-scale capital entailed by a programme of rapid industrialisation soon alienated the largely English urban working class. This group began to drift towards the Nationalist Party with its traditional anti-business stance. By 1924 the process was already far advanced, and after a shock defeat for Smuts's South Africa Party at the Wakkerstroom by-election, the Prime Minister opted for a general election. Lord Athlone, the Governor-General, experienced mixed feelings at this decision. He recognised its political logic and felt that its 'bold and courageous' quality resembled Smuts's heroic handling of the great Rand strike in 1922, whilst it was unlikely that the Nationalists, once in power, would attempt to revive the republican question.[42] But the prospect of losing Smuts struck a despairing note in Athlone's mind:

> one of the worst consequences would be the loss to this country for five years, and possibly for all time, of the services of her greatest Statesman who fought for his country's predominance until he realised the futility of that ambition and whose subsequent career has been devoted to the loyal fulfillment of the Treaty of Vereeniging and the realisation under the British Crown of a great and united British South Africa.[43]

Hertzog duly displaced Smuts when the election took place in June 1924, and although his early statements and his Cabinet appointments seemed not to threaten the British position, it was not long before doubts crept in. The early release of the Afrikaner extremist Maritz and Hertzog's clear intention of effecting the movement of Dutch moderates from the South Africa Party caused particular concern.[44] When Smuts responded to Hertzog's tactics by accusing him of attempting to re-divide South Africa on racial lines, Athlone reported

> The question whether General Smuts has not been somewhat impulsive in thus openly exposing the possibility of the disintegration of his party is open to discussion, and it can be argued that his statements amounted to a confession that the danger is real and that the integrity of his party is vulnerable.[45]

The prospect of Smuts's political destruction and the unification of the Dutch under the Nationalist emblem touched an ancient nerve in the British official mind.

At least South Africa remained an ordered community; Ireland in the 1920s bore the stigmata of anti-British rebellion followed by a bloody civil war. These stages in the Irish tragedy were marked off by the 1921 Articles of Agreement. These Articles represented Lloyd George's conclusion that British coercion of the nationalist south was no longer a viable policy. The last gamble of counter-terrorism in the shape of the Black and Tans had failed to stifle the military effort of the insurrectionists, public opinion in the UK and Dominions had been offended by the ruthlessness of British methods whilst, perhaps most importantly, the Anglo–Irish struggle had become a stumbling-block in good relations with America. But was there a mechanism available which could satisfy the South's desire for self-rule without prejudicing essential British interests? Lloyd George calculated that the British Commonwealth provided such an option, with an Irish Free State enjoying the same rights as Canada. This, however, entailed a partition of Catholic south from Protestant north, and the underlying question was whether a sufficiently coherent group of southern politicians could be found to operate such a truncated version of their objectives. The London talks in October 1921 were concerned with this political exercise,[46] and finally Cosgrave assumed the burden of converting a rebel–republican organisation into a legitimate Government within the Commonwealth. The de Valerists opposed this and civil war followed. This situation cannot be fully treated here. The important point is that Lloyd George had sought to approach the historic Irish Question by bringing it within the framework of the Commonwealth. In this way the Commonwealth itself became much more of a volatile political institution. And although British officials took some time before they really accepted the Irish Free State as an authentic Dominion, they did not fail to appreciate that a Commonwealth with Ireland was a very different and more complex phenomenon than one without.

Political change in the Commonwealth after 1920, then, had been rapid and fundamental. It was not easy, from a British vantage point, to define what all these changes actually amounted to. Perhaps they meant that the long battles for South Africa and Ireland had been lost, and that the central British aim of assimilating diverse societies within the democratic, consensual and pragmatic political culture of modern Britain had been smashed on the rocks of older divisions. Perhaps they meant, on the contrary, that in a transforming world, where the main themes were economic and political interdependence, even Afrikaner and Irish nationalism (let alone the modest dissidence of Canadian liberalism) could be absorbed within the Commonwealth nexus. One point, however, could not fail to be understood. The Commonwealth had become a political framework within which very diverse forces existed. It was a fragile and problematic coalition of interests which required continuous management. It was in this important sense that a 'Commonwealth problem' really dates from the mid-1920s. The establishment of the Dominions Office in 1925 is therefore a useful benchmark in our analysis. But before looking at that event a broad view of the inter-war Commonwealth will be presented.

2 The Inter-War Commonwealth: a British Perspective

The underlying theme of this book is that the organisation of Commonwealth was one way that the British state attempted to stem political and economic decline after 1918. Some attempt must be made, therefore, to look broadly at how the Commonwealth became relevant to the preservation of British power. Some early clues to this lie in the prominent role given to imperial reorganisation in the post-1918 reconstruction debate. In particular, it was a useful weapon in the hands of those who criticised the orthodoxies of nineteenth-century political economy. The flavour of this emerges in Ellis Barker's *Economic Statesmanship*, published in 1918 and reprinted in 1920, which was typical of a whole spate of revisionist literature.

> The teachings of the British economists have profoundly affected British policy. For the benefit of the capitalist, the middleman and the speculator, the State was to remain absolutely passive in economic matters. . . . Production was sacrificed to speculation. The unrestricted enterprise of company promoters, userers and swindlers of every kind was considered more important than the welfare of producers who create the national wealth. National strength and security was sacrificed to speculation. The Stock Market was considered more important than the great industries. Paper wealth was placed above real wealth. The development of the great Imperial domain was left to chance and tö the tender mercies of cosmopolitan financiers, who, under the pretext of developing the Empire, tried to fleece the British investors. No attempt was made to direct the huge stream of British emigrants towards the empty lands of the Empire, for money was considered more important than men. . . .[1]

Where the nineteenth-century consensus in Britain had seen the free market as a life-giving organism, for an increasing range of UK economic interests after 1900 it was seen as a cancer. For most of the nineteenth century British industrial costs had proved responsive to market forces, capital had accumulated and the factory classes (owners,

24

managers and workers) had been willing to move from stagnating industries into new ones with more advanced technology and therefore higher productivity. The physical and financial resources which resulted were used to expand the import and export trades with primary-producing areas elsewhere in the world; and in this way Britain had become the centre of a vast mercantile system. But by the outbreak of World War I, the market economy was no longer operating so effectively in the UK. Too many vested interests had grown up around the particular technologies of the mid- and late-nineteenth century. The institutional growth of the trade union movement meant that the labour market was affected by political rather than economic criteria; whilst the staple export industries had grown to such a scale that, when their turn for reduction came within the development process, they resisted with a corporate determination unknown to the handloom weavers of the early Industrial Revolution who had tamely accepted their fate. Thus by the 1920s British industry was fast losing its 'modernity' in that it was ceasing to respond to the processes of market change. The consequence was an inevitable loss of competitiveness in international markets.

There were two possible ways of dealing with this situation. The first was to reinstate the authentic working of the market. This required two changes. Internally, it necessitated bringing industrial costs – above all wage rates – down into line with requirements for profitability. Externally, it necessitated a restoration of the gold standard to bring sterling into an accurate relationship with other world currencies and thus restore competitiveness. But would the social system withstand the pressure of discontent among the workers and managements so drastically affected by the situation? The alternative response to market renewal was to seek some means of disengaging from the international system while taking a large enough slice of it to ensure supplies of food and raw materials on the one hand and markets for manufactures on the other. But did the UK have enough leverage on other economies to weld them into a new system of trade, and would that system be broad enough to finance the growth in living standards which democratic politics made vital?

These were difficult and complex choices, and the reasons why some specific interests moved one way and some the other is beyond our terms of reference. The relevant point here is that for those who sought to escape the workings of the market the Empire seemed the logical connection around which to shape new tariff arrangements; and, because of the size of their economies, it was – not surprisingly – the Dominions rather than the Crown Colonies which were the focus of attention. Before and immediately after World War I this view was largely restricted to narrow and specifically Empire-minded pressure groups. The break came about 1922 with the intensification of world competition in manufactures. The sudden prospect of deflation had forced manufacturers throughout the industrial nations into dumping their surpluses, and in these circumstances it was always the British market, hugely vulnerable to international fluctuations, which became the most heavily glutted. From this point on industrial support in the UK for ideas of an imperial economy grew rapidly, and the return of sterling to the gold standard in 1925 at the old parity of $4.86 (a policy determined by financial interests, the Treasury and the politicians, not the industrialists) gave an added push by reducing the average competitiveness of British goods a further 10 per cent. Still, the balance between free trade and protectionist forces within British industry was still not entirely clear, even in the late 1920s. Whereas automobile interests were now articulate and aggressive in their espousal of an imperial trade strategy,[2] other industrial groups were still making profits from international sales and remained sceptical.

What finally produced a tariff consensus was a rapid deterioration in the overseas payments position in mid-1930. Even the Federation of British Industries, which had avoided taking a position ever since its establishment in 1916, openly called for duties on foreign goods. The industrial campaign which followed was intense. By May 1932 the iron and steel makers were suffering so greatly from disorganised trading that they arrived in Montreal demanding a stabilisation agreement with the Canadians and threatening to join a European consortium unless it was promptly delivered.[3] The politicians, desperate to retain some credibility in economic policy, were also being constrained into imperial postures. The Ottawa Conference which took place in August 1932, and which established a bilateral series of deals between Commonwealth members, was the culmination of the post-war emphasis on Empire development. This rhetoric was deceptive. For many of its advocates, an Empire strategy was attractive precisely because it was anti-development, a policy which protected the domestic industrial structure from new conditions in the world economy. Whatever the underlying motives, however, it should be clear that the idea of Commonwealth had a significance in that it was held to offer elements of stability for a metropolitan economy whose growth was rapidly contracting.

But the imperial economy in the 1930s proved to be an inadequate answer to the enormity of Britain's economic malaise. The industrial leadership, deep down, always believed that at some point 'social readjustment' (lower wages, reduced social services and longer hours) were required for any fundamental up-turn in economic performance. Nor did the British and Dominion economies fit in the way that imperial enthusiasts contended. The scale of Dominion surpluses in key commodities (Canadian wheat, for example) meant that the British market could never fully absorb them, and the Dominion producers were ultimately bound to gear their operations to world, not merely imperial, markets. Because Dominion agricultural output rose during the

Depression, with farmers suicidally trying to offset falling prices by increasing productivity, this logical fault in the Empire trade concept became only too clear. It was underlined further when, after 1931 and the passage of the Wheat Act, the British Government began to protect and expand UK agriculture. The motives for this were complex; the need to appease agricultural pressure groups, to create a more balanced social structure, to move towards a better long-term balance of payments. The effect was clear; it shocked and embittered Dominion governments who depended on easy access to the UK consumer.

If the fit of the Commonwealth economies was so bad on primary produce, it was even worse when it came to manufacturing. Imperial trade development hinged on a continuing specialisation of production in its geographical parts, and in particular that the Dominions did not develop industries to compete with Britain. But already urban industrial development was the chief growth element in much of the Dominions.[4] In all these societies, indeed, industrialisation had become such a critical part of the political and social nexus that it could not be constrained into an imperial pattern. This situation became vastly more difficult during the Depression because the Dominions attempted, like all the other great agricultural exporters, to shift their rural unemployed into the factories. This cut their dole queues and reduced their international deficits, but it was also another blow to the British exporter. By the mid-1930s the UK industrial community had become distinctly antagonistic to the Dominions. In some trades where Dominion competition had begun to be felt, manufacturers called for a new tariff system which treated Empire competitors like any other foreigner.[5] Many went even further and called keenly for an embargo on capital goods exports to the Dominions which would prevent their creating a secondary infrastructure.[6] Dispassionate observers pointed out that Dominion development could mean a bonanza for British industrialists if they themselves were to concentrate on more specialised products, but this point was rarely heard above the din created by lost export orders. Even the Board of Trade, which consistently sought to modify protectionist excesses, became acutely conscious that the UK (with net imports of capital and a static population growth) could not go on bearing the strain of Commonwealth development, a strain which involved rises in UK imports of merchandise to absorb increases in Dominion productivity.[7] The Anglo–American Trade Treaty of 1938, although concluded for a variety of reasons, marked the point at which the UK establishment as a whole relegated the Commonwealth in their scale of economic priorities.[8] Most importantly, this Treaty indicated that by the end of the 1930s the UK was seeking stability not through imperial protectionism but through an international liberalisation of trade modified, where necessary, by cartel arrangements to protect vested interests. British industrialists, indeed, had been busy ever since 1936 defining areas of possible cooperation with their German counterparts as well.[9] Although World War II intervened to limit this trading front for Western industrial nations, the tracks of a new alignment in international economic affairs was clearly visible at the time of its outbreak and quickly reappeared in 1945; and inevitably this meant a reduced role for the Commonwealth as an economic entity.

The economic rationale of Commonwealth after 1918 was therefore an important factor governing the British world picture. But the real force of this rationale will be missed unless it is linked to changes in international politics. Most imperial economic rhetoric was, as we saw in the last chapter, a rhetoric of the state. In Europe, state expansion was the institutional expression of an intensifying conflict among rival groups for economic and social power. These groups, indeed, were as much regional as national, so that by 1914 Western, Central and South-Eastern Europe (whatever their internal differences) were distinct political formations. Moreover, World War I, whilst testimony to the lasting divisions among European groups, simultaneously undermined Europe's collective control in those other continents on which she depended for raw materials and investment returns. European dominance in the Orient had been severely curtailed by the emergence of Japan as a Great Power demanding her slice of the Chinese pie. Nationalism in India, Egypt and the Middle East had created a businessman's nightmare of 'uncertainty'. Finally, the old fears that American economic growth would be translated into a competing *Weltpolitik* had by 1919 become something of a reality.

Taken together these developments represented a reallocation of power within the world system, and they convinced British commentators that the future shape of conflict lay between large 'blocks' competing to control the finite sources of primary wealth available. There were differences of opinion as to whether there would be two or three blocks in Europe, how far the Russian sphere would penetrate southern Asia and what extensions the US would make to the Monroe Doctrine, but the assumptions were generally the same. Whereas Darwinist thinking along these lines had been distinctive of the Tory Right before 1914, it now spread across the political spectrum. 'America is at the moment the chief enemy of the human race. Japan, after absorbing China, will be', Bertrand Russell told Clifford Allen in 1919, 'I believe that the conflict between the white and yellow races will come one day.'[10] Russell's view of World War I as opening a new stage in the world struggle was common. Another, less distinguished, writer declared in a tract entitled 'Australia – White or Yellow' that

It has yet to be fully recognised that the impulse to swarm and to find new homes is as natural and fitting in men as in bees . . . that the time for swarming has come; and that the nations are revolting against the

restrictions which are placed upon their movements by their more
fortunate rivals. . . . The future of the Empire which encloses the
greater part of the coveted regions inevitably depends upon the nature
of its response to this affirmation.[11]

From early on in the inter-war period, then, there was a new global
perspective to international conflict. This conflict was increasingly
related to access to raw materials. Not surprisingly, it was felt that the
British Empire was very near the heart of these developments because it
contained such rich resources and racial diversity. Here were great risks
but also great opportunities, and it is this duality which goes some way
towards explaining the pathology of imperial advocates such as
Amery – one minute calling the nation to arms to prevent imminent
collapse, the next vividly portraying a future in which imperial
development would exceed the nineteenth-century successes of the US.
Either way, it was clear that the UK would have to mobilise economic,
technological and political resources on a new scale. Recognition of this
went far beyond the Milnerite connection and coloured attitudes
throughout the political public. Thus imperial reorganisation was a
response to the heightened sense of competitive nationalism in international politics.

This emphasis on an imperial block, however, was contradicted by the
salient fact that the war had integrated the UK more closely than ever
into a European system. Financially there were the huge war debts owed
to Britain by her European allies, particularly France, and the
reparation payments owed by Germany. Strategically, the advent of
aircraft and the submarine had made it irrefutable that Britain was part
of Europe's military problem. Diplomatically, Britain's role in the
establishment of the League of Nations had institutionalised her
involvement in European affairs. Economically, the industrial interests
of Western Europe increasingly impinged on each other. To reverse
these processes to any extent required a programme of expenditures and
upheavals which the post-war electorate was in no mood to face; and, as
Michael Howard has rightly stressed, the inter-war years are not least
important because they saw the emergence (for good or ill, and it was
often the latter) of 'public opinion' as the critical consideration in policy
evaluation.[12]

Any analysis of the Commonwealth situation, then, has to take
account of the dichotomy between Empire and Europe which confronted British policy-makers. What was the nature of this dichotomy?
It was not that *in principle* Britain's European and Imperial interests
were incompatible, but rather that the restricted availability of resources
created a situation in which a conflict of priorities did emerge. Reinhard
Meyer, a German historian, has put this succinctly

Out of the necessity of matching the demands of home defence and Europe with those made by the defence of the Empire evolved those political endeavours aimed not only at the large-scale avoidance of entanglements in Continental Europe, but also at the confinement of the British role to that of an 'honest broker' mediating between the European revisionist and status quo powers.[13]

The real difference within the higher echelons of the British establishment lay between those who thought such brokerage provided an effective means of coordinating British interests, regardless of the gap between resources and obligations which might arise in a purely hypothetical war situation; and those who thought that the broker function would break under the strain, and that it was necessary to concentrate on those areas where Britain retained a unilateral capacity to act. This was part of the divide that separated Baldwin and Amery, a divide whose emotional width was increased by its relationship to factional struggles within the Conservative party. In 1928, when Baldwin, speaking at the Lord Mayor's banquet, concentrated his remarks on the improvement in the European atmosphere, Amery (who had been appointed Colonial Secretary in 1924) castigated him for getting his priorities wrong:

This particular speech (at the annual Lord Mayor's feast) goes back to the days when the only part of the world outside these islands that really mattered was the world of foreign powers. Today the part of the outer world that matters most for us, whether for trade, for defence, or for any other purpose, is that part of the world which is comprised in the nations of the British Commonwealth. Obviously, then, in the world as it exists today the great annual speech of the Prime Minister ought to say at least as much about the Empire outside as about the outer world of 'Dutch and Dagoes'.[14]

It is tempting, in its clarity, to articulate these two main approaches in terms of 'Continentalists' and 'Isolationists'. At times the application of such categories would be justified; when back-bench MPs tried to trip up Austen Chamberlain's foreign policy in the House of Commons they were certainly acting like archetypal isolationists.[15] In the same way, Michael Howard traces the ambiguity between a British diplomacy increasingly sensitive to European security issues, and a Service leadership which continued to see itself as principally concerned with the policing of an Empire; and he shows how the latter were forced in the end to recognise a continental commitment.[16] It would be possible, therefore, to relate the events of the 1930s in terms of a Europeanisation of British power in which diplomats, politicians and military leaders came to accept that British interests were really part of a European pattern. This would be misleading, although not enormously so. What happened after 1918 was rather an *internationalisation* of British power, a process by which British actions came to be subject to veto by a wide range of international circumstances, as much American as European. Not everybody, however, saw a sharp clash between Britain's imperial and her European, or even international, roles. Whitehall officials – in an atmosphere where attitudes were not polarised by the party political struggle and who instinctively sought the *via media* – found it easier to assume a practical accommodation between them. But if we should be wary of rigid divisions between Continentalists and isolationists, it can be positively asserted that British opinion as a whole after 1918 was deeply equivocal on European matters. Such equivocations frequently hardened into isolationism, and the Commonwealth idea was able to breed off this psychology of doubt and anxiety.

It will have been noticed that, in the evidence so far presented, several references have been made to racial factors. Did racism, like isolationism, constitute a strand in the formulation and working of Commonwealth? It is difficult, but vital, to distinguish the different levels of this problem. During these years race became a popular model for communicating political anxiety in general. A mass literature built up on the subject, and it need only be said that T. H. Stoddard's *The Rising Tide of Colour* was typical.[17] Between the wars, as Hugh Tinker emphasises in his broad survey of race in the twentieth century,[18] the white ideal of Empire reached its zenith. Even the great ceremonial of Empire had become bound in a white veil. William Macmillan, the South African historian, complained poignantly to Lionel Curtis

I am old enough to remember the Jubilee of 1897. Black Africans and West Indians remember too – and mark the change in 1935 – and the touching 'loyalty' still alive in them (but deeply shocked) is a thing you really ought to see and feel. It is being endangered.[19]

The fact that, as in Kenya, the articulation of the settler ideal was couched in terms of aspirations to Dominionhood indicates that Commonwealth membership had become for many a synonym for white supremacy. Admittedly, India was a participating member of the Imperial Conference, and at the 1923 meeting the Indian representatives were able to embarrass Smuts by confronting him with their demand for equal rights for their nationals in British overseas possessions.[20] But, in fact, India was never really regarded as one of the 'club', and it was fully realised that any attempt to appease Indian nationalism through the application of Dominion status would have been outrightly opposed by South Africa and possibly other Dominions too – a special clause had to be inserted into the 1931 Statute of Westminster preserving the UK's unilateral right to extend Commonwealth membership.

It would be easy to ascribe these racial themes to Dominion rather than UK assumptions as to the Commonwealth character. But any cursory reading of Amery's writings shows that the concept of race was deeply embedded in his Empire ideology. One of his motives in establishing the Dominions Office in 1925 was, as he put it to Dawson of *The Times*,[21] to eliminate 'the legend of Colonial Office officials writing to a nigger one minute and then turning round and writing in the same strain to Dominion Prime Ministers'.[22] He told Garvin[23] of *The Observer*, at the same time, that he hoped thereby to avoid the embarrassment of Colonial debates at Westminster in which 'the grievances of black men in Kenya, of dockyard workers in Malta, of Chinese in Malaya and highly constitutional problems of inter-Empire relationships are all jumbled up together'.[24] Amery, although perhaps distinguished by a certain vulgar directness, was not alone in the racial colouring of his views. The Foreign Office struggled valiantly to uphold the thesis, supported by voluminous evidence from the Metropolitan Police, that black riots in South Africa were the product of Comintern propaganda rather than economic hardship.[25] The Dominions Office, because its very nature involved it in the domestic politics of the Dominions, was, if certain episodes are taken in isolation, actively involved in running the Commonwealth as a race alliance. Thus there were many instances where British influence was used to protect the discriminatory policies of Dominion Governments from external pressures.

One such event took place in 1935 when B. K. Basu,[26] en route to attend the League Assembly as India's delegate, harangued Harding about the Indian Government's demand for equal rights for her nationals in the Empire. Harding was determined to dissuade him from a public campaign along these lines and contended that the difficulty 'was really one of economic relations and necessities . . . rather than . . . "racial superiority" '.[27] Basu was not so easily pacified and pointed out that the Japanese community in British Columbia were accorded a better status than Indian residents – an unacceptable example of one Empire Government discriminating against the citizens of another Empire Government in favour of the foreigner. Amery had to intervene. He assured Basu that a full day's debate would be given to the topic, but, as Harding privately admitted, this was a 'shelving attitude' for no day could possibly be made available.[28] Basu left London deeply irritated, whilst the Dominions Office hurriedly warned the External Affairs Department in Ottawa to prepare a case should the issue of Indian rights in Canada be raised at Geneva.[29] Because instances such as these multiplied during this period, it is impossible to avoid the conclusion that there was a politics of race subsumed within the Commonwealth mechanism.

But to say that racial assumptions were generally prevalent in inter-war political thought, and that the Commonwealth association at points helped to reinforce Governments committed to discriminatory action, is not to contend that the Commonwealth had, for Britain, a racial *role*. What had made the Dominions central to British perspectives of Empire was not their whiteness but their production capacity, their growing value as markets and their manpower. In trying to avoid differences among Commonwealth members, or in trying to keep intra-Commonwealth issues out of international forums, or just in trying to prove to the Dominions that British diplomacy was vital to their perceived interests, officials inevitably became implicated in the tactics of the white settler communities. But they did not themselves have specifically racial objectives in the making of policy. Their own tactical priorities, indeed, made British officials just as likely to adopt liberal postures on race matters as reactionary ones. Thus both the Colonial and Dominions Offices became increasingly critical of South African domestic policies as they threatened to disrupt colonial stability elsewhere in Africa, and by 1936, as we shall see later, the Dominions Office was musing on the long-term advantages of a multi-racial Commonwealth which could keep India and Egypt to the British connection.[30] British management of the Commonwealth relationship, then, meant a recurring involvement in racial politics, but the pattern of that involvement was one determined by essentially non-racial factors.

If, to some Olympian observer, the Commonwealth seemed to be definable as a white system of dominance, at ground level its various Anglo–Saxon parts were remarkably ignorant of, and insensitive towards, each other. Once the pressures of world war receded, the different Commonwealth publics returned to the local introspections which had always characterised them. Thus the Dominions always saw colonial policing as a responsibility for the UK. Even worse, they sometimes spoke and acted as if to disassociate themselves from the whole colonial enterprise. Canadian magazines and newspapers in the 1920s began to replicate traditional American anti-colonialism, much of their coverage of India coming from 'undesirable sources' in the US.[31] When Amery had set up the Dominions Office in 1925 he was, therefore, determined to promote a sense of integrated Commonwealth interests. 'That Dominion public opinion should be interested in the Colonial Empire', Amery minuted in 1929, 'is of very great importance as affecting the Dominion outlook on our problems and responsibilities.'[32] One tactic designed to bring this about was the attempt to stimulate a steady flow of personnel from the Dominion universities into the Colonial Service. The Canadian response proved disappointing, and although more success was had in Australia and New Zealand, the recruitment scheme never got off the ground.[33] The problem was that increased exchanges at such elite levels were never likely to effect the restructuring of public attitudes that Amery had in mind. One official recognised that the challenge was one of the masses or, as he put it, 'How to make the plain people of the UK and the Dominions well acquainted with each other?'.[34]

Hitherto the press in each Dominion had carried very little on the outside world, and what little there was tended to be about Britain rather than other Commonwealth members; whilst the British press was rarely to be seen reporting on Australian wool-shearing or the progress of the Canadian harvest. The development of communications technology seemed to create an opportunity to transform this situation. Wireless, for example, was thought to possess great 'imperial' potential, and a scheme was devised by which a 'first-class journalist' would be installed in each Dominion whose task was to set up an information flow among Commonwealth partners.[35] But, as one Whitehall critic warned,

> If the British Official Wireless is to be widely and regularly used [by the Dominions] the first essential is that it should be interesting. Could a daily supply of the right stamp be assured? It would not do to give second-rate stuff, or to have to announce 'Special Imperial Bulletin: no news tonight'.[36]

A lack of material scintillating enough to compare with the latest Paris scandal or the power struggle in Berlin was not the only barrier. There was the possibility that any manipulative tinkering with the media would only serve to provide nationalist propaganda in the Dominions with evidence of an imperial conspiracy. Thus the DO ensured that the appointment of journalists involved in the scheme took place under the non-official auspices of the Empire Press Union,[37] whilst Whitehall personnel were carefully instructed that no suspicions must be aroused that 'an attempt was being made to fill them [the Dominions] up with propaganda'.[38] Such suspicions would, of course, have been well founded. Stephen Tallents,[39] for example, told Whiskard that over the preceding years wide experience had been gained by the DO in the 'placing of articles overseas which we now do successfully on a fair scale. Ryan established personal touch with the leading Canadian papers when he was at the Toronto Exhibition a year ago, and he is now doing the same in South Africa. . . .'[40] There is no poll data which would allow us to calculate the effect of these actions, but it is safe to conclude that by 1939 the Commonwealth publics were markedly better informed about the world in general, and each other in particular, than they had been in 1914. This increase in dialogue, however, was almost certainly more effective in promoting the density, rather than the clarity, of political relations.

Wireless was not the only important innovation in communications during this period. Cable transmission was also extended, and the Imperial Communications Company was set up to counter the growing

US monopoly of international cable lines. But the most significant technical development was naturally the aeroplane. At first, aviation development was viewed in terms of its impact on military strategy, but during the 1920s its economic and more generally political implications took shape. Any country which could make itself the radial focus of international air communications was clearly in a position to reap considerable benefits. The UK seemed well placed to exploit these possibilities because having British populations dispersed on several continents provided the passengers and mail to make long-distance air travel commercially viable. The aviation challenge underlined the fact that international competition required the mobilisation of technical skills, finance and access to facilities on a new scale, and that if Britain were to respond to this situation Commonwealth cooperation was vital. The main UK aviation combine was therefore appropriately labelled 'Imperial Airways', and its Managing Director spoke of a 'great Imperial cooperation to handle all the big through inter-imperial routes'.[41] Equally, the Dominions came to depend on the UK for their access to updated models, and during the 1930s this was a major factor which tied Dominions to British foreign policy. But if British air-frame production capacity provided a technological nexus which reduced the Dominions' freedom of manoeuvre, the failure to create an 'All-Red' air route in these years also proved that clusters of local political and economic interests would always prevent a Commonwealth 'system' in this or any other field. The 'All-Red' route was intended to permit air travel from Australia to the UK without touching foreign territory. But, although Bruce hurried through completion of the Rangoon–Australia section, the construction of the Karachi–Rangoon branch lay fallow. Despite Bruce's constant pleas, the India Office adamantly held that Indian revenues could not stand the strain.[42] Meanwhile, the South African government was concerned with African, not imperial, security, and the key to this lay in railways rather than in aeroplanes; indeed, any diversion of traffic to air services would undermine the precariously balanced finances of the South African rail network.[43] Thus, although the DO tried to solicit Pretoria's cooperation by granting the managership of the southern African route to a protégé of Smuts, providing South African capital with a lucrative role in the financial arrangements, and by hinting at large UK subsidies, Imperial Airways were never allowed to go farther south than Johannesburg.[44] In the case of selecting a transatlantic route, moreover, it was the UK which saw its interest as lying outside the Commonwealth framework. Canada wanted the UK to collaborate on a northern route linking the Canadian East Coast cities, Newfoundland, Greenland and the UK, thus making Montreal 'the real entrepot station of the North American continent instead of, as at present, New York'.[45] But the UK aviation interests and the Air Ministry recognised clearlythat the really profitable route lay between the UK, Bermuda, the Azores and New York; and to this consideration was added the political factor that any UK involvement in Canadian manipulations of the local balance in the American North-East would throw Pan-American Airways into powerful collaboration with French and other European aviation combines.[46] The DO criticised this failure to satisfy Canadian desires for an 'imperial' policy, but with little effect. The threads of British power were too deeply knit into the fabric of the non-Commonwealth world (what Amery was pleased to term 'Dutch and Dagoes') to permit the strategy of an integrated Empire anything more than the occasional flash of substance.

Several references have already been made to the emergence of America as a world power. By the late 1920s the American economy was almost double the size of the British, and was bigger than that of Britain and Germany combined.[47] Anxiety as to how to respond to American dominance, and how to bring about some accommodation of Anglo–American interests, affected Whitehall thinking throughout the inter-war years. Anti-Americanism and the Commonwealth idea, indeed, were closely related in that they were rooted in the determination of British policy-makers to retain some unilateral initiative in world affairs. As late as 1933 Admiral Massingberd,[48] objecting to the inclusion of France as a possible enemy in a military planning exercise, burst out 'If we start dragging in other possible enemies, why not introduce America? Personally I would sooner go to war with America than I would with France.'[49] The conflict of British and American interests was evident in almost all the main issues of the day – naval power, trade policy, access to raw materials, the containment of Japan, and so on. But its most characteristic expression was a topic rarely dealt with in subsequent histories, but which is littered throughout the British records, public and private: the export of American culture and its head-on clash with 'British values'. Post-war imperial rhetoric reached its most strident note when it focused on these cultural questions. Predictably, it was around Hollywood and its near-monopoly of the popular film market that these fears crystallised. Thus, whilst the British and Australian publics were bitterly divided by their common love of cricket (the 'body-line' test controversies of 1932–3 were a landmark in the politicisation of sport), the Australian and American publics were united in their mutual adulation of Jean Harlow.

Official concern about these developments reached the very highest levels. In 1926 an American cinema company produced a film of old Australian convict life replete with vivid scenes of 'English brutality' culled from Marcus Clark's best-selling novel, *For the Term of his Natural Life*. A UK visitor to the Antipodean Dominions wrote in haste to the Boy Scouts International Bureau in London

If this film does get abroad, it will be used to condemn England in the blackest possible manner, and do more towards smashing up the Empire than anything so far attempted. . . .[50]

A personal friend of Baldwin's, Sir Francis Newdegate, petitioned the Prime Minister in the same vein, warning that the production would undermine Australian loyalism which hitherto had constructed 'a most progressive, right-thinking and patriotic British Race'.[51] Meanwhile, the Home Office, gripped with its usual departmental compassion, was attempting to persuade the DO into action on the grounds that the film would cause distress to, and revive Anglophobia amongst, convict descendants 'who are now in many cases in good positions in Tasmania and Australia'.[52] It was finally decided that Amery would have a quiet word with Bruce at the Imperial Conference, in the hope that the Australian authorities would take the appropriate action. The result is not known, but the episode, apart from its intrinsic humour, does usefully illustrate that the psychology of Commonwealth extended well beyond the conventional boundaries of economic and political matters. Whenever the stimulation of a UK film industry was discussed in subsequent years, it was always placed in the context of shoring up British values in the face of cheap cultural competition from the US.[53]

It was in their changing perception of America that Whitehall officials revealed much of their underlying judgements on the state of the Commonwealth. Not surprisingly, this interaction underlay the anxious attention given to the question of Canada's future. A stream of British observers travelled across the senior Dominion nations in an attempt to find out what kind of society was emerging there. In 1925, for example, the War Office despatched Captain T. B. Trappes-Lomax[54] on such a trip. His report is worth recounting because it encapsulates many of the nuances of tradition and change in inter-imperial relations shortly after the end of the World War I. The Captain's immediate terms of reference were to evaluate Canada's capacity to resist an invasion by the US. His conclusion was that the geographical bottlenecks along the border would allow effective delaying tactics if the Canadian air forces could be expanded.[55] But he stressed that military annexation was less of a threat than the cultural and economic penetration of American influence. Trappes-Lomax, however, felt some confidence on this score. This was partly because he shared the common expectation that quite soon the US economy was bound to suffer the 'normal economic ills' of surplus production and to grind into the sort of prolonged recession which had affected the UK since the 1870s. Trappes-Lomax, however, was typical in seeing economic factors as only one determinant of power. Thus, whatever the economic superiority of the US might be, the moral superiority of British culture was a guarantee of political resistance in Canada. He observed the average Canadian . . . thinks in the way an Englishman thinks. He does not share the American admiration for abstract ideas, for doctrinaire theories, for rigid solutions. Thus none of the articles of the American faith – neither the abstract idea of Human Equality, nor the doctrinaire theory of Representation, nor the rigid solutions of political machinery which is in their constitution – appeal to the Canadian mind . . . whereas the Canadian welcomes the conception of a gentleman, the American dislikes it by instinct.[56]

Canadian resistance to American expansion, Trappes-Lomax stressed, had to be nurtured by the export of rugby and cricket teams as an 'Imperial asset', and by the teaching of 'Imperial civics' – especially in Quebec. The Captain recognised, however, that the 'British' quality of Canadian thought did not mean the simple continuance of old-fashioned and sentimental loyalism. A political nationalism expressed in the rhetoric of 'Canada First' was defining itself after the War as a shared assumption throughout Canadian affairs. This meant that Canadian 'imperialism' was taking on more diluted forms. 'Its object', said Trappes-Lomax in commenting on Canada's imperial loyalties, 'is rather the soil, the trees, the houses, and the people from which a man is sprung.'[57] But even in this less specific, heavily localised and almost metaphysical shape, Trappes-Lomax felt that the imperial impulse would prove strong enough to mobilise Dominion assistance if the UK were to become involved in major hostilities. He recalled that in 1921, 5000 Canadians had volunteered to join the British forces facing Kemal Ataturk. Given Canada's potential for industrial growth and a population projected at 30 million within the next twenty years, Trappes-Lomax predicted that the Dominion could play a vital role in providing Britain with the resources to continue its stabilising function within international politics. In the meantime a 'holding operation' was required in which Canadian sensitivities were delicately handled and her latent anti-Americanism manipulated. Any crude imposition of 'rigid Imperial Federationism' would prejudice these long-term goals, and the Captain's final recommendation was that political benefits would follow if the legal relationship between Canada and the UK were re-defined in the former's favour. In this his views meshed neatly with those of Leopold Amery as he prepared for the meeting of the 1926 Imperial Conference.[58]

This chapter has sought to describe, in a general way, the forces shaping the concept of Commonwealth after 1918. That idea took on substance and colour because it appeared to have a new relevance to the variety of problems facing UK policy-makers. In a world where it was desirable not to be totally dependent on international trade, where political conflict was necessitating the large scale organisation of resources, where all who were able to distance themselves from Europe's problems sought to do so and where the populism of American culture threatened to overwhelm the identity of British values, the appeal of Commonwealth was distinctive and powerful. It was, it must be said, an appeal to political imagination rather than fact. There was not a Commonwealth system any more than there was an international system, or a Western system or any other kind of system. Coalitions of power in the world were too complex, too contradictory, too overlapping for such abstractions to have an easy validity. But, however illusory they may have been, such ideas were important if people (policymakers, bureaucracies and electorates) were to make sense of their political environment and formulate their self-interest. The inter-war Commonwealth had precisely this 'articulating' significance for Britain. It is with this general function in mind that we can turn to an essentially chronological study of Whitehall and the Commonwealth.

3 1925: The Establishment of the Dominions Office and the Locarno Treaties

The year 1925 marks a watershed in post-war British history, and most of this book is devoted to the years which followed. The forces making for such a truncation require some brief reflections. We have already seen that a 'Commonwealth problem' had crystallised by the mid-1920s. This general development roughly coincided with the return of Baldwin as Prime Minister in 1924, an event which marked the reconstitution of traditional, anti-coalitionist conservatism. Leopold Amery's influence within the new political arrangements meant that he could succeed in his objective of cutting the Dominions Department out of the Colonial Office structure and setting it up as a separate office; and as there is no more certain method of perpetuating a problem than to establish a body to look after it, the Dominion–Commonwealth was bound in subsequent years to loom large in official thinking. But 1925 was a critical point in international affairs also. The Locarno Treaties were thought to have finally liquidated the war mood in Europe, a mood which had shown a macabre resilience even into the 1920s. But Britain had to pay a price for this achievement. Locarno marks the point at which Britain recognised a responsibility to police West European stability; after this, no easy definition existed as to where 'British interests' began and ended. This chapter attempts to examine these developments and their imperial significance.

The Establishment of the Dominions Office

To put the administrative change of 1925 into perspective it is necessary to describe in outline how the previous bureaucratic arrangements had evolved.[1] The Dominions had always been the responsibility of the Colonial Office. Organised on a geographical basis, the Colonial Office in the late nineteenth century included a North American and Australasian Department and a South African Department, which together covered most Dominion business. The permanent officials had consistently opposed any tampering with this geographical approach, and they managed to thwart those (such as Lord Carnarvon in 1870) who had contended that a clear distinction should be made between the strictly 'colonial' aspect of office business and the more 'political' aspects of the Dominions.[2] After 1900 the pressure for change came chiefly from Dominion politicians, such as Deakin of Australia, who saw in a large and unwieldy Colonial Office (as much concerned with the Gold Coast as with the Antipodes) a barrier to their own influence. The 1907 Imperial Conference was followed by reforms leaving three departments within the Office: a Dominions Department, Crown Colonies and Legal and General. Even this did not satisfy such enthusiasts as Leopold Amery, and it was at this time that the latter (whilst touring Kenya and Uganda) began to call for a complete separation of Colonial and Dominion affairs. The Colonial Office succeeded in warding off the reformers at the 1911 Imperial Conference, but behind the institutional facade the shape of Anglo–Dominion exchanges was changing. Both the Foreign Office and the Committee for Imperial Defence, for example, were involving themselves with Dominion matters, and by 1913 the Dominions Department was beginning to be lampooned as merely a 'sorting office' for others.[3] This was inaccurate, but war organisation between 1914 and 1918 further cut into the Colonial Office monopoly of Dominion business. Direct communication was arranged between the Prime Ministers of the Empire. In actual fact this did not reverberate very much on Colonial Office authority because Lloyd George practised his direct communications with the Dominions through the Colonial Office. Of more lasting significance, however, was the fact that the UK Cabinet Secretariat developed responsibility for the Imperial Conferences. Ever afterwards the Dominions Department (and after 1925 the Dominions Office) had to work closely with Hankey. Lord Milner as Colonial Secretary, characteristically acting against the advice of his Civil Service advisers, tried to ensure after 1918 that Commonwealth matters were largely dealt with at Cabinet level. But in this he failed. The end of military conflict had taken the pressure off the need for enticing immediate Dominion cooperation, whilst the Dominion leaders themselves were now concerned (externally and internally) with larger matters than merely the institutional set-up in London. The Colonial Office was therefore able to restore a large measure of its control over the administration of Empire relations;[4] and it is likely that the old pattern of a Dominions Department within the Colonial Office would have continued through the following decades had it not been for the simple fact of Amery's elevation to the Colonial Secretaryship.

As the Dominions Office was almost entirely the creation of Leopold Amery, it is important to define his motives. His commitment to an ideology of imperial development has already been stressed. This partly arose, no doubt, from the mere chance that in the early 1900s he fell in with the group surrounding Lord Milner, and shared in their South African apotheosis. More generally, however, Amery developed a keen awareness of resource-supply and its economic ramifications; he saw that the Empire constituted a resource bank whose deposits could be skilfully employed by the UK. But Amery, despite this, was not primarily *homo economicus*. He was a British nationalist whose key objective was to maintain Britain's ability to act in her own interests. He was really interested in the unilateral exercise of political power.

Amery's political style, however, was very different from that of his early mentor, Joe Chamberlain. Chamberlain, for all his reservations about the inefficiency of democratic politics, was a man who liked to take an issue 'on the stump'. Empire reform, he thought, could be effected by operating at a mass level. Amery's instincts and qualities were different. He was at best a mediocre public speaker, and was incapable of stirring up a Parliamentary audience – let alone an open-air meeting. Chamberlain had spent much of his life outside national politics and was as happy (in the sense of being 'unmuzzled') outside of office as in. Amery, in contrast, was, like his fellow-Milnerites, bred to power and accepted the equivocations which went with it. His activism was ministerial, not mass. It is therefore typical that, whereas Chamberlain's approach to imperial reform was political (so that he left the Cabinet and fought a protectionist campaign for control of his party), Amery's was essentially administrative. He felt that a separate Dominions Office, working with an enlarged influence within the institutions of government, could succeed where Chamberlain's disruptive tactics had failed.

But although Amery was not a populist, he was keenly aware of the need for a sustaining ideology, and he saw very explicitly a relationship between the imperial idea and the party politics of the day. Where Chamberlain had disjointedly criticised the factionalism of liberal politics, Amery developed a coherent and systematic critique of the nineteenth-century consensus. Free trade, he argued, had spawned a pervasive individualism which fragmented the social polity and bereft the ordinary citizen of group-identity. Socialism had been a natural result of this, returning to the working-man his sense of a fixed place in society. The conservative intellect would be destroyed by this socialist force unless it reversed its earlier mistake of attempting to modernise itself on the false basis of individualism. It had to locate an idea which could 'kindle the imagination of the working man' and put constructive conservatism in control of the democratic system.[5] This idea Amery found in imperial development. Indeed, perhaps his aspirations are best described broadly as 'a politics of imperial order'; individualism would be replaced by social cohesion, unstable economic cycles by a corporately planned economy, involvement in European tensions by a cautious quasi-isolationism. Amery's imperialism, then, was a fairly sophisticated blend of responses to domestic and international pressures after 1918.

Amery's views led him to see as many enemies within his own Party and Cabinet as on the Opposition benches in the House of Commons. As the second Baldwin administration got under way, Austen Chamberlain's conduct of foreign policy and Winston Churchill's management at the Treasury both took on internationalist colours. Amery later recalled

> It was Churchill's ascendancy over weaker-willed colleagues and his obstinate Free Trade convictions which, for me, constituted the real danger to the future of Unionism as a positive progressive force.[6]

The Colonial Office alone had little chance of standing up to the combined weight of Treasury and Foreign Office. What Amery needed was greater institutional leverage within Government to stop the internationalist rot: a separate Dominions Office would go a little way towards providing this.

This interpretation of Amery's motives is speculative. The problem is that the arguments produced for and against a Dominions Office assiduously avoided the fundamental issues. The Conservative leadership was only very slowly knitting itself together after years of defeat and coalitionism, and nobody was rash enough to articulate internal differences in any aggressive way. Instead, the various lobbies boxed each other on shadow issues. Churchill's opposition to a Dominions Office rested on the contention that the historic place of the Colonial Office in the Whitehall establishment would be correspondingly reduced.[7] He also rejected Amery's view that the Colonial Office was too busy with Crown Colonies to deal effectively with the Dominions, pointing out that the delegation of power to Crown Colony governments in recent years had greatly reduced the CO's burdens. He stated sharply

> So far as the Dominions are concerned they have not the slightest intention of being interfered with in any busy way. The number of questions arising in this sphere from month to month is very small. An examination of the Office records would show how few papers of consequence have been passing through the Dominions Department, apart from the war period, in the last twenty years. There is, it is true, a most important theoretical side to the question i.e. the study of the whole development of our Dominions for the closer constitutional unity of the British Empire. These are questions which do not require a large number of administrative persons, but rather the deliberate and reflective study of two or three selected and experienced officials. I deprecate the unnecessary creation of an important and numerous

staff in this sphere whose expense would not be justified either by the volume or character of the work they had to do.[8]

Amery would not have dissented that the old Dominions Department had been small and restricted in its conceptions. His point was that the pressures of the situation required something bolder. The weakness of Amery's position on the question lay not in past deficiencies but that in the present he could not point to any effective support for his scheme. The Dominion Prime Ministers of the mid-1920s were not, in fact, keen to develop alternative sources of communication and were actually suspicious of any new bureaucracy which might cause them political embarrassment. Amery had to refer back to 1907 and 1911 to gather evidence that Dominion opposition to Empire cooperation was 'really based on the one desire of getting away from the Colonial Office', and that a Dominions Office would dispel that 'historical complex' which had hitherto thwarted an effective pooling of Commonwealth resources.[9] The truth was that Amery was alone amongst the major political figures in his desire for administrative change. Both Churchill and Chamberlain feared that Amery, or the Dominions themselves, might seek to interfere in foreign or economic policy by using the new office for their own purposes, and these suspicions spilled over into the civil service committee which reported negatively on the proposal.[10] Amery was forced in the end to make a plea direct to the Prime Minister. He wrote somewhat stridently to Baldwin:

> If I am to do any good work in this office, whether at home or getting into personal touch with the Empire outside, I must have an adequate instrument to do the work. . . . Do not think that I am petulant about the delay or wish to blame anyone. I daresay it was inevitable. But it has postponed things badly and diminished by several months the time that may be given me to carry out a big work in the Empire.[11]

In the end Baldwin used his authority to give Amery what he wanted. Again, there is no evidence to prove precisely why he did so, but it is safe to assume that on both policy and factional grounds he was keen to gratify the Colonial Secretary; that way, he offset the internationalist trend in Government policy, re-establishing the *via media* he instinctively favoured, and pleased the 'imperialist' wing of his party so well represented on the back-benches. The new Dominions Office, however, was to be a very truncated affair. It was to have no services of its own, and had to rely on the secretarial and library resources of the Colonial Office; whilst the Permanent Under-Secretary of the Dominions Office was to receive a lower salary than his Colonial Office equivalent as an open reminder of the bureaucratic pecking order.[12] Nor could Amery publicise the new Office in the way that he would have wished, because an emphasis on boosting Empire cooperation might have elicited nationalist responses in the Dominions. He emphasised racial objectives when selling the project to the Press.[13] The only people he could reveal his real thoughts to were the civil servants involved in the changeover. He told them that the new Office's role was that of 'chief of staff's work' and he described the Office personnel as 'Dominions "General Staff"'.[14] The use of terminology indicates his sense of the Commonwealth relationship as one concerned with the organisation of force in an age of conflict, and his belief that with shrewd management the Dominion auxiliaries could be woven into an Empire-wide strategy. Indeed, looked at in a larger context the new DO could be seen as part of a general attempt to reinforce Government machinery in the mid-1920s, along with, for example, the setting-up of the Chiefs of Staff Committee in 1923[15] and the establishment of the Civil Research Council as a domestic policy counterpart to the Committee of Imperial Defence. But Amery's administrative model could only work if his underlying political assumptions proved correct. They did not, and the DO had to come to terms with a continued commitment to international, not just imperial, responsibilities by the UK authorities. The Locarno negotiations, ironically contemporaneous with the birth of the Dominions Office, indicated the limited terms of reference within which the Office had to work.

Before dealing with Locarno, it is appropriate at this point to jump ahead of our story and look at the growth of the DO after 1925. It was to remain dependent on Colonial Office services even after the two offices ceased to share the same Secretary of State in 1930.[16] At its establishment the DO had only thirteen administrative class officials (a Permanent Under-Secretary, an assistant under-secretary, three assistant secretaries, four principals and four assistant principals) and eighteen other staff, mostly registry clerks.[17] This hardly made it a bureaucracy in its own right, and restricted size was one factor explaining why the Office was never badly split by internal policy differences. Always under the same roof, Harding, Batterbee and their colleagues never lost touch with the traditions and perspectives of the Colonial Office. Even where, logically, differences might have revealed themselves, as in southern Africa where the DO's priority was the improvement of Anglo–South African understanding whilst the CO was determined to avoid the expansion of Pretoria's influence, the two Offices worked pretty much in tandem. Thus the smallness and essential subordination of the DO compared with its Whitehall partners meant that its departmental culture was very much one of flanking movements, the deflection of attacks and the search for compromise, rather than a forthright advance towards defined objectives.

The DO of the later 1930s, nonetheless, was a more considerable affair than ten years previously. Its staff had more than doubled. Under the

Permanent Under-Secretary were now two assistant under-secretaries, five assistant secretaries, thirteen principals, ten assistant principals and thirty-eight other staff.[18] To these could be added the members of British High Commissions established in the Dominions after 1928. These were largely staffed by, and came under the control of, the DO. If this expansion of the staff roll differentiated the department more clearly from the CO, the High Commissions also meant that the DO was no longer completely without leverage in its relations with the Foreign Office, even though the latter (with its patrician humour) never ceased to make disparaging jokes about its poorer cousin. Office business, too, had developed along more sophisticated lines. The balance was tilted much more towards a subject basis – constitutional and nationality questions, civil aviation, international economic questions, inter-imperial trade and so on. In short, as the 1930s progressed the DO developed an authentic group identity within the Whitehall jungle and acquired a style and tactics adapted to its specific experience.

The Locarno Treaties

When the new Dominions Office was debated in the House of Commons, it was described by one speaker in a phrase that subsequently stuck: 'a Foreign Office with a family feeling'.[19] But almost simultaneously the Locarno episode provided the first major indication that Britain and the Dominions did not possess a common approach to international questions. Before clarifying this, two points must be emphasised about Austen Chamberlain who, as British Foreign Secretary, had played the vital bridging role between Gustave Stressmann and Aristide Briand. First, Chamberlain was under great personal strain at Locarno, and the apparently successful outcome seemed all the more triumphant to him; he believed that a genuine obstacle had at last been raised against a recrudescence of war. Second, the Locarno experience convinced Chamberlain that the chief cause of European instability lay in German intransigence;[20] Chamberlain always understood the justifiable character of French neuroses on security matters.

It was to sever the roots of French anxiety that the Foreign Secretary had agreed to pledge that Britain would guarantee both the French and German borders. Without this UK commitment to participate in the responsibilities of policing West European stability, Locarno would have been impossible. The problem that arose, from a British viewpoint, was whether these responsibilities really could be limited to west of the Rhine. The complex interdependence of politics and economics throughout Europe meant that a Russo–German war in the East could all too easily lead to military movements in the West, and so necessitate British intervention. Austen Chamberlain recognised and accepted this indivisibility of the European political problem and the price it imposed on British diplomacy. He sought to promote no unsustainable distinctions between a defence of the Channel ports and a role on the Continental landmass. He told Amery firmly

> All our history shows that the Channel and the Channel ports have a vital interest for us. . . . It is not unlikely that if the position of the British Empire had been clearly defined in the early months of 1914 that we might have escaped war. . . . If we withdrew from Europe I say without hesitation that the chance of permanent peace is gone and that the world must make up its mind that sooner or later – perhaps in a couple of generations – a new disaster will fall upon us and civilisation itself may perish. The suggestion for a mutual pact offers the one way out. . . .[21]

But Dominion opinion did not share these insights. For them British power was not a reflection of buoyant international trade but of naval mastery, and as such the Channel appeared to them a natural *limit* to 'imperial interests'. Unlike Britain, the Dominions exported only a very minor proportion of their goods to European countries. The electorate in every Dominion, indeed, included a high percentage of families whose only European memory was the loss of fathers and brothers. It is therefore not surprising that Dominion opinion exhibited in extreme forms that intense Francophobia which typified the post-war years. It would have been impossible under these circumstances for Austen Chamberlain to have carried the Dominions along with him in the Locarno process. Instead he simply ignored them. When critics of Locarno in the House of Commons tried to undermine the treaties by calling for the publication of inter-imperial correspondence, thereby revealing deep differences of opinion, the DO noted 'In actual fact, there was practically no such correspondence. The Dominion Governments were not formally asked for their views.'[22]

It is important to understand the Foreign Office refusal to consult the Dominions over Locarno. It did not reflect a 'moving away' from an imperial foreign policy.[23] Such a conclusion would make nonsense of the manoeuverings during the following years. Rather, it arose from a real anxiety that Dominion involvement in British policy-making on such a contentious issue would seriously restrict Britain's ability to play the mediating role which the Versailles system had thrust upon her. Certainly, during the negotiations the Foreign Office paid serious attention to packaging the Locarno policy in as imperial a shape as possible. Article 9 of the Treaties thus allowed for the Dominions to associate themselves with the UK's new commitments at a later date if they so wished. Afterwards Article 9 formed the basis of the FO's attempt to define a relationship between Britain's obligations to West Europe and Dominion obligations to Britain. The article, the department asserted, was not a conventional adherence clause which could have applied to any specified country.

> Article 9 . . . is obviously a provision which prevents certain consequences following from the Treaty which would follow automatically if this provision were not there, and it provides that such consequences shall not follow automatically but only if . . . notice is given by certain designated 'Governments'.[24]

This technical rendering was designed to create a definite impression that behind Britain's new Continental commitment lay a reservoir of Commonwealth support, in peacetime held up by the sole UK signature of the Treaty but which, in an emergency, would flood across the Channel through the sluice of Article 9. This determined attempt by the Foreign Office to fit Locarno into a Commonwealth context arose partly from the need to pilot the policy through Parliament, where many MPs strove to appear as good 'imperialists' and were therefore certain to focus on the wedge that had apparently been driven between Britain and her family partners. But it was not just a matter of tactics. The break in the continuity of 'Empire Foreign Policy' had genuinely shocked the Foreign Office into reflections on the actual substance of Commonwealth obligations in a war situation. It was concluded that

> It is impossible to define the nature of this 'duty' (to assist the U.K. in war). It is not a 'duty' existing under international law, nor under any British or municipal law. It seems to be . . . a moral duty.[25]

This righteous conclusion cannot be separated from the general revolution within the world of diplomacy since 1918, whereby moral argumentation had become an essential element in a nation's political armour. In a situation where political leaderships everywhere were hurrying to wrap themselves in the angelic garments of League loyalty, the FO sought to root Dominion commitments in the solid earth of 'moral duty'. It must be stressed that because it was British interests which above all hinged on the preservation of peace, the UK's diplomatic language relied more heavily on ethical nuances than that of any other nation; so that 'Commonwealth equality' and 'collective security' were both part of a moralisation of the British official mind.

The Foreign Office failed to pre-empt the criticisms of those who opposed European involvements. *The Round Table*, almost the official organ of the 'imperialist' wing in Britain, damned the Treaties with faint praise.[26] Tory backbenchers afforded them a rough Parliamentary passage.[27] More disturbing, however, was the stringent opposition that

Dominion leaders privately expressed. Stanley Bruce contemptuously dismissed Locarno as 'merely a gesture to French public opinion', and argued that French security was 'a purely Continental question'.[28] Any extension of the UK role in Europe would, he added, intensify the old Dominion fears of being pulled along in the British wake. 'This would throw us back' Bruce angrily concluded 'to the position we were in in 1914 when the War broke out.'[29] At least Bruce did not seem to doubt that if a 1914 situation were to arise the Dominions would still follow. Smuts went a good deal further and, although now relegated to Opposition, his reputation continued to carry considerable weight in London. Smuts concentrated on what was the most sensitive part of the Locarno arrangements: Eastern Europe. In view of the French connection with the 'successor states' in the East, he held that a guarantee of the Rhine was equivalent to a guarantee of the Volga. He warned Chamberlain

> I am afraid the Dominions will keep out of this Pact and will look upon it as a precedent to disinterest themselves in future more and more in the foreign policy of Great Britain. Thus for the Empire too the Pact will become a new departure.[30]

Smuts's motives here were complex. For one thing, he probably knew very well that it was impossible for any Dominion to 'disinterest themselves' in British foreign policy; the interdependence of trade, finance and strategy was too great for this. In effect, Smuts was telling Chamberlain that, unless British policy was reshaped according to Dominion criticisms, those particular elements which were antithetic to other Commonwealth governments would not be supported. Commonwealth relations had moved into the stage of bluff and counter-bluff. Smuts was also endeavouring to increase his bargaining power when, as he fully expected, he was returned to power in South Africa. By laying claim to a distinct South African foreign policy, he would then be able to contest Hertzog's monopoly of nationalist rhetoric. His objectives in attacking Locarno were therefore very different from those of Amery. Nonetheless, the Dominions Secretary was able to weave Smuts's critique into his plan to undermine Austen Chamberlain. Amery had, in the early stages of Locarno, refrained from intervention because he could not have afforded to instigate open conflict with his Cabinet colleague whilst the departmental reforms in Whitehall were still under consideration. But with the Dominions Office now operating, and emboldened by Bruce and Smuts, he put a warning shot across the Foreign Secretary's bows

> I must confess to you that I have acquiesced so far as I have a good deal because I have thought that in the end what we shall commit

ourselves and the Empire to is something so remote and contingent that we are not likely in fact ever to be called upon to intervene, and that the Pact will consequently, from the imperial point of view, serve as a warning rather than create the kind of danger Bruce fears.[31]

Chamberlain did not take any of these criticisms lightly. He recognised that diplomatic and strategic cooperation in the Empire hinged on a common view of priorities. This meant, in his opinion, that the Dominions had to be brought along the same weary road that he had travelled, until they arrived at the conclusion that the key to peace lay in French public opinion. Bruce's disparagement of any move to appease Poincareism in France betrayed a fundamental misunderstanding of the linkages in modern European politics, and Chamberlain sought for effective means of persuasion. He suggested to Amery, for example, that Lord Cecil,[32] an old friend of Smuts who had once acted as South African Delegate to the League Assembly, might be used as an intermediary with the Opposition leader. Amery shuffled off this suggestion by arguing that Cecil's temperament made him unsuitable – he was 'an ingrained sentimentalist whilst Smuts's own sentimentalism is more in the nature of a luxury emotion which he never allows to interfere with his practical conclusions'.[33] Certainly the Dominions Secretary did not attempt to use his own influence with Dominion leaders to 'sell' Locarno. It is safe to assume that he enjoyed seeing Chamberlain under Dominion fire for his European ways, for Amery never shunned from using Commonwealth ammunition in the bureaucratic fracas at home. In fact he now saw an opportunity to assert the existence of a Dominions Office, and the Commonwealth factor in policy-making that it represented, by demanding that the coming Imperial Conference should clarify the exact nature of imperial obligations in a European war.

The Foreign Office's reaction to Amery's new move is interesting because it reflects that department's attitude to both the Dominions Office and the Dominions. First of all, however, it is important to stress that ever since 1916 the FO had feared losing its authority in the making of foreign policy. Lloyd George had used his own inner advisors as decision-makers on international issues. Baldwin had returned to the FO something of its old powers, but the department remained very sensitive on questions of responsibility. The Commonwealth aspect of Locarno touched these raw bureaucratic nerves because it held out the prospects of the Dominions, or Amery acting as their self-proclaimed proxy, demanding a sustained role in the policy process. Thus, although the FO was engaged privately on examining the character of Commonwealth obligations, it was not prepared to broaden the discussion of this at a Conference. The Dominions Office was therefore tersely informed that there was no value in further dialectical incursions into the niceties entailed by adhesion or non-adhesion of the Dominions to the Pact. It would, in fact, we feel, be a capital error to dogmatise on so highly speculative and controversial an issue. . . . If a threat to peace under the treaty arises, the Dominions will *all* as a matter of course be consulted. But *our* actions under the Locarno Treaty will not – indeed cannot – be dependent on the unanimous imprimatur of all the Dominions. We shall act as the British Parliament of the day decides; in short it will be the Locarno procedure over again; the Dominions will follow as their Parliaments decide. Is not this the common-sense of the matter.[34]

In other words the Foreign Office wanted to get on with running foreign policy without other Commonwealth Governments or Whitehall departments interfering. Their position here was strengthened by Hertzog's support of Chamberlain's policy. At first sight this support appears odd. Hertzog was more bitterly anti-French than Smuts, and he might have taken the opportunity to have attacked the British obsession with meddling in European power-politics. But this temptation was offset by the fact that Britain's unilateral negotiation at Locarno could rather be applauded as a final acceptance that 'Empire foreign policy' no longer existed. Hertzog therefore congratulated the UK government on choosing policies according to its own needs, without seeking to impose them on Commonwealth partners.[35] The unusual sight of a South African Nationalist leader warmly approving a British Conservative government made it difficult for Amery to sustain his anti-Locarno tactics. The Dominions Secretary continued to need the Foreign Secretary's cooperation on a number of other questions;[36] whilst moderation was made even more necessary by the almost universal approbation which crystallised around Locarno once it appeared that Europe had indeed been stabilised on a basis of interlocking guarantees. To stand out against this seemed to be to stand against the deepest needs of the time. Amery therefore somewhat equivocally assured Chamberlain

> I am quite sure that we shall be able to get over the difficult years during which we have no definitely recognised system of shaping our Empire foreign policy, if the policy of the British Government is such as justifies itself on merits to the Dominions. That certainly has been the case with Locarno. . . .[37]

It was the Locarno situation, indeed, which preoccupied the UK in their timing of the Imperial Conference in late 1926. Austen Chamberlain wanted to carry out his parliamentary promise to put the Treaties before the other Empire Governments before ratification;[38] Bruce had insisted that any postponement of the Conference until 1927 would be used as evidence that the UK did not take foreign policy consultation seriously;[39] whilst the Dominions Office wanted an early Conference to head off potentially divisive Locarno debates in South Africa and Canada.[40] If, therefore, the 1926 Conference was later to be famous for its constitutional conclusions enshrined in the Balfour Report, it can only be properly understood against this background of concern with the divergent foreign policy perspectives of Commonwealth partners.

4 The Balfour Report and Constitutional Change 1926–1930

The story of the Balfour Report has frequently been told. Indeed, a mini-controversy has taken place as to who can be credited with its achievement; Hertzog as the man who initially raised the matter of a constitutional definition before and during the Imperial Conference of 1926, Mackenzie King as the mediator who brought the South Africans and British together, and Balfour[1] as the draftsman of the document, have all found their champions.[2] A more recent work has contended that it was above all the Irish Free State delegates, especially O'Higgins,[3] who ensured that Hertzog's original demand was heeded, even when the old Boer General was inclined to forget about it.[4] But, whoever can properly claim the parentage of the 1926 declaration, it is clear that the relationship was of a foster nature, for there was nothing original in any of the statements contained within it. As Duncan Hall noted some time ago, the standard phrases such as 'autonomous nations', 'continuous consultation' and 'an adequate voice in foreign policy', had been in circulation since 1911.[5] Indeed, there were some who felt that by 1926 the time had come to reverse, rather than commence, the implementation of equality. Lord Selborne[6] forwarded to Amery a South African loyalist petition condemning the 'colossal blunder' of equal status, and he expressed the hope that Baldwin:

> will be very cautious and have before his mind the loyal subjects of the King who will be . . . hanging on his lips – This letter shows how thoroughly they now realise the disastrous consequences of Lloyd George throwing off pregnant phrases without attempting to think out the implications.[7]

Amery assured Selborne that the UK had no intention of taking any constitutional initiatives at the forthcoming Conference. Although the Colonial Secretary certainly did, in a general way, look forward to some constitutional declaration on Commonwealth relations, there does not seem to be any good evidence that the British Delegation approached the Conference with a solid plan of 'settlement'. Rather, as Wigley points out,[8] the British prepared for the Conference in a defensive fashion, thinking of ways to meet the Dominions on minor matters (such as the appointment of Dominion consuls abroad) in order to fend off any penetration of sensitive constitutional areas. In fact most of the Dominion leaders were in no position in 1926 to lead a constitutional campaign. The Irish Free State leaders, hardly recovered from a civil war, could only hope to assist some other Dominion whose leverage within the Commonwealth was more developed. They were disappointed if they thought that Mackenzie King would play a dissident role. The Canadian premier had only just emerged from his dispute with Lord Byng,[9] and having won a decisive parliamentary majority by using slogans of constitutional 'freedom' he was too astute not to realise that his interest now lay in quietness and stability. Mackenzie King remained deeply suspicious of the British and was quite prepared to reap the benefits of a middleman position in Commonwealth disputes, but he was not prepared to take any initiatives himself. The only Dominion Prime Minister, in fact, who was determined to test the volatility of the constitutional question at the Conference was Hertzog of South Africa.

Since 1924 Hertzog's ascendancy had rested on an uneasy Pact between the Nationalists (overwhelmingly Afrikaner) and Labour (largely English), and it was not long after the Pact had entered office that the fragilities of this relationship became plain. Hertzog's only hope of limiting the threatened fragmentation was to settle the constitutional question which had accentuated Nationalist–Labour differences. But in seeking to take up the middle ground there was a danger that he would appear to be adopting positions long held by Smuts. Hertzog's answer to this dilemma was on the one hand to step up the old accusations that Smuts had aimed at a British 'superstate' whilst on the other establishing the case that a co-equal Commonwealth was compatible with South African independence. In two key speeches before the Imperial Conference in the Assembly during April 1926 and at Stellenbosch in May Hertzog pushed this line, attacking Smuts for questioning South Africa's right of secession and yet contending that within the Commonwealth South Africa was 'completely independent . . . just as free as England itself'.[10] Meanwhile, he attempted to persuade Amery that a constitutional settlement would permanently stabilise Commonwealth politics. He told the Colonial Secretary:

> In order to let you see how much we shall achieve if these ideas (of constitutional progress) are given effect to, allow me to mention a small incident which took place the day after my Stellenbosch speech. A colleague of mine in the Cabinet, a man of great influence with those in the country whom General Smuts in the past has so often stamped as secessionists and rebels, came up to me enthusiastically saying 'General, if the people could only be made to understand what our

status is – such as you explained it at Stellenbosch – you will not hear of secession again!' The day after, his words were repeated to me by another colleague from the same province. Only this morning, upon being shown Smuts' memo [of 1921] and your approval of it, he exclaimed 'Then why don't they say so openly. All disagreements would at once vanish.'[11]

Thus Hertzog came to London hoping to obtain a constitutional agreement but determined to seek it with a conciliatory mildness which would avoid any public confrontation between Commonwealth states-men likely to polarise, rather than unify, the South African domestic scene.

Given the fact that Hertzog was willing to work within a Commonwealth framework, it is not surprising that the Conference debates failed to divide aggressive 'radicals' against stubborn 'con-servatives'. Hertzog put his case in its most moderate form, basing his argument on the Smuts memorandum of 1921 and repeatedly stressing that he wanted nothing more than a political recognition of what in fact already existed – nothing more, indeed, than what 'responsible Englishmen' had themselves admitted ever since 1917.[12] He focused his requests, moreover, not on the delicate matter of the Crown's in-divisibility, but on the status of the Dominions within international affairs. Hertzog's position was much stronger than Smuts's at the earlier Conference simply because the old conservative bloc of 1921 had broken up. For Australia, Bruce did not have Hughes's pugnaciousness even though his instincts were against change; for Canada, Mackenzie King was not likely to tarnish his new 'nationalist' image by opposing the South Africans; whilst the presence of the Irish Free State delegates, largely silent and hesitant though they were, altered the centre of political gravity. Finally, in explaining the absence of ideological conflict at the Conference, it is necessary to stress the softening, even disintegrative, effects of power on established leaderships. O'Higgins commented, for example, that Hertzog showed signs of being very tired and 'whilst a very decent, likeable kind of man, has not been a success – he talks a lot and none too clearly', whilst he felt that since 1923 Mackenzie King had 'gone fat and American and self-complacent'.[13]

The British response to Hertzog's demands were mixed but rarely hostile. Amery, although careful to conceal his motives, seized on it as an opportunity to legitimise Commonwealth even in the eyes of 'leftist' parties in the Dominions; he had, in short, accepted Hertzog's private rationale of the situation in full.[14] Of the other British Ministers on the inside of the Conference, the most concerned was Austen Chamberlain. Because Hertzog had defined Dominion autonomy in terms of treaty-making, the attendance of international discussions and political representation abroad, it was the Foreign Office alone which felt its position threatened. This, coupled with a dose of traditional metropolitan arrogance towards 'colonials', was reflected in the Foreign Secretary's initial reaction

> We have never endeavoured to conduct our domestic negotiations with Irishmen, miners, transport-workers or any other section of the community in plenary meetings of the Cabinet.[15]

This remark indicates that Chamberlain's concern was not with a loosening of legal ties but with what he perceived as an awkward and unwarranted intrusion into the making of British policy. Indeed, to say that the Foreign Secretary feared that Dominion leaders were trying to get *into* imperial decision-making rather than to get *out* of it would not be a mere cynical aside. His main criticism of Hertzog's suggestions, for example, was that the Locarno negotiations would have been impossible if Dominion attendance had been allowed to complicate the talks and divide the British position.[16] Linked to this, his underlying anxiety was not what Hertzog might do in South Africa with a declaration of equality, but that Amery might use it to sharpen his claims to a greater influence in Whitehall. There was a good deal of substance to this concern. The Dominions Secretary had assured Chamberlain that a constitutional agreement would have no implications for the Commonwealth's role as a single unit in international affairs, and that 'anything in the nature of a formal communication to individual foreign powers, or to foreign powers generally' must be studiously avoided;[17] but meanwhile, behind Chamberlain's back, he was privately canvassing Dominion Prime Ministers to permit their High Commissioners to be circulated with UK State Papers.[18] Confident of controlling the High Commissioners, Amery saw this as a way of driving his own wedge into the traditional prerogatives of the Foreign Office. Chamberlain, sensing that his own authority was under threat, exploded to his Cabinet colleague

> You have committed me without consultation and I must submit but I respectfully and very decidedly protest against your assumption that you had a right to take action so intimately affecting me without consulting me; and I record my opinion . . . that you have made a great mistake.[19]

Chamberlain's animus, then, was not directed at Hertzog's public claims but at Amery's private machinations. He was careful to involve himself in the drafting processes of the Conference. The ebb and flow of these debates cannot be treated at length, but they are best described as a delicate compromise in which the participants worked hard at meeting each other's needs. Mackenzie King certainly played a large part in formulating the terms of the consensus, although to picture him as a 'broker' wrongly implies a polarity between Hertzog and the Irish on the one side, and the British on the other. In the end the Conference issued a statement emphasising the themes of autonomy and equality and decided on recommendations for consular appointments, the status of Governor-Generals (they were in future to be the representatives of the monarchy, not of the British Government) and treaty procedures. Chamberlain was able to enthuse to Hankey

> Between me and you we have I hope wiped out the prejudice against the words 'British Empire' by removing the misapprehensions as to its import which existed in the minds of Hertzog and O'Higgins. Keep British Empire therefore everywhere where you can and get rid of 'British Commonwealth of Nations', which is not a term of art.[20]

What stands out from a reading of the Conference material is not the clash of different constitutional or political conceptions of Commonwealth, but precisely this general atmosphere of liberated camaraderie among the various delegations. Even the Free Staters, according to one Irish historian, were affected by a gathering of 'unusual warmth and friendliness'.[21] And when, years later, de Valera seemed to move to the brink of a Republic, DO officials remained convinced that had he, like Hertzog, been present in 1926 and participated in its curious spirit of reunion, he would never have taken the secessionist route to power.[22] The great increase in the number of social events compared with previous Commonwealth meetings was one index of this political relaxation.[23] Amery later recalled the long series of intimate dinner parties which distinguished 1926, and particularly one reclusive weekend with Mackenzie King 'when Baldwin was at his best, walking us through the beech woods in their autumn glory'.[24] Amery, even more than Chamberlain, was convinced that the Conference marked a new departure in Empire relations. He believed that Balfour's formulation had laid to rest the old fears of a British superstate which had long haunted the colonial mind, and that the way was open to a systematic approach to imperial cooperation. Above all, Amery was obsessed with the thought that historic grievances had been liquidated. Just as the 1921 Treaty had pacified the tribal hatreds of Ireland, so now the Boer War had been obliterated from the South African mind. He sought to symbolise this occurrence by restoring to Hertzog, amid the reconciling pleasures of a Lord Mayoral dinner, President Kruger's travelling wagon.[25] He wrote to the South African Prime Minister and ex-rebel of 1914:

> After all as between ourselves we can afford to talk with pride and mutual respect of past encounters but we do not need to cherish

trophies of those in which one of us happened to be successful over the other.[26]

This is an evocative example of the appeasing psychology of the British leadership after 1918.[27] Amery's belief that the concentration camp image of the Boer War could be expunged from the Afrikaner memory and replaced by folk-recollections of an amiable fracas, a public-school encounter on the cricket pitch ending with mutual hurrahs and back-slapping, must rank as one of the more naive optimisms of his time. But it does reflect the widely felt sense that modern Britain had to disassociate herself from the repugnant necessities of nineteenth-century expansion and reformulate her international leadership in terms of equity and the peaceful resolution of disputes. The same yearning was evident in Amery's claim to have converted Hertzog during a Conference interlude to a hearty acceptance of Commonwealth membership by proving by means of the *Encyclopaedia Brittanica* that the word 'Empire' connoted not a 'centralised authority' but a 'complex political mechanism'.[28] Even the stolid Cabinet Secretary, Hankey, was not immune to the sense of imperial reaffirmation. 'There is always some Dominion that gives trouble', he noted confidently after the various delegations had gone home, 'but it is hardly ever the same one twice running.'[29]

The difficulty with the 1926 Conference, therefore, is not in defining the origins and character of the Balfour Report, but in explaining the reconciling psychology which lay behind it and governed the proceedings as a whole. The immediate factor here appears not to have been internal to the Commonwealth association at all, but lies in the wider context of Britain's international policies. Locarno, by easing tensions in Europe, had also eased tensions within the Empire because, for the first time since 1911, an Imperial Conference was taking place at a time when British foreign policy did not carry with it the immediate threat of involvement in a European conflict. It was the sense of relief as the War period finally seemed to have ended which explains the quality of the 1926 Imperial Conference. The 'Locarno spring', indeed, revived millenarial impulses which had been bred out of the 1914–18 experience but subsequently repressed by the continuation of a crisis mood in Europe. League internationalism was the chief of these, but among them also was the prospect of a reorganised and coordinated Commonwealth. 'We believe that there is a real though undefined unity of purpose [in the Empire]', the *Round Table* editorialised in the ethereal cadences of the time, 'and that the forces animating it are so powerful that no Dominion Government can ignore them.'[30] The Balfour Report, like the Kellogg Pact, can only be understood in this context of political romanticism, a romanticism mortgaged to the continuance of Continental stability and the prevention of war.

As Selborne had warned Amery earlier, however, it was impossible to 'fling off pregnant phrases' at an Imperial Conference without granting hostages to the changing fortunes of Dominion domestic politics. Inevitably the Balfour Report was quickly absorbed into the party political conflict in South Africa and Canada, and given a shape and dynamic not originally contemplated in London. Thus Hertzog returned home from England flourishing Balfour's formula as proof that South Africa was at last 'free and independent'.[31] Smuts, increasingly the captive of the English-speaking rump of the South Africa Party, felt compelled to disrupt the deal between the British government and Hertzog by denouncing the document as an 'adroit way of deceiving the *back-veldt* into believing that they had gained their independence when in reality their status remained unaltered'.[32] Thus before long Bede Clifford, the UK representative in South Africa after 1928,[33] was reporting to Amery that the Conference statements, far from settling anything, had only served to revive what had been the dying embers of antagonism between the two white tribes of South Africa.[34] Similarly, in Canada, R. B. Bennett,[35] leader of the Conservative opposition, responded to Mackenzie King's projection of the declaration as a 'nationalist achievement' by beating the loyalist drum and asserting the inviolability of the British North America Act.[36] British officials in fact resented these aggressive statements of the conservative case because they prevented the general stabilisation of Anglo–Dominion relations which was a precondition of imperial cooperation. Smuts and Bennett, whose political interests lay in unsettling the governing parties, were a liability in this crucial respect. Thus the UK High Commissioner in Ottawa, for example, finally took Bennett aside and attempted to throw a cold douche on his loyalist zeal. He stated

> it was abundantly evident that there was no pretence or *arriere pensee* about Great Britain's action in joining the declaration of 1926. It was surely clear that the existence of overriding powers, which was freely admitted and discussed in the Inter-Imperial Relations Committee, did not mean their exercise; and if Canada wished for modification of the British North America Act, it seemed very unlikely, as things are, that the British Parliament would refuse.[37]

But if British officials wished to curtail conservative extremism, they were just as determined to 'head off' radical interpretations of what had taken place. But what did the UK consider vital and what expendable in the field of constitutional change? Good evidence on this point is provided by an episode immediately after the Conference. An article appeared in *The Sunday Times* stating that, because Empire Governments were now co-equal, the UK Cabinet could neither in fact nor theory be held to function as a mechanism by which advice was transferred from the Dominion Governments to the King, and that direct transmission of advice from the Dominion governments to the person of the monarch logically implied recognition of a separate 'Kingdom' in each part of the Commonwealth.[38] But by undermining the indivisibility of the Crown, this argument automatically threatened the undivided character of statehood within the Commonwealth association and with it the root principle that 'When the King is at war, the Empire is at war.' Amery was particularly concerned because the article's author, Sir Sydney Low,[39] was about to publish a new edition of his textbook, *The Governance of England*. The Dominions Secretary, acting quickly to prevent error crystallising into academic orthodoxy, remonstrated to Low

> The one fatal heresy to guard against is the idea that there are many Crowns and that the King is King in different parts of the Empire in different senses.[40]

Low's retort, however, was not comforting. He commented

> I gather that there is no intention to make any innovation either in practice or theory. I had derived a somewhat different impression from the Report; and so apparently have others, if I may judge from observations made in the Canadian Parliament, and elsewhere. It looked as if it were contemplated that the present conception of an Empire–Realm under the Crown should pass to that of an alliance of separate nation-states or Kingdoms. General Hertzog seems to convey the same impression when he says 'All that remained was a free alliance of England and the six Dominions . . . forming their own League of nations.'[41]

Low's distinction between an Empire–Realm and a free alliance was precisely the point at issue. The one indicated a state-unit which, however devolved its peacetime government may be, always acted indivisibly in a crisis; the other indicated at least the right of members to opt out of emergency measures. Much of the subtle confusion in Commonwealth thinking, indeed, arose from the fact that what the British might regard as an acceptable mode of operation in peacetime would not be so acceptable in wartime.

Amery responded to this problem by attempting to balance a municipalised sovereignty against the assumption of indivisible statehood. He did this by interpreting sovereignty as the legislative competence of Dominion Parliaments, and indivisible statehood as the single monarch who embraced all these local jurisdictions within his own constitutional authority. This strategy had, suggestively, formed in his mind during the Locarno episode. His idea here was that, although the

Dominions were not party to the specific European obligations involved, they could still, when a crisis came, be held to be bound to act with Britain by virtue of a general underlying obligation based on common allegiance to the Throne. 'What emerges generally', Amery had written after the Locarno debate had subsided, 'is the importance in these matters of laying stress on His Majesty as the High Contracting Party.'[42] Amery ever afterwards spoke of the Crown with a mystical reverence,[43] whilst the Lord Chancellor (Lord Sankey) in Ramsay MacDonald's second administration felt drawn to remark that

> At the present moment the Crown is the last surviving link and it is one of the odd things of history that after the power has been diminishing through the generations from being an absolute to a constitutional monarchy, he should become the most important factor in keeping things together.[44]

The peculiar resilience of the Crown in twentieth-century British politics is partly attributable to the role it played in this restructuring and maintenance of imperial relations. After 1926 British politicians and officials were, on the whole, prepared to witness the unravelling of parliamentary anachronisms on which Westminster authority had come to be based (such as the repugnancy, reservation and disallowance of Dominion legislation) providing that no Dominion trespassed on the critical area of the single Kingship. No Dominion did so until de Valera after 1932, and then both economic and political sanctions were not long in coming.[45] On this basis of a straight 'swap' – devolved parliamentary sovereignties for a residual undivided monarchy – constitutional reform proceeded in an orderly manner between the Balfour declaration and the 1931 Statute of Westminster. Even the UK Law Officers found it relatively easy to provide a rationale for the limitation of Westminster authority which appeared to fit neatly with the pragmatic continuity of English legal traditions. Risley[46] thus stated that

> English institutions formed the model on which the Colonies have developed – There was no place in the Constitution of England for anything equivalent to the power of reservation. If there had been it might well have been argued that it extended to Colonial legislatures as they came into being – But it seems difficult to maintain that the prerogative of disallowance in its application to the Colonies contained within itself a sort of 'half-way' procedure unknown to the English Constitution.[47]

There were naturally practical problems involved in the abolition of long-standing parliamentary devices such as disallowance because various interests had become encrusted around them. UK shipping interests feared that the Dominions, hitherto bound by the Merchant Shipping Law of 1894, might henceforth legislate for lower mercantile standards, undercut their UK rivals and yet still claim the international goodwill attaching to the category of 'British ship'.[48] City interests and the Treasury were opposed to the continued admission of Dominion stocks to the London Exchange on a favourable basis if the British Parliament no longer had the power to reserve Dominion legislation which affected financial values, a concern given real point by the defaulting policies of the Lang government in New South Wales.[49] Indeed, a formidable coalition including J. M. Keynes, the *Investor's Chronicle* and *The Times* had for some time expressed the opinion that Australia and Canada had received larger amounts of credit through the mechanism of the Colonial Stocks Act of 1900 than their small populations warranted.[50] Finally, the War Office was determined to avoid a situation where the discipline of British troops in the Dominions did not come under Westminster jurisdiction because, if India ever did become a Dominion, large numbers of Imperial forces in a crucial theatre might be affected.[51] But the dynamic of political compromise was too strong for legal or even financial considerations to preclude solutions. On the question of Dominion stocks, for example, an agreement was reached at the 1929 Conference on the Operation of Dominion Legislation whereby the power of reservation vested in the Westminster Parliament should continue in relation to legislation which affected equity values.[52] This did not permanently resolve the problem and it recurred at regular intervals later, but broadly none of the Commonwealth partners were prepared to allow side issues to detract from the overall picture of a steady move towards a new constitutional and political equilibrium. Indeed, the idea of a single piece of imperial legislation enacting all the legal changes decided at the 1929 Constitutional Conference had formed in Amery's mind even before that meeting had assembled. 'In some ways I am rather attracted by the ambitious conception of a comprehensive releasing Statute of Westminster', Amery minuted, 'There are great possibilities in this.'[53]

The process of constitutional change is best seen, therefore, as a political bargain between the British Government on the one hand, and the South African, Canadian and Irish Free State Governments on the other. The British Government was prepared to dismember Westminster's imperial functions so that Mackenzie King, Hertzog and Cosgrave[54] could appease their nationalist supporters; the Dominion leaders were prepared to equivocate on the indivisibility of the Crown so that the UK could go on playing the Empire card in its international policies. This deal was implicit in the 1929 Constitutional Conference. The key concession that the UK delegation extracted from these talks took the form of a declaratory convention that none of the Empire

Parliaments would legislate on the Royal Succession without the consent of the others. Not everyone, however, viewed the risks involved in these adjustments with equanimity. Their most prestigious critic was none other than George V who, far from seeing the Succession clause as a welcome guarantee, disliked the monarchy being used as a bargaining counter. Ramsay MacDonald, who had succeeded Baldwin as Prime Minister in May 1929, had a difficult task obtaining royal approval. 'He [the King] has the assurance of the Law Officers', the Prime Minister stated, 'that the arrangement may be accepted as being satisfactory to the Empire whilst at the same time allaying and defeating tendencies which, unless headed off, might become seriously disruptive.'[55] George V, being a simple and honest character, had a healthy suspicion of the direction in which political tactics led. 'I cannot look into the future', he replied, 'without feelings of no little anxiety as to the constitutional unity of the Empire.'[56] But George V could not ultimately obstruct politicians and officials driven by a desire to insulate the Commonwealth association from the volatility of party politics in divided colonial societies such as South Africa.

In 1929, however, nobody in Whitehall yet appreciated just how far it was necessary to go in order to attain such stabilisation. They soon found that whenever one Government reached an agreement with Britain, its parliamentary opposition was bound to attack its terms as detrimental to the electorate's interests. This meant that in 1929, even more vigorously than in 1926, the oppositions in South Africa and Canada, both of which happened to be conservative on status questions, tried to disrupt the balances achieved at the Conference. Smuts did this by attempting to upset the quiet passage of the Conference Report through the South African Assembly, arguing that under the Succession clause Hertzog had *de facto* accepted the illegality of secession.[57] Hertzog certainly wanted the British to believe this to be true; but he equally certainly did not want his more fervently nationalist supporters to observe that he had broken with the Kruger traditions of the party. The Assembly debate, as Smuts had intended, erupted in dispute

> Mr Havenga said that if General Smuts' view was correct it would only be the beginning of secession and whilst the Nationalists were loudly cheering, General Hertzog looked towards General Smuts and said 'If you are right, then the struggle will now begin.'[58]

But if Hertzog had thus to adopt a public mask of radical anit-imperialism, in private he assured the Political Secretary to the British High Commission, Houston-Boswall,[59] that his response had been a tactical necessity induced by Smut's irresponsible and self-interested behaviour.[60] The most diverse of political personalities, indeed, were brought together in their disapproval of Smut's intervention. Houston-Boswall reported

> Duncan[61] felt that he ought never to go away and leave Smuts alone again for he was in Swaziland when it all happened! The Prime Minister [Hertzog] said what a pity it all was as he had been quite sure of securing the assent of Parliament to the Report with which . . . even the Irish Free State were content.[62]

The Political Secretary expressed concern that Smuts's 'temerity in resuscitating the dead dog of secession' might prevent Hertzog being cooperative at the 1930 Imperial Conference,[63] and Hankey quickly worked himself into a panic that Hertzog would use the secessionist weapon to break up the imperial gathering.[64]

These short-term obsessions were to subside, but such episodes were beginning to effect a basic reorientation of British attitudes to constitutional issues which went beyond the limited tactical compromises of 1926 and 1929. Huston-Boswall, for example, included in his despatch on the Smuts incident a long-range view of how Anglo–South African relations should develop. His key recommendation was that no constitutional limits should be applied to South African governments. The whole tangled problem of 'rights' which had for so long obstructed understanding between London and Pretoria should be thrown overboard. This view was explicitly based on the assumption that Smuts's South Africa Party (with its old-fashioned loyalism, its associations with Jewish big business on the Rand, its alleged liberalism on the native issue) was a spent force. Instead the UK should seek an alliance with the Nationalists, an understanding which could evoke support not only tacitly from its leadership but from its factions too. This meant conceding on both the secession and the neutrality questions. Only such a surgical act could cut Commonwealth membership out of the party political spiral in South Africa. Houston-Boswall recorded approvingly an argument put to him by Hertzog's recent (and, it was rumoured, anti-British) appointment to the Department of External Affairs, H. Bodenstein.[65]

> He said that he [Bodenstein] was a lifelong Republican but had been converted by the Imperial Conference of 1926. Many of his friends were still Republicans and like all South Africans enjoyed political discussions and argument. He had found that the best way to meet them was to quote Bonar Law's pronouncement to the effect that any member of the Commonwealth was at liberty to secede therefrom if it wished to do so. That being admitted, it was possible to argue dispassionately the pros and cons for remaining within the Empire. But, he said, if you start by assuring the Republican that he would

always have to remain a subject of the King, then calm discussion becomes impossible.[66]

There was a compelling psychological logic to this contention. By taking the imperial factor out of South African politics and reducing the debate to a scientific analysis of costs and benefits it would become clear that the British connection was a net asset. Nor was Houston-Boswall the only British official to be pressing this point on his London superiors. Just as he was recognising the political strengths of Hertzogite nationalism, Peters[67] (the Board of Trade representative in Dublin) was reporting the steady progress of de Valera's Fianna Fail in Irish Free State politics. He remarked to Batterbee, recently promoted to Assistant Under-Secretary of State in the Dominions Office:

I am inclined to think that a very clear statement of the right of the Irish Free State to secede if it so wishes would bring the Fianna Fail up against a rather difficult problem. The fact that the Cattle Traders Association should have passed a resolution supporting the idea of Empire Free Trade is significant in the sense that it shows that the farmers, on whose support the Fianna Fail party at present largely depends, may have strong views on the question of cutting loose from the Empire.[68]

Robert Hadow,[69] an advisor on the British High Commission staff in Ottawa, also pressed on the Dominions Office that apparently 'radical' statements by Liberals and other anti-Conservatives represented an instinctive antagonism to Bennett and his Ontario clique rather than any considered rejection of the British connection.[70] Government and opposition antics on the constitution, he pointed out, were determined by political, not ideological, considerations and that, in the end, the guarantee of that connection lay in the attitude of the French population of Quebec 'who cling to the right of appeal to the UK Parliament and to the Privy Council as to the best bulwark of their special privileges'.[71] Hadow was not as clear-cut as Houston-Boswall or Peters in his advice, but the general implication was clear: constitutional interpretations of Commonwealth not only obscured the essentially political character of that association, but could (because it was Quebec, not Ontario, which ultimately necessitated the continued operation of the British North America Act) make friends out to be enemies and enemies to be friends.

By 1930, then, Whitehall was being insistently advised by its overseas representatives to 'de-constitutionalise' the Commonwealth. This advice, however, was not digested whole. If all legal and constitutional connections were cut, Commonwealth membership might indeed find itself less of a target for aspiring Dominion politicians, but what would the *substance* of membership then actually amount to? After all, the ultimate objective for UK officials was not to keep Hertzog from a Republic but to ensure that in another war South African resources would be part of a 'Commonwealth effort'. Fron London's larger perspective it was harder to give up the Smuts ghost to a Hertzogite future, especially when the former had just returned from a North American lecture tour in which he had extolled Commonwealth reorganisation and the establishment of the League of Nations as the major post-war achievements in world politics. 'The main effect (of Smuts's visit) was . . . to revive the faith of Canada', Clark,[72] the new British High Commissioner in Ottawa, told Lord Passfield, who had been appointed Dominions Secretary in the Labour government of 1929, 'a faith which has undoubtedly been shaken of late by the persistent tales of hardship and difficulty'.[73] However flexible Hertzog might prove to be, it was difficult to imagine him ever uttering such welcome sentiments. Houston-Boswall's advice, in fact, credited the Hertzog leadership with an ability to control his anti-British right wing which South African history hardly justified. Whitehall's hesitations were reinforced during 1930 as the international atmosphere worsened and the economic, diplomatic and defence divergences within the Commonwealth became more pronounced. The DO, although its own instinct was to opt for stable relations regardless of the repercussions in such concrete areas of policy as defence, could never move far ahead of the Whitehall consensus. Only the shock of the Irish crisis after 1932 was to push the DO into articulating a new approach to Commonwealth. In 1930 Batterbee sought to reject Smuts's conservative interpretation of the Succession clause in the 1929 Report, without daring to move towards any acceptance of secession as a legal possibility. 'Whether secession would be a rightful act', he stated, 'depends upon other factors and [the Report] leaves those factors unaffected.'[74]

   Whatever the limits to change, however, Whitehall had learnt that the constitutional debate was merely a front for the shifting alignments of Dominion domestic politics. This meant that the 1926 idea of a 'settlement' was illusory. The most that could be achieved in a situation where the political struggle for power, not ideological consistency, prevailed was a working ambiguity. The idea of 'Dominion status' became less relevant to the actual management of Commonwealth relations, and the DO was henceforth to be irritated by the work of such constitutional scholars as Arthur Berriedale Keith[75] who wrote endless tomes of legal paraphernalia. The politics of constitutionalism in the 1920s became not a confrontation but a stately minuet in which the various Governments sought to effect polite compromises which would allow each to meet its own particular needs. It was only where constitutional reform seemed to threaten the Empire's potential unity in war, as it clearly did whenever a Dominion leader tweaked the secessionist nerve in the British official mind, that the UK sprang to the defence of what it perceived as a fundamental interest. As the inter-war period progressed it was the unity of attitudes on international issues, and the preservation of a 'British dimension' in international affairs generally, which preoccupied UK departments concerned with the Dominions.

5 The Problem of Diplomatic Unity

The thrust of Dominion nationalism in the 1920s was not a crude movement towards secession but an attempt to manoeuvre into a position where commitments to assist the UK in diplomatic and military crises became optional rather than obligatory. Hertzog and Mackenzie King could have secured this objective by laying formal claim to rights of neutrality in a future war. But although such claims were sometimes made on the political platform, especially by the former, neither did so in official discussions or at an Imperial Conference. Both were too conscious of the relationship between the Commonwealth association and their own internal political stability, a relationship largely to be explained in terms of large English populations, to adopt such a radical separatism. For Britain, too, the chief significance of Commonwealth relations lay in its international dimension. Beneath all the verbiage of Whitehall discussions lay the fundamental concern that Dominion assistance in war should be protected from erosion, whatever else might be conceded to 'modern times'. The UK could have countered the political implications of constitutional change by an outright rejection of those neutralist and secessionist principles so often culled by Dominion politicians from the Balfourian mixture. Such action, however, would only generate a politics of confrontation which the British officials were determined to avoid.

Even before the 1926 Imperial Conference Amery had been thinking of ways to graft the Dominions into the policy-making process. The establishment of the DO alone was not enough to ensure that British and Dominion policies were kept in line with each other. Understaffed from the beginning, the DO could only deal with issues which had already reached the highest government levels and where preconceptions had already formed. What was required were subsidiary channels of liaison which could ensure coordination of views before any problem took on the proportions of a critical 'issue'; and, in addition, some means of controlling the sort of information which was being pumped into the decision-making bureaucracies in the Dominion capitals. Amery saw the Dominion High Commissioners as potentially playing a vital role in this process, and immediately after the formation of the Dominions Office he had instituted a weekly session at which the Dominions

68

Secretary was 'at home' for the High Commissioners to call and receive a progress report on British policy-making.[1] Chamberlain, too, saw the necessity for such innovations. In 1924 he had cooperated with Bruce in establishing an Australian junior liaison officer, Richard Casey,[2] within the Whitehall system, with ready access to the papers and personnel of both the Foreign and Colonial Offices.[3] He wrote to Lord Stonehaven,[4] Governor-General of Australia, in May 1926:

> I am glad you have told Bruce something of my ideas of imperial reorganisation in London. They may or may not be acceptable to him, but what I am anxious that the Dominion Ministers should realise is that, if they are not in their own opinion *sufficiently consulted* on foreign affairs, it is not the result of unwillingness or carelessness on our part, but is due to the fact that we have not at present in existence a machinery for this purpose capable of working in the conditions which prevail in international affairs. All Parliamentary Governments are faced with the same difficulty. How can they adjust parliamentary control to the need for rapid and sometimes instantaneous decision?[5]

Like Amery, Chamberlain saw the High Commissioners as a basis for this machinery, and they conspired together on how to manoeuvre the High Commissioners 'into the position of being able to deal with us on matters of common imperial concern with the kind of full knowledge that Casey has possessed, but with the authority of their senior position'.[6] But the two Ministers were confronted with considerable opposition to their plans.

First of all, a majority of the British Cabinet were unwilling to accept innovation. Involving Dominion personnel in the policy-making process held out unpleasant possibilities of Irish or South African filibustering, disrupting executive action as Parnell had disrupted parliamentary business in the 1880s. The scheme was thus voted down, although Baldwin encouraged Amery and Chamberlain to consider the proposal merely 'adjourned'.[7] Secondly, there was mutual rivalry and suspicion between the Foreign and Dominions Secretaries. They differed as to the conception of inter-imperial liaison. Chamberlain saw it more in limited terms of the UK consulting the Dominions but retaining unilateral discretion in determining what form 'Empire Foreign Policy' took; whereas Amery envisaged a more convoluted process in which imperial policy was the subject of continuous debate or 'horse-trading' from which an acceptable consensus would invariably emerge. This difference of opinion was rooted in their opposed views on Britain's proper international role. Amery the isolationist wanted to use the Dominions as a check on Britain's European involvements; Chamberlain, the architect of Locarno, wanted to make certain that the

UK government retained its ability to influence Continental affairs. Chamberlain's vigorous reaction to Amery's attempt to establish a liaison system under his own aegis reflected not merely a jealous protection of his departmental prerogatives, but a determination to mould the policies which emerged from Whitehall in the Locarno image. Hence his annoyance, noted below, when Amery tried at the Imperial Conference to act independently of the Foreign Secretary in arranging access to State Papers for the High Commissioners.[8]

The third constraint on Commonwealth liaison was the unwillingness of all the Dominions, if for different reasons, to sanction the kind of reforms which Chamberlain and Amery respectively hoped for. To begin with, no Dominion Prime Minister was prepared to reduce his own control over imperial and foreign relations by unleashing their High Commissioners amidst the insidious trammels of the Whitehall bureaucracy. Even the New Zealand government gave little real scope to London representatives in their contact with British officials.[9] Amery recognised the force of these Dominion objections more accurately than Chamberlain. The Foreign Secretary, for example, was 'taken in' by Mackenzie King's apparent desire to see a British High Commissioner appointed to Ottawa, and by the Canadian Prime Minister's assurance that if such an official had existed in 1925 his Dominion would have found it possible to enter into Locarno obligations.[10] Where Chamberlain interpreted this as showing an evident intention to cooperate on a broad front in future, Amery appreciated that Mackenzie King's strategy was to ensure that whatever cooperation and liaison had to be accepted should be done under his own nose in Ottawa and not in London. Amery explained that Mackenzie King really intended

> to do the least consultation possible . . . . What I think he is most timid about is the idea of the High Commissioners meeting you or me collectively, lest out of that there should in some way or other grow up some sort of Imperial Council.[11]

Both British and Dominion opposition, then, limited the usefulness of Dominion High Commissioners at the London end. As such, liaison at the Dominion end as suggested by Meckenzie King was preferable to no liaison at all, and the main purpose of Amery's Empire tour in 1927 was not so much to explain the changes of the 1926 Conference (as he claimed) but to facilitate the appointment of British officials in Dominion capitals. His talks in New Zealand, for example, revolved completely around this topic, for Prime Minister Coates[12] and his Cabinet colleagues bitterly opposed a scheme which they feared would allow Canadian Liberals, South African Nationalists and Free Staters of any political complexion to drive a separatist wedge into imperial unity.[13] Thus Bell,[14] the Minister for External Affairs, warned Amery that his strategy of penetrating Empire governments by a network of 'upgraded Caseys' would boomerang because it meant 'trusting the confidence of a series of Cabinets' – a confidence he, like most of Amery's Cabinet colleagues in the UK, considered totally unjustified.[15] Bell, in his attempt to dissuade Amery, went so far as to threaten that a Labour administration was certain to come to power in Auckland in the near future, and that it would use the existence of an official British presence as a justification for treating the UK as a foreign country and destroy the still prevailing assumptions of 'Empire Policy'.[16] But limiting the destructive effects of nationalist governments in the Dominions was exactly the objective which Amery calculated such inter-imperial representation could achieve. He replied,

> The more natural and automatic the supply of information the more likely that such a Government would keep straight and continue on the lines of its predecessors . . . he knew the great value that the Civil Service had been to the Labour Government when in office in Great Britain.[17]

This was a revealing analogy. Amery was typical of UK official opinion in seeing Dominion nationalism, like socialism at home, as an aberrated response to modern conditions. Both would disappear in the long term as their detrimental effects became evident. In the meantime, as electorates felt drawn to experiment with novel ideas, the permanent bureaucracies had to act as a check to the logic of mass politics.

Certainly New Zealand objections were not enough to deter Amery. If New Zealand had had her way, indeed, there would not have been a Balfour Report in 1926 nor a Statute of Westminster in 1931, and a political crisis in Commonwealth relations might have been incurred over points that did not touch vital British interests. After his return to London, and this time in discreet collaboration with Chamberlain, Amery put before the Cabinet a comprehensive scheme for UK representation in the Dominions.[18] Canada was to receive a High Commissioner, South Africa an Imperial Secretary, and Australia and New Zealand junior liaison officers on the Casey model. But the Cabinet majority had not changed its stance despite the 1926 Report. That Report, in fact, had even augmented their fears of imperial dissolution. The Lord President thus felt that the innovations suggested by the two Ministers would 'play into the hands of the Canadian separatist element' and would encourage nationalism in the Dominions generally.[19] The Treasury, under Churchill's control, attacked the plan on 'general grounds' whilst making the specific complaint that the projected expenditure of £40,000 'was no less than three times the amount of the saving by the proposed changes regarding the Ministry of Transport, the

Mines Department and the Department of Trade';[20] but equally relevant, no doubt, were Churchill's suspicions of Amery's intention to use Dominion pressure in a campaign for protection. The President of the Board of Trade was also unhappy since he clearly resented Amery's desire to usurp control of the British Trade Commissioners in the Dominions.[21] This opposition – a compound of inertia, Tory reaction, retrenchment and a healthy dislike of Amery's constant intrigues – was sufficient to stall the scheme yet again.

What in the end made it possible for Amery and Chamberlain to overcome these obstructions was, as so often in British imperial history, the necessities imposed by external factors rather than any dispassionate re-evaluation from within. The crucial event in this case was the appointment of an American Ambassador to the Canadian Government. This revitalised traditional fears of Canadian gravitation towards the US and connected with that intense anti-Americanism which marked British political circles in the later 1920s. But more broadly, the American appointment also brought home the fact that an international market was forming for Dominion friendship. Thus Lord Willingdon,[22] the Governor-General of Canada, was loud in his denunciations of American intentions, and he played a vital part in converting one of the most rigorous critics of Amery's plans, George V. The US, Willingdon warned the King,

> had the fixed purpose of working on in this manner so that in time the Canadians will feel that the American is from all points of view a better friend to Canada than the Englishman, and if they can bring this state of mind about, it would obviously have a very serious effect on the stability of the Empire. . . .[23]

Later, Willingdon pressed the same arguments on Baldwin, pointing out that the recent visit by Lindberg, the transatlantic airman, to Ottawa, the dominance of the New York syndicated press in Canadian journalism and the continued flow of US industrial investment were all part of a well-planned penetration of Canadian society by American interests.[24] Robert Vansittart,[25] Permanent Secretary at the Foreign Office, added his considerable weight to these pleas, stating that the appointment of Ambassador Phillips had had a 'profound effect' in Canada and that any failure by the UK to match it

> would not only be seriously detrimental to Imperial policy generally but would from the very outset be construed by Canadians as implying that we do not take as great an interest in Canada as Americans do. . . .[26]

Any argument which could bring together an imperial proconsul like

Lord Willingdon and a Europeanist such as Vansittart clearly possessed considerable cogency, and the Cabinet duly authorised the Chamberlain–Amery package.[27]

Although Chamberlain and Amery had succeeded in establishing new channels of liaison, however, the uneasy cooperation between them soon ran into difficulties. Both wished to appoint a 'creature' of their own choosing. Again, this competition reflected an essential conflict on the functional character of the Dominions Office. Chamberlain continued to see the Dominions Office not as a 'thinking department' which formulated an independent view duly fed into the policy-making process, but as a mere collecting-house for the attitudes of others. He therefore demanded that the British High Commissioner in Canada, which was the first of the appointments to be made, should be a Foreign Service officer.[28] Amery had wider conceptions not only of his new department's role but also of the British officials who were to be sent to the Dominions. 'It was important to have liaison not only on foreign policy but also on inter-imperial and defence questions', Amery told Chamberlain, 'An all-round man was required.'[29] If Empire liaison could be interpreted in this way, Amery was clearly in a good position to influence almost all British policies. Baldwin, however, was careful to steer a middle course between two such dominant members of the Government as Amery and Chamberlain, and a compromise candidate finally emerged in the form of Sir William Clark, a Board of Trade official with considerable international experience.

Clark's objectives in Canada (like Bede Clifford's[30] in South Africa, Crutchely's[31] in Australia and Nicholls's[32] in New Zealand) were not just those of linking the Empire Cabinets more closely than before. He was also to spread 'discreet propaganda', supervise the 'feeding of the press' and correct 'misapprehensions' as to the state of the British economy. These activities have to be seen, too, in the context of other attempts to ensure that 'imperial interests' remained a working assumption throughout the Commonwealth. The concern for a managed press and an imperial communications system,[33] Amery's eagerness to involve the Dominions in the work of the Committee of Imperial Defence[34] and the considerable effort put into filtering British policy at the League through regular meetings of the British delegations were all part of this overall strategy. Amery, indeed, felt that by 1928 a set of arrangements had been instituted capable of making 'Empire Policy' a reality. 'The house is wired, the lights are in', Amery enthusiastically informed Smit,[35] the South African High Commissioner in London, 'All that General Hertzog needs to do is to turn the switch.'[36]

The machinery which British Ministers hoped would integrate the organisation of imperial interests, however, was capable of being used by other Commonwealth politicians for their own purposes. If a Dominion Prime Minister decided, for example, to treat a British High

Commissioner not as an intimate counsellor but as a formal Ambassador, he would be putting the UK on the same diplomatic footing as foreign countries. Thus, when Clark paid his first visit to the Department of External Affairs, Skelton immediately raised the question of Clark's 'promotion' to ambassadorial status.[37] Clark evasively responded that he 'had not given it much thought as it seemed a hypothetical question'.[38] Behind these exchanges lay the question of Dominion diplomatic identity. For as the British government was finally constrained into sending its representatives to the Dominions, the Dominions were establishing representatives in foreign countries. Whether these two lines of movement were parallel or divergent soon became a matter for argument in Whitehall.

The Extension of Dominion Diplomatic Representation

'Among the consequences that have flowed from the Imperial Conference of 1926', the Foreign Office commented in July 1929, 'none has been more important than the extension of the system of direct representation of individual Dominions in foreign countries'.[39] In fact the principle of Dominion representation had been conceded as early as 1920, when the Canadians had obtained permission to appoint a Minister to Washington. This Minister was to be a member of the British Embassy and second-in-command to the Ambassador. Moreover, and vitally important in the later dispute over Dominion representation, none of the terms which Borden had negotiated in any way restricted the Canadian appointee's terms of reference. Borden never actually got around to filling this post, but the negotiated precedent remained, and in 1924 the Irish Free State made use of it by sending Professor Smiddy[40] as their American representative; three years later the Canadian Government finally exercised their right and filled the Washington vacancy. The Irish and Canadian appointments to the United States, however, had been seen by UK officials as special cases where the volume of business relating to those particular Dominions, as opposed to questions which concerned the Commonwealth as a whole, was considerable. Indeed, Esme Howard,[41] British Ambassador in Washington, was glad to shuffle off responsibility for Irish and Canadian matters to people who knew the intricacies involved.[42] Where these conditions did not exist and Dominion representatives were likely to meddle with the general political business of the British Embassy, the response of UK foreign service personnel to Dominion diplomatic aspirations was consistently one of mixed astonishment and resentment.

One typical example of a recurring situation must suffice. In this instance the Irish Free State Trade Commissioner in Brussels, Count

O'Kelly,[43] had persistently laid claim to membership of the diplomatic corps. As one British Embassy official commented,

> My personal impression is that Count O'Kelly has persuaded his Government . . . who are quite ignorant of these matters, to call him 'Representative of the Irish Free State'. They have done so in the same spirit in which they would at home call the 'odd man' the butler if it made him happier. . . .[44]

O'Kelly did not smooth the passage of his own pretensions by absenting himself from Queen Alexandra's funeral service, flaunting his bogus title and adopting mannerisms which even the Secretary of the Free State Delegation at the League agreed were those of a 'cocky little beggar'.[45] Grahame,[46] the British Ambassador, concluded that it was 'a case of La Fontaine's fable, a frog trying to puff himself out'.[47] But Grahame's anxieties were not merely those of an outraged social exclusiveness. He warned the Foreign Office that O'Kelly was misleading the Dublin government with 'exaggerated reports' as to the commercial and political benefits of representation, and that, unless the Foreign Office intervened, there would be a flood of 'pseudo-Irish diplomatists with all the troubles and controversies to which equivocal situations . . . give rise'.[48] The Foreign Office shared these apprehensions and informed the Dominions Office that the time had come to end the 'troublesome farce' in Brussels.[49] The Dominions Office, however, took a different view, which was symptomatic of its response to the politicisation of Empire relations. Far from seeing the Free State Government as either ignorant or devious, the Office sympathised with it as the victim of political circumstances. These circumstances meant that the Dublin authorities could not deal severely with anti-British freebooters and careerists such as O'Kelly. The Dominion Office's information showed that they had tried 'roundabout ways' to restrict O'Kelly's activities, but that any direct action – such as a recall – would only play into the hands of the de Valerists. The departmental conclusion was that, until the 1921 settlement had fully stabilised, the British government had to accept the limits to Free State control over its own personnel.[50] Amery's advice to the Foreign Office was that a private complaint rather than a formal demand should be made, and with this the latter had to be satisfied.[51] O'Kelly's antics continued and he was, it seems, instrumental in persuading other Dominion officials (such as the Canadian Trade Commissioner in Buenos Aires) to duplicate his behaviour.[52] All this clearly did the Count no harm, for years later he became the President of the Irish Republic.

Providing, however, that the diplomatic posturings of Dominion personnel were restricted to a few such localised instances and did not become an explicit part of governmental programmes, little damage could result. But ambitious individuals like O'Kelly apart, the economic growth of certain Dominions and the character of their domestic politics was propelling them into a much wider and more complex set of international relationships. This threatened to define much more clearly a national and regional perspective which was antithetic to the total concept of 'imperial interests'. And almost immediately after the 1926 Imperial Conference a minor fracas between Mexico and Canada pointed to the dangers of diplomatic fragmentation implicit in this process.

The events here can be briefly told. The Catholic establishment in Canada strongly criticised the visit by a team of Canadian railway experts to reorganise the Mexican transport system. This culminated in a publication by Bishop Fallon[53] condemning the anti-Catholicism of the Mexican Revolution. The Mexican Consul-General in Ottawa promptly responded by presenting a defence of his Government's policies in the *Toronto Globe*, and pressure immediately began for his recall.[54] Mackenzie King, contending that the dispute threatened to revive old denominational controversies in Canada, insisted that the Foreign Office effect the Consul's departure by, if necessary, breaking Canadian–Mexican relations.[55] In fact Mackenzie King was manipulating this affair to confront the UK with a dilemma – how could Canadian–Mexican relations be distinguished from Anglo–Mexican relations whilst maintaining the principle of imperial unity? The latter had only recently returned to a normal footing after the long freeze of the revolutionary period, and the Mexican government made it perfectly clear that they for one would refuse to make the distinction Mackenzie King required and that British as well as Canadian interests would be affected if the Consul were asked to leave.[56] Mackenzie King remained unmoved by the Foreign Office's pleas that religious division in Mexico was infinitely more complex than in Canada and some understanding of the necessities that arose from this was vital.[57] Instead, he took the narrowly legal ground that as the official request for withdrawal would be on the advice of Canadian Ministers, there was no valid reasoning behind the Mexican intention to involve the UK; and behind this pointed legalism lay the political threat that, if the matter exploded in the Canadian Parliament before the Foreign Office had performed the surgery required, Mackenzie King would do the job himself.[58] Tensions eased, however, after February, and by June a compromise had emerged – Mackenzie King quashed the parliamentary debate whilst the Mexican Government moved the Consul to a new posting. Nonetheless, the Canadian Prime Minister had made his major point that the Foreign Office had to be prepared to function as the tool of the Canadian as well as of the British Government.

The official mind in Britain was certainly jolted by the possibilities this episode conjured up of a permanent fracture in imperial interests. The

Foreign Office took to analysing a hypothetical situation where Dominion–foreign relations could be cordoned off from those of the wider Empire, and concluded that

> Such a state could only exist on the hypothesis that His Majesty is, for international purposes, something other and different in relation to Canada from what he is in relation to this country and the rest of the Empire . . . and it would seem to follow logically that some of them [the Dominions] might be at war with that country whilst others are not. It is obvious that if this is so the British Empire has ceased to exist as an international entity.[59]

Yet, at the same time, it seemed politically impossible, after 1926, to deny a Dominion which requested the Foreign Office to arrange on its behalf separate representation in a foreign capital. The key to this dilemma in the Foreign Office mind was to concede representation but to protect the paramountcy of the British Ambassador in the capitals concerned. Warning that Dominion practice might one day apply to India and thus affect British diplomacy throughout the Middle East and Asia, it was therefore asserted that the British Ambassador 'must remain . . . the King's Imperial Representative who acts as the mouthpiece of all His Majesty's Governments . . . on the greater political issues'.[60] Effectively, Dominion representatives should only have competence in matters which directly and solely affected them individually and take a 'back seat' whenever wider imperial interests were at stake. Stamfordham[61] wrote strongly to Amery in this sense,[62] whilst Lord Cushendun,[63] Chancellor of the Duchy of Lancaster, stated categorically, whilst staying at the British Embassy in Paris, that British diplomacy was unworkable if some necessarily vague inter-imperial consensus had to be thrashed out during important international negotiations.[64] 'We consider it impossible', Cushendun impressed on Amery, 'to conduct our business on such lines.'[65]

Amery himself had been concerned at the implications in the Mexican affair. 'I don't quite like to say it is not possible to pursue a foreign policy separate and independent', Amery remarked to his Permanent Under-Secretary in the Dominions Office, 'it is not justifiable or consistent with the principles on which alone the Empire can work.'[66] But his approach was fundamentally different from that of the Foreign Office. Amery's essential idea was to bind the Dominions as closely as possible into the formulation and execution of British policy. In this way the concept of imperial interests could be deepened and freed from suspicions of being a front for the UK's particular needs. Dominion External Affairs Ministers would find it much harder to distance themselves from British policy in a particular area if their own representative had collaborated in all the initial moves with the British Ambassador. Foreign countries would be the more impressed with the reality of a united Commonwealth and give up the old calculations as to its imminent collapse if the 'full chord' – as Harding phrased it – of Empire diplomacy could be struck.[67] Finally, Dominion diplomatic expansion would obviously help Amery develop the Dominion Office's leverage within the Whitehall bureaucracy and would particularly help him to push British policy in the isolationist direction which he favoured. The Dominions Secretary, therefore, did not wish to restrict the role of Dominion Ministers overseas to purely Dominion business. And in arguing his case, Amery was able to make effective use of precedent. The chief of these was the initial failure in the Free State and Canadian appointments to Washington to limit their terms of reference. But there was also the important recent precedent of separate Dominion adhesions to the Kellogg Pact which, by any reckoning, was one of the greater political initiatives of the time. Ironically, it had been the insistence of the Foreign Office on a rapid signature of the Kellogg Pact which had made it necessary to give up the time-consuming attempt to synchronise an 'Empire' signature, and the Dominions Office had complained of having to deal with 'important constitutional matters' in too much of a hurry;[68] now the consequences of that decision worked to Amery's advantage. He told Lindsay,[69] the Permanent Under-Secretary at the Foreign Office,

> We have surely accepted the position that the powers and responsibilities of Dominion representatives . . . cover all subjects. if the Secretary of State for Foreign Affairs ever speaks for the whole Empire, it is only after having assured himself that he is in a position to do so . . . on the principles of the Imperial Conference we cannot hold out for any definition of local and common interests. The essence of the position is that every one of His Majesty's Governments has an unlimited field of authority coupled with a real measure of responsibility for the common interest . . . . Foreign Governments, knowing where the centre of gravity is, will in fact on all the big issues go to London or to the British Ambassador at their capital.[70]

Within the departmental hierarchy of Whitehall, Amery (even through he combined the Colonial and Dominion Offices) could not 'bulldoze' the Foreign Office. But he was able to offset this bureaucratic weakness by merging his own objectives with the pressures exerted by Mackenzie King, Hertzog and Cosgrave. This interaction can be illustrated by the establishment of a Canadian Legation in Paris, for it was around this appointment and the formal description of the Canadian Minister's responsibilities that the question of the 'Washington basis' (that is, whether new Dominion representatives overseas should share the unlimited scope which Smiddy enjoyed in the United States) reached a climax. In September 1928 Mackenzie King visited Europe, partly to speak in Geneva, but also, he hoped, to personally open the Paris Legation. Dining in Paris with Cushendun, the Canadian Prime Minister made it quite clear that he would brook no alteration of the Washington formula.[71] King's temper frayed even more when he arrived in Geneva and was informed by his aides that the British had been trying to block the Paris scheme, at least temporarily, by putting protocol difficulties in its path.[72] He vented his illwill on Price,[73] the Dominions Office representative at the League. Price informed Betterbee

> He appeared to take the matter as a personal slight to himself and implied that no one interested himself in the matter at all. In this connection he referred caustically to 'shooting in Scotland' . . . .[74]

Alienating King was bad enough, but there were clear signs that UK procrastination was prompting the creation of a radical front among Canada, South Africa and the Free State. It appeared, for example, that the Canadians and Free Staters in Geneva were working together to define a common attitude to the whole question of overseas appointments;[75] whilst Hertzog made it plain to Amery that he stood by Mackenzie King on the Washington terms.[76] Overruling the Dominions Office, therefore, also meant clashing with Dominion leaders on a point they considered vital to their interests. The Foreign Office backed down, and the credentials which the Canadian Minister finally presented at the Quasi d'Orsay contained no limiting clauses.

But if Amery and King had interacted on the issue of credentials, their objectives remained fundamentally divergent. Some indication of this emerged when King, returning to England aboard the SS *Ile de France*, voiced his ideas on foreign policy liaison. He told Liesching,[77] who served on the UK High Commission staff in Ottawa, that he envisaged all Empire representatives in a foreign capital functioning as

> . . . a small council in the closest contact, who would discuss with each other the questions arising with the foreign country concerned and inform each other of the points at which such questions bore especially on the interests of their respective Governments. In this way as he foresaw things, the present long-range consultations between Governments would in some cases be dispensed with, and in others much diminished as the result of the ground being cleared by personal discussion on the spot . . . . Dr. Skelton . . . touched on the same subject in much the same terms when I was talking to him in Paris.[78]

Mackenzie King, in other words, wished to use his overseas Ministers as instruments to dislodge broader inter-governmental consultation in the

Commonwealth. If this could be done it would me much easier to distance Canada from hypothetical commitments to Britain or even an actual war in which Britain was involved. In contrast, Amery conceived of Dominion Ministers abroad as another piece of coordinating machinery which would permit consultation in precisely that long-range sense which King deprecated. Amery and King, then, found themselves in occasional alliance despite totally opposed assumptions as to the political direction in which the Commonwealth was headed.

But, although Amery and King had their differences, so did King and Hertzog. The different texture of dissidence in the Dominions was, in fact, as important as Whitehall's tactical pragmatism in preserving the consensual, non-ideological pattern of Commonwealth politics. At the level of platform politics, and sometimes even of leadership self-image, it did occasionally seem that a Dominion–radical front was emerging. Ever since 1911 Canadian and South African statesmen had pictured themselves as working together to decentralise British imperialism and on various matters had assisted each other's arguments. But the different contexts of Canadian and South African politics ultimately led to mutual misunderstandings. In July 1928, for example, Hertzog announced his intention to appoint a South African Minister to serve simultaneously in the United States and Canada.[79] His motive in this unusual arrangement was partly cut-price diplomacy, but it was also designed to have the clear effect of blurring the differences between inter-imperial and international relations. Overlapping as it did with Mackenzie King's troubles over the Paris Legation, Hertzog no doubt expected strong Canadian support. In fact Mackenzie King turned him down flatly, leaving Hertzog deeply surprised and angered.[80] The South African proposal had implied, however unintentionally, the Americanisation of Canada and could have embarrassed King in domestic politics. Hertzog never understood how the economic and political pressures in Canada which arose from American regional hegemony structured perceptions of the Commonwealth in a very different way when compared with the South African case. Internal political conditions therefore determined the limits of Dominion nationalism just as positively as they circumscribed the possibilities of imperial integration, although it was not until the 1930s that British officials recognised the force of this point.

Baulked in his plan for a single North American representative, Hertzog contented himself with a less controversial scheme to appoint two Ministers to European countries: the first to cover Italy, France and Portugal, and the second Germany, Holland and Belgium. Although Hertzog spoke of these appointments as an assertion of a separate South African identity in international affairs, he was careful to adopt a lower profile when negotiating with British officials. He told Harding, for example, that South African representation in Europe was required for specifically commercial purposes because Trade Commissioners lacked the political 'clout' to extract concessions.[81] Bede Clifford, Britain's newly appointed High Commissioner in South Africa, saw no reason for opposing the Nationalist leader. Clifford agreed that Hertzog's motives were not just commercial but part of an 'independence programme' stemming from the 1926 Imperial Conference.[82] But did such a programme really conflict with imperial interests? Clifford was convinced, like Amery, that the facts of economic and political power ensured that extended South African participation in international affairs would assume an imperial expression. He had been impressed by Bodenstein's admission that South Africa did not have the trained personnel for diplomatic work, so that recruits would have to be attached to the UK Foreign Office and Embassies for instruction. The Imperial Secretary advised Amery that

> Our best plan would be to encourage them and offer facilities which will result in these young men being trained along lines which will inculcate in them an appreciation of the benefits of Empire association and the importance of maintaining diplomatic unity amongst the Dominions, rather than by discouraging the proposal we should compel the Union to educate these young men in a secessionist environment.[83]

Clifford's willingness to collaborate with Bodenstein was part of his more general optimism regarding Hertzogite politics. In October 1928, for example, Hertzog had delivered a major policy speech in which the old anti-imperialism was brusquely discarded. The Nationalist leader now 'took the Republican element severely to task', and went on to enumerate the benefits of the British connection such as use of the UK Embassies and Consulates. 'His attitudes on this occasion', Clifford prophesied to Batterbee, 'may in my opinion mark a turning point in the constitutional position in this country of considerable significance.'[84]

His Whitehall superiors, however, did not follow the Clifford recommendation. The outcome of the dispute over Canada's French legation had only decided the credentials of a Dominion appointment; it did imply automatic British agreement to such appointments in the first place. Moreover, although they were careful never to say so, Whitehall officials were never as ready to extend to South Africa advantages already accorded to Canada. In 1928 especially two developments had occurred which made the British nervous over the direction of any South African diplomacy. Firstly, Hertzog negotiated a convention with the Portuguese authorities in Mozambique without effective consultation with the Foreign Office; and secondly, there was the South African–German Trade Treaty which threatened to dismantle Imperial Preference altogether. Together these events implied that South Africa was intent on diversifying out of the Commonwealth relationship. Clifford was therefore ordered to dissuade Hertzog from making his European appointments. When he tried to do so, the South African Prime Minister responded by re-stating his claims in an ideological style. He told Clifford that the Locarno Treaties, and more recently the Anglo–French Naval Agreement, in which the UK had incurred obligations apart from the Dominions, had destroyed the convention of an Empire-state in any shape or form.[85] The Imperial Secretary tried to steer the exchange back to simple pragmatism. 'Insistence on our individual independence', Clifford stated, 'could be carried too far, particularly in our relations with foreign powers. The effect would be an isolating of the Dominions and that of the Empire in international affairs.'[86] This argument, that any Dominion which sought to act outside the Commonwealth framework would quickly find itself considerably weakened, was to gain in authenticity through the 1930s. But in 1928 world conditions remained relatively stable, and Hertzog brushed Clifford aside. He accepted the need for 'solidarity', but thought that ' "unity" . . . implied a concrete or too rigid an association'.[87] The tactics and ultimate ambiguity of this confrontation typified the Anglo–Dominion exchanges of the period.

Although it is probable that South Africa would have gone ahead anyway with its European representation, what broke the log-jam was again a Canadian action. In this case it was the appointment of a Canadian Minister to Japan. Unlike any previous Dominion representation, it was clear that a Canadian presence in Tokyo could only be justified on the most general political grounds. It would hardly be possible after such a move to deny other Dominions representation wherever they liked. The Japanese episode, however, is important also because it shows the problems and limits to Dominion diplomacy. Psychologically the Dominion personnel involved were very much at a disadvantage entering a world of rigid protocol and procedures. This situation was not helped when Mackenzie King selected for the Tokyo post an old political supporter, Herbert Marler,[88] whose experience in the fixing of provincial politics was not always appropriate in the more ritualistic sphere of international relations. Hadow, for example, was clearly amused at the farce which took place in Ottawa when the British High Commissioner invited the new Minister to a reception.

> I met Mr Marler at Government House a few days ago, just after he [Marler] had entirely failed to realise whom Sir William Clark was or why Sir William had made a polite effort to speak to him. Tall, and slightly taciturn, he was extremely apologetic for having made this gaffe and impressed upon me for a good half an hour the fact that he was 'entirely new to the game of diplomacy'.[89]

Marler's initial sense of insecurity was so great that, without even being asked, he requested to be briefed in London by the Foreign Office, and once there proved eager to learn his lines.[90] The fact that the British Government changed hands during his stay did not make this task any easier. Even at this point everything might have gone smoothly if Mackenzie King had coordinated his plans with the Japanese. In fact the Japanese turned out to relish no more than the British the prospect of 'British' diplomats 'taking divergent views whilst speaking on behalf of the same Empire'.[91] The Japanese Foreign Minister lectured the British Ambassador, Tilley,[92] on the danger that a Canadian presence would only focus attention on the problem of Oriental rights in British Columbia.[93] The right-wing Tokyo press was already demanding that the Canadians be denied representation until the question of Japanese exclusion from the Dominion was cleared up.[94] This anti-Canadian campaign mounted until Mackenzie King, too far advanced in his plan to risk a humiliating retreat, agreed to a new immigration agreement. 'It is not very often', Harding wryly commented after Mackenzie King had been forced into concessions, 'that the Foreign Office speaks in such complimentary terms of action taken by Canada in the sphere of foreign relations.'[95] Certainly Mackenzie King had learnt at first hand that setting up a legation involved political costs as well as benefits, and afterwards the Canadian Government was not eager for Marler to adopt a vigorous style which might generate further demands. It was thus Skelton, ironically, who remarked happily to Harding that the main function of the Canadian Legation in its initial months of operation had been to supervise a baseball match between the Japanese Foreign Office and the US Embassy.[96] If the chief of the Canadian External Affairs Department could be so disdainful of his own protegees, it was not surprising that British officials continued to harbour equivocal sentiments as to the status and field of operations of Dominion diplomats. 'On general grounds I think that we should wish to uphold that a Canadian Minister is a "British Ambassador"', Stephenson,[97] Assistant Secretary in the Dominions Office, minuted, 'but I see no objection (in fact some advantage) in treating any particular case as a possible exception to the general principle.'[98]

In the story of Dominion diplomatic representation, as in so much else, 1929–30 was a watershed. As international markets contracted, the commercial benefits of representation decreased; and as budgets tightened, the money for establishing Legation properties and personnel was just not available. But more broadly, the essentially political attractions of creating a Canadian or South African presence in international affairs decreased with general destabilisation in international affairs. Representation in a 'Locarno world' was one thing; in situations likely to fall apart in chaos and possibly war at any moment it was quite another. Similarly, as international conditions worsened,

British officials became increasingly intolerant of Dominion action which complicated the task of defending imperial interests. In these respects the failure of the proposal for a Canadian Legation in China marks a turning-point.

The China scheme surfaced in early 1930, when Herbert Marler visited Shanghai and informed the British Consul-General that the Chinese were pressing for a Canadian Legation.[99] Marler claimed to be 'instinctively' opposed to this, but the Consul suspected that in fact Marler, who was openly dissatisfied with the position accorded him in Japan, sought to add China to his diplomatic portfolio and augment his claims to full ambassadorial status.[100] Although Marler had appeared to agree with the Consul's repeated arguments that there was a 'danger that too many cooks might end by spoiling the broth', he soon returned from Nanking clutching an official request for a Canadian representative.[101] The Consul hurriedly warned Lampson,[102] the Ambassador in Peking, that Marler was being manipulated by the Chinese.[103] 'Hitherto the British Empire has spoken with one voice in China', he remarked, 'but the possibility of pitting one of His Majesty's Ministers . . . against another in such a matter as a commercial treaty, must have appealed to [the Chinese] as a piquant development of their diplomacy.'[104] Lampson's mind was working even more darkly. If the Canadians set up a Legation, he told the Foreign Office, 'they might well find the Chinese trying to deal with them as a *non-Treaty Power*.'[105] Marler had become a very minor pawn in the Chinese attempt to crack the Treaty structure. Even the Dominions Office admitted that Canadian diplomacy was beginning to threaten not only traditional procedures but the substance of imperial interests.[106] The Ottawa Department of External Affairs was subsequently bombarded with arguments the drift of which was that a Canadian representative should not be 'pitched into the present Chinese mess'.[107] Skelton, however, seems to have supported Marler's plan as a device to keep the new Conservative Prime Minister, R. B. Bennett, on a nationalist course, and in June 1931 Marler returned to Ottawa to help the External Affairs Secretary push the appointment through the Cabinet. The bait of a Canadian contribution to the Imperial Navy was held out to Clark, and the High Commissioner pressed the attractions of such a 'deal' on the Dominions Office.[108] The Office, however, was only irritated at Clark's apparent innocence, and Clutterbuck[109] commented,

> Mr Marler was full of it when he called here before taking up his present appointment in Tokyo. If Canada really wants to show gratitude the best way of doing so is to refrain from action which our experience indicates could only lead to embarrassment.[110]

Clutterbuck's remarks indicate the critical disillusionment with which many British officials were beginning to perceive Commonwealth relations. The optimisms had been stripped from imperial as well as European affairs; there was a fresh emphasis on fundamentals and an intolerance of side-issues. Thus, when Skelton tried to shunt the China Legation through the Canadian Cabinet without a discussion, Clark acted on his instructions and intervened, firmly confronting Skelton in King's presence; the High Commissioner stated flatly that any attempt to redefine imperial interests into its Dominion components was a luxury for quiet times and untroubled places; where the real question at issue was getting 'British' rights as a whole recognised and protected, it was irrelevant.[111] Skelton's machinations continued, but Bennett, by refusing any further debate on the matter and backing Clark to the full, had effectively put a halt to Canada's diplomatic manoeuvres. Marler had to drag out an unsatisfactory period of service in Tokyo, pathetically trying to establish his claim as superior to the Chargé d'Affaires in the hierarchy of the British Embassy. Unsupported by Ottawa, he had little success. 'Marler must be made clearly to understand', Mounsey, the Assistant Under-Secretary in the Foreign Office, was firmly declaring by 1934, 'the position of the Canadian Legation in the Imperial family.'[112]

The political effects of the 1926 Imperial Conference, then, can be divided into two identifiable themes. The first was the attempt by British officials to find an effective response to the new situation. The key problem here was to protect the concept and operation of a 'British' force in world affairs which was greater than the UK alone. But if there was agreement in the UK on this objective, there had not (even at Cabinet level) been agreement on the means. The establishment of British High Commissioners emerged as a partial solution, and as a system it greatly increased the UK's information about, and sensitivity towards, Commonwealth politics. These staffs became a minor bureaucracy in their own right and from early on developed approaches distinct from those dominant back in London. Thus, partly through tactical design and partly under the impact of bureaucratic expansion, Anglo–Dominion relations had become subject to a new set of managerial institutions. The second theme was the progressive interaction of the Dominions with the non-Commonwealth world. The British, both in Whitehall and serving in foreign capitals, found this process difficult to handle, and their suspicions of Dominion diplomatic intentions were acute. They did develop a set of tactics for this situation, such as the paramountcy of the British Ambassador, but it was not so much their flexibility that limited Dominion experimentation as the latter's lack of personnel, psychological restraints, the political costs of aspiring to an international role and, ultimately decisive, the hostile diplomatic climate after 1930. But the problem of the Empire's diplomatic unity from 1926 onwards must also be set against a background of deepening intra-

Commonwealth tensions. The sense of disillusionment which came to colour British perceptions of the Commonwealth in the later 1920s must now be described.

6 The Alliance under Strain 1926–1930

The imperial rapport of 1926 was gradually undermined in the following four years, and by 1930 a more acute sense of doubt as to the long-term prospects of Commonwealth prevailed than at any time since the War. In 1929 Arthur Ponsonby,[1] shortly after his appointment as Parliamentary Under-Secretary for Dominion Affairs in the new Labour government, remarked

> I cannot help feeling that we are drifting too much without plan on the various questions connected with the position of the Dominions. . . . While up to a point it may be wise to deal with problems as they arise it is conceivable, and indeed symptoms are not lacking, that we may find ourselves confronted one of these days with a serious dilemma.[2]

This anxiety over tactics was, as we have already noted, endemic. But Ponsonby was referring here to more than the problems created by Dominions' representation abroad and the attempt to fashion some workable method of consultation. He was aware that the whole structure of economic and diplomatic relations in the Commonwealth had become more complex and vulnerable to internal contradictions. British official opinion generally was pushed by events into asking whether the Commonwealth remained (as the intensive propaganda of the Great War had taught them to believe) a coherent political force. Sources of doubt on this issue can be described under two headings: international relations and economic problems.

International Relations

The Foreign Office quickly became disillusioned with the idea of a coordinated 'Empire Foreign Policy' even in the limited shape it had previously assumed in Austen Chamberlain's mind. This was not because the Dominions showed signs of staking out any defined foreign policy which clashed with that of the UK. Occasionally, it is true, Dominion opinion ventured to criticise the British government on some major policy decision (so that the Canadian press bitterly attacked the Anglo–French Naval Agreement of 1928 because it was concluded in the face of US opposition[3]) but generally the approach of Dominion governments was to take as vague and uncommitted a line as possible on such 'high diplomacy'. In many minor ways, however, the welding of a 'Dominion factor' into the management of Britain's international relations had made the Foreign Office task much more difficult. The Anglo–Chinese negotiations in 1928 can be used as a case in point. The Chinese, asserting that under the 1926 dispensation the Dominions were as responsible as the UK for British foreign policy, contended that they could not commit themselves to non-discrimination against British citizens unless they received reciprocal rights not only in the UK but in the Dominions also.[4] Because Asiatics were discriminated against in Canada, Australia and South Africa, this was clearly a problem. The British negotiators struggled hard to explain the Balfour Report to their Chinese counterparts and emphasised that it did not mean there was any way of standardising racial policies in the Empire, but if the precise sense of that declaration was not clear even in London, it certainly did not make itself readily comprehensible to officials in Peking. Meanwhile the Dominions Office had to excise carefully all information of these negotiations from documents sent to Commonwealth governments, for it would only 'show the trouble we are having over questions concerned with their [the Dominions'] position, and might indeed prompt them to take a larger hand themselves'.[5] This was typical, as Ponsonby himself admitted,[6] of how the UK had to resort to subterfuge in order to conceal the impracticalities implicit in an 'Empire policy' and, in retrospect, it is clear how the necessary use of such stratagems soon led to an attitude of disillusioned pragmatism towards the whole problem of managing Anglo–Dominion relations.

The intention of some Dominions at least to 'take a larger hand themselves' was indicated by the expansion of their External Affairs Departments. Certainly the heightened influence within Dominion governments of departments and officials with foreign political functions caused considerable concern. This concern was partly expressed in terms of an irritation with muddling amateurs whose activities complicated the task of professional diplomats elsewhere. Liesching, following a conversation with one of Mackenzie King's Private Secretaries on the working of the Canadian Department of External Affairs, thus reported to the Dominions Office:

From the account he gave me, unless he exaggerates the ignorance which appears to exist of elementary matters of procedure, it seems almost a miracle that they ever get anything done at all, or if they do, that some important interests are not prejudiced.[7]

But to this mild if patronising critique was added slightly more disturbing political considerations. Dominion Prime Ministers, for example, were thought habitually to staff their External Affairs Departments with civil servants and politicians of separatist leanings. This suspicion seemed to be confirmed when Hertzog appointed H. Bodenstein (who, according to Birch Reynardson,[8] 'has . . . the reputation of being intensely anti-British'[9]) to be Secretary of the External Affairs Department in 1927 even when other more 'suitable' candidates were available. An inquiry was immediately made into Bodenstein's allegedly treasonous activities in Holland during the War[10] and, although none of these allegations could be confirmed, Bodenstein was subsequently seen as the 'wicked uncle' who pressurised the unsuspecting Hertzog into dissident acts.[11] Similarly Skelton, who in his capacity as Secretary of the External Affairs Department dominated Canadian foreign policy from 1924 until 1938,[12] was consistently seen as the 'villain of the piece' whenever Mackenzie King did anything which annoyed the British government.

It was in terms, then, of a separatist conspiracy that the Foreign Office especially tended to see Dominion actions which embarrassed the UK. One such standing grievance was the Canadian practice of publishing confidential foreign policy documents which they received as part of the consultative arrangements agreed in 1926, a proclivity again attributed to Skelton's mischievous influence.[13] The Dominions Office in these situations invariably sought to avoid confrontation by explaining the Dominion position as innocuously as possible to other Whitehall departments. In this case (which concerned the Anglo–French correspondence on the naval treaty) it held that Mackenzie King had to be able to defend himself against parliamentary criticisms by producing the necessary documents just as the UK government occasionally had to do.[14] The Foreign Office, not surprisingly, took such arguments as proof that the Dominions Office could not recognise plain separatism even when it stared them in the face. 'It is a principle which should be decided once and for all,' Chamberlain stated firmly. 'If the Prime Minister of Canada wishes to be free to publish all our communications, we must in future be as cautious and uninformative in what we say to him as he habitually is in what he says to us.'[15]

As perturbing as such unexpurgated publication of state papers by Dominion Governments, however, were their continuing attempts to by-pass the UK in their international negotiations. Foreign Office patience on this point gave out when Bodenstein tried to start a direct dialogue between Pretoria and Washington on the subject of the Kellogg Pact, an attempt which failed because the US was not prepared to alienate the UK authorities for the sake of South African goodwill. 'We find it difficult', Koppell,[16] a Foreign Office official, explained to the Dominions Office in rejecting the latter's call for flexibility, 'to see where a line could be drawn if we relax the procedure still further and we think therefore that it is better . . . to rest at the point now reached.'[17] By the end of 1928, therefore, the implications of such catchphrases as 'consultation' and 'equality' as the guiding principles of a workable system of Empire policy were being seriously questioned.

So far the irritations felt by the UK might be dismissed as relatively minor and of a procedural rather than substantively political nature. But the tendencies outlined have to be set against the background of accumulating evidence that certain Dominions were gradually defining their interests as regional rather than imperial, and that within those reduced orbits they were seeking to assert their ability to take over diplomatic roles hitherto the preserve of the Foreign Office. Not only did this challenge Britain's traditional authority to determine what Empire policy was, but it threatened to create situations in which UK and Dominion interests openly clashed. As an example of this we can look at South Africa's attempt to exert greater control over her relations with the Portuguese colonies in 1927–8.

Competition for labour and railway traffic in southern Africa had continued to grow more acute during the 1920s. South Africa, especially, had become more dependent on its work-force drawn from Portuguese Mozambique and on the port of Lourenço Marques as an outlet for its goods. In 1927 the Portuguese–South African Convention governing these matters came up for renegotiation. The first point which emerges from the events which followed is that even such a dissident Dominion as Nationalist South Africa did not wish to forgo British assistance altogether when bargaining with foreign powers. Hertzog, for example, sought British help to undermine Portugal's request for a reconstruction loan from the League, for the money would clearly be used to cover the losses involved in stopping the flow of labour to the Rand.[18] Clifford was eager that the British government should co-operate on this since it would be proof that South Africa continued to receive concrete benefits from Commonwealth association,[19] and the Treasury subsequently agreed, if somewhat reticently, to 'let the views of the Union Government be known in the right quarter'.[20] But the South African approach was to put strict limits on British involvement in their regional diplomacy. Thus as far as the specific problems of labour, transport and port facilities were concerned, Hertzog was determined to 'freeze' the Foreign Office out of the discussions. In attempting to do so, he was testing the limits of South Africa's political capabilities. Did the Nationalist Government possess the leverage it required to extract concessions from a colonial regime notoriously resilient to pressure? Amery, confident that this was not the case, was prepared to refrain from action and let affairs take their course. He told Chamberlain with undisguised delight that the Pretoria officials were indeed learning their lesson

The other day he [Hertzog] received thirty sheets of contemptuous and studied insolence in which all the misdeeds of Boers and British were lumped together in a long catalogue of Portuguese grievances.[21]

To the Foreign Office this appeared to be typical of Amery's complacency. Whatever lessons Hertzog might be learning, in the process South African unilateralism would exacerbate relations throughout the southern region. Moreover, Chamberlain felt that the continuance of the Anglo–Portuguese alliance was a more important consideration than seeking Hertzog's goodwill. He told Balfour

The Dominions Office appeared to think that we had discharged our whole duty by, to use their own words, 'manoeuvring' ourselves into a favourable position, but they seem to have no conception of working the Empire as a partnership in which we should make the South African case our own, and in so doing help to prevent a row between South Africa and Portugal in which we should occupy a very dangerous position.[22]

Chamberlain had not grasped the differentiation of interests which made it impossible for the British and South African cases to be integrated. Intent on by-passing Amery, the Foreign Secretary impressed on Hertzog that, whilst labour quotas from Mozambique could be settled 'on the spot' (for he was quite happy to disassociate himself from the Union's recruitment policies), the proposed convention raised questions of an 'international character' regarding railways and harbours which Britain had a right to supervise.[23] Chamberlain suggested that negotiations take place in Lisbon where South African and British officials could work more easily together than in the partisan atmosphere of Johannesburg.[24] He attempted to pressurise Hertzog into this scheme by warning him that the Portuguese Opposition were spreading rumours that Pretoria was about to take Mozambique labour away by force if necessary, and that only the presence of South African delegates in Lisbon could calm this situation.[25]

Events, however, had already gone beyond British control for the Governor-General of Mozambique had been invited to Pretoria, presumably with the intention of steamrolling an agreement which could then be presented to the Foreign Office as a *fait accompli*. Clifford tried to disrupt this strategy, arguing that the Nationalist Government could only defeat Smuts at the following election if it had secured favourable terms from Portugal, and that only by collaboration with the UK could such terms be obtained. So much for British non-interference with Dominion domestic politics, although it is noteworthy that such interventions were as frequently biased towards Dominion 'nationalists' as towards their 'loyalist' opponents.[26] In fact Roos assured Clifford that Hertzog intended to reserve the key questions for Lisbon, and that the Governor-General's visit was only intended as an exercise in 'entertaining, flattery and making pleasant speeches'.[27] This was bluff, and the Imperial Secretary soon found that, once the Portuguese delegation arrived, he was kept from any information on the negotiations. What scraps of news he did receive, in fact, came from the Portuguese.[28] Thus the Convention, which was finally signed in Pretoria on 11 September 1928, was one in which the UK had played a minimal role. Behind this fact lay a complex interaction of conflicting objectives, misunderstandings and deceptions which was eroding the Anglo–South African relationship.

The Foreign Office disillusionment over the state of Anglo–Dominion relations, and more specifically with the role of the Dominions Office, was shared by those officials in the UK whose concern was defence rather than foreign policy. For the Service departments the basic assumption in Commonwealth affairs was the 'common responsibility' for Imperial Defence affirmed at the 1923 Imperial Conference, and this principle was seen as especially vital because the UK's resources failed increasingly to match the strategic obligations facing her. The Dominions Office tendency, therefore, to dilute imperial obligations by concessions designed to conciliate Dominion separatism met with sustained criticism. This reached a peak over the Kellogg Pact.

The South African government had exploited the pact by arguing that, because it was at least theoretically possible for another Dominion to be an aggressor, South Africa could not be automatically obligated to support her Commonwealth partners in war, and the Dominions Office (having great difficulties in arranging a simultaneous adherence to the Pact by the Dominions) had agreed.[29] This admission appeared to undermine the root principle of the Empire's indivisibility in war. To Chamberlain, the Foreign Office and the military departments, the DO's preoccupation with the delicate management of nationalist Dominions distorted its judgement as to the whole *point* of the Commonwealth relationship, and made it incapable of recognising when resistance to change was necessary. MacReady,[30] Assistant Secretary to the Committee of Imperial Defence, thus complained bitterly to Hankey of the DO's concession.

> This, I suggest, is a very pernicious doctrine, and is not in accordance with the basis of present day imperial defence arrangements. It has been recognised for years that the defence of the Empire is a 'common responsibility' although Great Britain still shoulders the main part. . . . If the principle of mutual support is not admitted, imperial defence would become an impossibility, since Great Britain can no longer undertake to defend the Empire as she did in the past.[31]

This general critique was followed up by a lengthy memorandum by Sir Charles Madden, the First Sea Lord and Chief of Naval Staff. In this paper[32] he pointed out that Commonwealth unity in war was not just a piece of symbolism of limited practical worth. Substantial and concrete interests were involved. An increase in the number of industrial and semi-industrial neutrals would increase the problem of restricting enemy trade; Dominion naval support would be forfeited in crucial areas such as the Pacific and Indian Oceans; whilst, above all, Dominion neutrality meant the loss of vital naval bases – Halifax, Cape Town, Darwin and Sydney.[33]

Hankey, as secretary of the Committee of Imperial Defence, usually found himself in sympathy with Service criticisms of Whitehall departments, and he shared this nervous apprehension regarding imperial relations. But he also had a realistic appreciation of the political limitations operating within the Commonwealth. In the military sphere, the main limitation was that active Dominion participation in a future war (such as the despatch of Dominion troops to the Continent, or South African troops being used in East Africa) clearly depended on the parliamentary consent of the Empire Governments at the time. Hankey accepted that Dominion cooperation in these 'offensive' roles could not be regarded as automatic, but at the same time he pressed on the Dominions Office a concept of 'passive participation'.[34] In other words, he felt there was a range of duties which a Dominion government could be expected to carry out which did not depend on the vagaries of its parliamentary majority. The South African government, for example, could arrange for Britain's Eastern trade to be switched to the Cape route should the Mediterranean be closed, whilst the Dominions generally could expand and mobilise their militia to prevent British troops having to be diverted for garrison purposes.[35] Such acts of cooperation with the UK meant effective belligerency, and Hankey insisted that such belligerency must remain 'an underlying assumption, and not say anything which tends to weaken the idea of common responsibility in such matters'.[36]

The Dominions Office, however, stuck to its view that any attempt to assert military obligations as implicit in Commonwealth association was a mistake. It was concerned with dealing with the Dominions in the current peacetime situation, not with planning for a hypothetical war which in 1928 still appeared an improbability; and that meant that its priority had to be forging a *modus vivendi* with some 'nationalist' Dominions who regarded military commitments of any kind as unacceptable. Diluting such assumptions as the Empire's indivisibility in war, therefore, seemed a worthwhile price for the political scope it gave for a more flexible Anglo–Dominion understanding. In defending this position, the Dominions Office had the advantage of being able to use the 1926 Report as a justification for their views. Harding therefore told Hankey bluntly that the UK could not escape the fact that under the new Commonwealth system the Dominions were to be 'the sole judge of the nature and extent of their cooperation' in war and that there could be no question of compulsory duties.[37] These differences of approach between the Dominions Office and their Whitehall colleagues were mirrored, in fact, in their rival attitudes to that Report. The Dominions Office regarded it (because Nationalists in South Africa, Liberals in Canada and all Governments in the Irish Free State regarded it) as a fundamental break in the political relations of Commonwealth. In contrast, other UK officials concerned with the Dominions as a by-product of their foreign political or military responsibilities, saw it as a tactical improvisation which could be breached or tacitly ignored if its implications were found to clash with imperial interests. Hankey therefore replied to Harding:

> I agree that the particular passages you quote from the Report of the Inter-Imperial Relations Committee do emphasise rather strongly the right of each Dominion to determine the extent of its cooperation in defence or anything else. I should, however, have been glad to avoid emphasising the point.[38]

Hankey's attempt to open up the question of defence cooperation, however, failed. This was not because the Dominions Office was able to impose its view, but because Baldwin intervened to silence a potentially disruptive debate; preparations for the Constitutional Conference in the following year were under way, and the Prime Minister was not prepared to risk the spectacle of a Conservative government presiding over a Commonwealth meeting split on basic issues.[39] Nonetheless, Baldwin assured Hankey that the time was near when an Imperial Conference would be required to reaffirm the overriding priorities of Imperial Defence. 'Our naval policy is entirely based on the existence of defended ports throughout the Dominions and Colonies', Baldwin stated, 'and on the existence in time of war of an Empire Navy.'[40]

Baldwin characteristically fastened onto the point of easiest compromise: the Dominions were not to be pressured into military arrangements in peacetime, but British planning for war should go ahead on an imperial basis. In 1929 the general stability of world affairs meant that this untested approach could roughly satisfy most groups. But beneath this surface consensus assumptions were being reshaped. Labour men often found this change easier to articulate than their Conservative counterparts. Ponsonby thus clearly understood that the actual content of international politics after World War I (above all, ideas of collective security) reacted on the rationale of Commonwealth. He noted that

As we approach to a more enlightened attitude towards arbitration and disarmament so do we weaken the formerly strong argument of the prime responsibility of the U.K. in matters of Imperial defence on which our supremacy within the Empire was based, and which therefore constituted an obvious excuse for our leadership if not our dictation. We still claim to be *primus inter pares* but even that may soon be challenged.[41]

Ponsonby had in mind here the inter-imperial difficulties which had attended the British signature of the Optional Clause of the League Charter in September 1929. The Optional Clause controversy, indeed, is perhaps the best illustration of the growing 'ungovernability' of the Commonwealth relationship and of how the Commonwealth factor was fitted into the making of British foreign political decisions. It is therefore worth relating in brief detail.

The Optional Clause Controversy

The Optional Clause had been part of the original Charter of the League. By signing it a state accepted the obligation to submit to judicial decision at the International Court at The Hague all disputes in which they were engaged. For a colonial power such as the UK this obviously posed problems; nationalists in any part of the Empire (colonies or Dominions) might take their case to The Hague or a neutral trader in a war situation might contest British exercise of Belligerent Rights. The British Cabinet was not prepared to see the UK's freedom to deal with her imperial problems further fettered by such legal restraints. They did not sign the Clause in 1919, and when the matter was discussed in 1924 it was again pushed aside. After the Locarno Treaties, however, the problem took on a sharper edge. 'The British Government had supported the principle of arbitration as regards the settlement of disputes between Germany and her neighbours', the Foreign Secretary explained to the Cabinet Committee, 'and was perhaps open to the charge of recommending others to adopt a procedure which she refused to follow herself.'[42] As yet, however, the UK did not feel sufficiently constrained by circumstances to prejudice vital national interests any more than (as the Attorney-General had pointed out) Canada seemed likely to accept an adverse judgement on its restrictions of Asiatic immigration.[43] The Optional Clause was therefore politely ignored. But once signs of instability returned after mid-decade, pressure built up for a 'forward move' at the League. The Dominions were deeply affected by this new current since their presence at the League was for all of them their most tangible evidence of new status, and they had benefited as a group from Canada's elevation to the Council in 1926. On the Optional Clause, therefore, Australia informed the British government that it was 'undesirable to maintain a *non-possumus* attitude very much longer',[44] whilst Canada indicated its readiness to sign the Clause with the qualification that Asiatic rights could not be considered within the competence of the Hague tribunal.[45] The Irish Free State, seeing an opportunity to embarrass the UK, went even further and announced its intention to come to separate arbitration arrangements with France, Italy and Spain if the UK did not stop its procrastination.[46] Here was a clear case for putting the post-1926 consultative arrangements to the test. But Batterbee was forced to admit

> I much doubt whether it is possible to reach agreement with the Dominions on arbitration [and] personally I do not think that we shall advance the matter much by bringing in the High Commissioners in a matter so complicated and important. There might be some advantage in e.g. Mr Smiddy growing familiar with the difficulties of the problem, but I doubt whether the High Commissioners would be able to contribute much towards the solution of them, or indeed would be allowed by their Governments to do so. A *via media* would be to ask Dominion Governments to send over legal experts to join in our discussion, but political issues are so tangled up with the legal issues that I doubt whether anyone short of the Dominion Prime Ministers is really capable to deal with them.[47]

Batterbee had implicitly touched on a central factor which increasingly obstructed Commonwealth planning of any kind. This was the politicisation of Empire relations. The political economy of the various Dominions had become so much interwoven with their relations with Britain that only the highest executive authorities could deal with issues of cooperation. But at these rarefied levels the political pressures were so great, and indeed contradictory, that anything so neat and tidy as a 'Commonwealth policy' was impossible. Most inter-imperial exchanges thus became little more than shallow exercises in which each leadership sought to evade commitments whilst sustaining the rhetoric. Empire foreign policy therefore constituted a set of incantations ('peace', 'security' and so on) rather than a detailed political strategy.

In this situation it is not surprising that the DO was reduced to 'manoeuvring' for position, leaving other departments with the impression that its personnel were sub-standard. Over the Optional Clause all the Office could do was attempt to delay any Dominion initiatives and stifle any public expression of intra-Commonwealth differences. Frequently these differences only leaked out because the Commonwealth had become part of the tactical interplay among Whitehall factions. The Foreign Office, which considered the Optional Clause another threat to its unilateral diplomacy, came to see in the Commonwealth aspects of signature a means of obstruction. It latched onto Bruce's suggestion that any British acceptance should carry a 'rider' that inter-imperial disputes were reserved from Hague jurisdiction, because it was clear that such a qualification would divide the Dominions and delay action.[48] The Dominions Office opposed the Bruce idea and pressed for a 'pure' signature. This was not because it had a view of the Clause one way or the other. It simply wanted to avoid embarrassing displays of disunity, and any attempt to verbalise the legal integrity of the Empire would certainly have led to such an incident. The inter-departmental conflict on this came to a head at a meeting in March 1929. The FO built up an elaborate picture of how the referral of Anglo–Dominion issues to The Hague would break the Empire, whilst the DO responded that no such risk existed because anti-imperialism had been expunged from Dominion politics.[49] The bureaucratic struggle was thus promoting different images of Commonwealth and inducting them into the policy process. As such, the association was becoming at times a polemical instrument within Whitehall rather than an extraneous influence from without. The likely effects of this in the longer term was to make any manageable consensus among Commonwealth leaderships impossible.

What was more disturbing from the DO's perspective, however, was how the Optional Clause controversy exposed Commonwealth relations to criticism in Parliament. Hitherto the British government had always used the easy excuse of inter-imperial consultation being 'in progress' to explain its immobility on League policy. Not surprisingly the pro-League lobby responded by caricaturing the Commonwealth connection as an obstacle to progress. The DO had to warn its political superiors that any further statements seeming to imply that Hertzog or Mackenzie King opposed the Clause would lead to public denials by them.[50] In the House of Lords debate at the end of May, however, the Government spokesmen rolled out the old formula of 'consultation', and there followed some biting Opposition attacks on Commonwealth orthodoxies. Cecil bluntly declared

> I think that this country must take the responsibility for recommending whatever course it thinks right, and if it be that some of our Dominions disagree with that course the best thing is that they should state it openly, and that the world should know who exactly is for it, and who is against it.[51]

Even more pointedly, Lord Parmoor,[52] the Labour leader in the upper House, drew the more general and dangerous conclusion that

> This Government has always proposed to give the units of our Empire the maximum of sovereign independence. I believe that is quite right;

but I doubt whether it is consistent with the continued practice of diplomatic unity.[53]

One of the DO's chief characteristics was its determination to keep Commonwealth issues off Parliament's agenda. It knew that the gap between the substance and rhetoric of Empire could only be bridged by ambiguity, and this ambiguity could never be strong enough to survive the crude analysis of a democratic legislature. The Optional Clause was one instance where Commonwealth was proved to be easy prey for politicians who found it cluttering their chosen path, and its vulnerability was to increase as economic conditions polarised attitudes on almost every question.

The DO, however, might well have hoped that the election of a Labour government in May 1929 ended its problems with the Optional Clause. The Labour party was committed to the principle of signature, and this meant that now all Commonwealth governments were agreed. In fact the achievement of this consensus only opened the way to much larger disagreements on what signature actually implied. Every Commonwealth member saw different priorities involved and drew the limits of Hague jurisdiction at different points. Bruce, for example, accepted the arbitration principle but decided on its limits with reference to Australian defence interests. Above all, this meant that it must not interfere with the viability of imperial communications. Because it was thought that Zaghlul Pasha, the Wafd leader in Egypt, would immediately take the UK to court on the question of the latter's right to maintain a military presence along Suez, the Clause issue was meshed into the net of Middle Eastern politics. Bruce demanded that the Egyptian matter be specifically 'reserved', and this fitted with the view of the British Foreign Office as it struggled to restrain Labour's foreign policy. 'Australia was extremely panicky', the Foreign Office reiterated in policy discussions, 'about anything in the nature of a forward policy in Egypt which would result in a lessening of British control.'[54]

In contrast, South Africa, Canada and the Irish Free State were all concerned to avoid involvements in colonial security and refused 'to have anything to do with a reservation of this kind';[55] and if the Foreign Office appeared to echo the anxieties of Canberra, the Dominions Office came to rest its position at some imaginary point between Dublin, Pretoria and Ottawa. Batterbee recommended that each Commonwealth Government should be able to adopt whatever attitude they liked on the 'British Monroe Doctrine' in Egypt:

it does not seem to us an insuperable objection that it [the Monroe Doctrine] would be acceptable to some of the Dominions and not to others. It is, of course, an axiom that the general scheme of the arbitration arrangements of the Empire should be the same . . . but the field of arbitration may well be different, as the practical problems of the various parts of the Empire are by no means identical.[56]

If any departmental extract could be taken to stereotype DO thinking, this would be it. Couched in the soothing style of bureaucratic practicality, open disagreement was crafted into a very generalised consensus. The fact that the resulting eclecticism in the arbitration arrangements of Commonwealth ruled out any common approach to the major institutional change in international organisation since the War did not, apparently, matter. Metaphorically, the DO considered that keeping the various Governments in the same nominal fleet was more important than any guidance of the direction in which the constituent vessels floated. Given the DO's total lack of leverage on the political problems it was charged with (not having, for example, even the Treasury's minimal capacity to act on the situation before it), this dilution of objectives was inevitable. It was, after all, the only way to preserve the concept of a Commonwealth 'system', and it was on the continuance of that concept that the DO – and the personal careers it included – depended for survival.

The problem, however, was that for some Dominions the specific interests at stake were simply too great for the bland evasion of complex choices to be acceptable. This was the case with the Australians and the New Zealanders on the Clause. For them, the right to their own Monroe Doctrine in Egypt given in Batterbee's formula was obviously worthless: the question was whether the one Commonwealth country with the resources to maintain imperial security (the UK) would actually do so. Antipodean fears on this score were so intense by 1928 that the Egyptian problem was soon being merged with the larger issue of Belligerent Rights. There were indeed signs that the British would give in to American pressures on this and yield her claimed prerogative of confiscating all neutral trade with an enemy power in wartime. In impinging on Belligerent Rights, the Clause question was further tautening the nerves of those whose security depended on Britain's long-range naval capacity. In a long memorandum, Carl Berendsen,[57] the New Zealand Prime Minister's external affairs advisor, argued that failure to cordon off League jurisdiction from sensitive military areas would be a tacit admission that 'Empire defence' no longer existed.[58]

It was precisely to reduce this scale of divergence that the UK had sought to develop consultative procedures. Far from developing into a means of policy debate, however, these procedures easily became a front behind which *faits accomplis* were prepared and executed. Privately, indeed, the Foreign Office was contemptuous of Bruce's claim that Australia had a right to hold up British policy until full discussions had taken place. One official noted that the UK was quite prepared to act alone or with the Dominions who are willing to fall into line with us. It would, however, probably be a mistake to say this now openly. We are in the process of consulting the other Governments . . . and their susceptibilities would probably be wounded if we made a bald statement to the effect that we were quite prepared to act without them if necessary.[59]

But Lindsay, the Permanent Head of the Foreign Office, now saw that the only way of blocking Clause signature was by inflating Bruce and consultation. He urged on Ramsay MacDonald the absolute necessity of keeping imperial issues out of the hands of European lawyer-politicians and Dominion separatists; Bruce's suggestion (that the Clause should be signed at Geneva, but that all reservations and ratifications should be left till later) was a 'weighty proposal'. Lindsay warned the Prime Minister that any failure to respond to Australia

would mean the end of joint action in future in matters of common interest as to which any difference of opinion existed, since the action of the U.K. would render it impossible in the future for us to object to similar independent action by the Free State or any other left wing Dominion.[60]

The FO's real objective in all this was to sink the Clause, not preserve Commonwealth unity. MacDonald's motives for surrendering to Lindsay are not clear, although he was habitually sensitive to Civil Service persuasions. Certainly, when a Cabinet Committee was hastily convened, he put Bruce right at the centre of his evaluation.

Australia has undoubtedly called 'check' and I see no way of moving further unless we are prepared to have a partial Dominion signature. This would be a mistake. . . . I think we can make a satisfactory appearance at Geneva with the Australian formula though it is not what I would like. Owing to constitutional developments we shall have to accept these impediments to the swift realisation of our will here. We must pay the price.[61]

This was the only occasion in the inter-war period when a British Prime Minister (ironically a Labour one) accepted that a Dominion could veto British action. It did not last. If MacDonald were susceptible to his Civil Service, he found it even more difficult to stand against his Party and the pro-League elements dominant within it. This group immediately organised a campaign which emphasised the reactionary influence of the Dominions. Cecil warned the Cabinet that if the Commonwealth connection continued to impede a peace policy in Europe there would be a deep public reaction against any future involvement of the Dominions in

British affairs,[62] and he told the Foreign Office that their tactics would end up by creating a 'Dominion *liberum* veto in Foreign Policy'.[63] But Cecil concentrated his remarks on the Prime Minister and created a picture of a general Dominion attempt to obtain a blocking-power over UK action. Bruce was, Cecil argued, using the arbitration issue as a means of extending this Dominion plan.[64] 'I cannot help feeling', he concluded, 'that if Bruce's thesis is admitted it will readily be extended to cover all important International Action.'[65] MacDonald was always quick to respond to any cry of 'internationalism in danger', and within days he swung round from his previous view. He now told Bruce that any failure by the UK to make an 'advance' at Geneva in the next Assembly session would stall the whole League experiment. 'If this entailed certain risks', he stated, 'we would still feel that they were risks which for the sake of stabilising peace we ought to be prepared to take.'[66]

Whilst the problem of the Commonwealth and the Clause had been elevated to the rarefied heights of Cabinet politics, the Dominions Office had, predictably, been squeezed out of the picture altogether. Now that the decision to sign had been taken, however, the department was drawn back into the proceedings and charged with the task of framing some approach which could allow MacDonald his moment of glory in Geneva without some Dominions jeering in the background. Much of the work of the Dominions Office, in fact, was of this nature – picking up the pieces of inter-imperial relations which had been broken by decisions taken by other departments. But now even the simplest procedural matters, such as convening a meeting of the Dominion representatives in London to discuss the form of the Clause signature, proved politically sensitive. The Irish Free State refused to send anybody at first on the transparent excuse that 'the subject is too complicated to brief the High Comissioner in the time available', and it was only after considerable persuasion on the part of the Dominions Office that Smiddy turned up at the last moment.[67] The Canadians firmly rejected the invitation and continued to do so even when the British officials sank to suggesting particular personnel who might be available.[68] Bruce agreed to send a representative, but made it plain that the latter's only authorisation would be to reiterate the Australian objections already made.[69] This was not the raw material out of which any convincing display of a united Empire could be wrought. The Dominions Office, however, was adept at technical devices which could add a cosmetic touch of unity. Passfield,[70] the new Dominions Secretary, suggested, therefore, that if all the Commonwealth governments could sign the Clause with a 'rider' that any one of them might attach reservations at a later date, MacDonald could make his signature whilst Bruce could still pretend that the UK might be persuaded to attach a reservation on Belligerent Rights and Egypt.[71] MacDonald urged this on the Dominion delegates who had finally assembled as a simple and comprehensive panacea, characteristically glossing over the differences which it concealed

> If we could not stand physically together the other nations would very quickly realise what had happened. . . . It seemed to him that all the Australian points were in the nature of additions to the reservations, and that such differences as existed might be smoothed over by mutual explanations. He wanted the door left open and if only each Dominion would agree to sign we could go ahead and interchange views, so that at the final act of reconciliation general agreement could be reached.[72]

MacDonald's urgent call for the Commonwealth to 'stand physically together' points to one of the central dilemmas in Britain's international policy. On the one hand the decisions that were taken increasingly reflected the degree to which the UK had become meshed into an international system; and yet a deep felt need remained to 'package' those decisions in terms of an Empire-state which still retained the power to act independently of the other major powers.

In the end both Coates and Bruce accepted the compromise worked out by the Dominions Office. This was not because they found McDonald's presentation convincing, but because, as Coates bitterly reflected, they realised that the UK's acceptance of the Clause was effectively binding on the whole Empire.[73] The strategic vulnerability of the Antipodean Dominions which made them oppose unqualified League arbitration also made it impossible for them to stake out independent positions on the matter. But clearly Australian and New Zealand confidence in the UK's ability and will to play an imperial role was declining rapidly by the later 1920s. Finally, MacDonald was disappointed in his belief that Bruce's conversion would secure a united Empire signature of the Clause. At the last moment the Irish Free State, refusing to contemplate a 'gentlemen's understanding' that inter-imperial disputes should be settled within a Commonwealth frame-work,[74] went ahead and signed alone and without any reservations whatsoever. Such public evidences of intra-Commonwealth disagreement had a real effect on the way other Powers viewed Britain and on the credibility of 'Empire Foreign Policy'.

Economic Problems

Whitehall's anxieties over Commonwealth relations in the later 1920s, then, chiefly arose from foreign policy dilemmas. Nonetheless, economic strains within the group relationship became increasingly important as the decade drew to a close. The Commonwealth comprised some of the great food-producing areas in the world, and those agrarian economies had moved into a crisis phase well before 1929 when the American stock market crash had such dramatic effects on industrialised nations. By 1930 each point of the 1923 triangle of Men, Money and Markets had been undermined.

The main author of the 1923 formula had been Stanley Bruce. His aim had been to meet mounting British criticisms that, ever since the passing of the pastoral age in the 1850s, Australia had failed to maximise the opportunities for UK exporters, investors or migrants. Britain, of course, had been central to Australian economic growth, but that growth had fallen well beneath metropolitan expectations;[75] and from the 1890s onwards British observers criticised Australian politicians for concentrating on raising living standards, rather than on generating the growth that would boost UK exports and migrants. Bruce now sought to link Anglo–Australian resources in a programme of development, not to please Whitehall, but because his domestic political strategy hinged on expanding jobs and productivity. His much publicised 1926 scheme for a group of leading British industrialists and financiers to visit Australia and draw up a 'blueprint' for growth was an attempt at that year's Imperial Conference to convince the UK government that he would keep his word.[76] He did not do so. Although development spending did rise appreciably in Australia during the 1920s (mostly through London borrowings), Bruce was unable to exert any political direction over expenditures. Whereas the prevailing image of imperial development implied that Dominion expansion should take place in the primary sector, in fact capital spending was concentrated on urban–industrial infrastructures; and, as Schedvin stresses in his fine analysis,[77] average productivity in the new secondary sector was less than in traditional rural activities, so that the general performance of the economy sagged.[78] Schedvin concludes

> Australia, unlike some of the larger industrial late-comers, found considerable early difficulty in achieving sufficient momentum for full 'take-off' into industrial growth. This was a function, in part, of size, of the unusually high living standard achieved prior to industrialisation, and of the timing of initial growth in the difficult inter-war years. Slow early growth, however, meant that Governments were required to play a more active part in industrial–urban development than would otherwise have been the case, not simply in providing adequate tariff protection, but also in creating much of the social capital on which this development rested.[79]

British public opinion did not understand the complexities of the Australian situation, but there was an awareness that the Australian economy was ceasing to fit neatly with that of the UK. Disappointed hopes quickly led to the apprehension of conspiracies, culprits and, it was hoped, some sort of corrective crisis ahead. By 1928 Hore-Ruthven,[80] Governor of South Australia, was denouncing the tacit alliance between Government and Unions in the Dominion which had, since 1918, built up yet another 'false standard of money, allowed people to live above their means and promoted the Communist notion that wealth could be created by legislation'.[81] The Queensland Governor was in full agreement on these points, although he was more hopeful about an imminent economic collapse which would force Australians out of productive activities which clashed with the UK.

> Personally I am of the opinion that sooner or later financial conditions . . . will compel a reorganisation of the whole industrial system [in Australia]. . . . It is courting failure for a man to come out to this country and forthwith his capital.[82]

British financial interests could not, however, be so complacent about the prospects of a downturn in the Australian economy because it was, ultimately, their money that was at stake. Indeed, during the 1920s Australia became the UK's largest overseas debtor, climaxing in 1927 when Australia had to find £47m for debt service, reconversions and new loan expenses in the UK.[83] The UK financial community had begun to question Australia's credit rating as early as 1924, but the Dominion's pressure on London money markets in 1927/28 sharpened the edge of criticism.[84] The political effects of the Anglo–Australian debt problem did not fully mature until the Depression, but by the late 1920s they were visible.

More generally, however, the 1920s witnessed a broad reassessment of the Dominions' economic potential. The War, with its rapid expansion of Dominion agricultural and to some extent industrial output, had led to exaggerated ideas of their likely economic development. In the 1920s, when all countries scrambled to recover their former markets, there followed an excess of productivity over demand in almost all trades, and primary produce prices were especially depressed. The agricultural economies of the Dominions came increasingly up against the need to contract rather than expand their operations. UK observers attributed this partly to the temporary problems of the world market, but it also led to a more realistic evaluation of the Dominions' long-term capacity. 'One fact is patent even to a layman', Nicholls explained to the Foreign Office after his first tour of New Zealand, 'viz. that the best land in New Zealand has been taken up and all the unoccupied land is now of second or third-class character.'[85] Archer,[86] a Principal in the Dominions Office, confirmed this new scepticism after travelling through the Antipodean Dominions in 1929: 'of great open spaces flowing with milk and honey', he reported, not without relish, 'I saw no sign either in

Australia or New Zealand.'[87] Canada was seen in much the same failing light. Indeed, the Canadian economy was particularly vulnerable because its prosperity during and after the War was based on wheat exports, and it was this commodity which more than any other was subject to competitive pressures. Although the wheat price did not 'dive' until 1929, the Canadian wheat pools had been struggling for years to locate adequate markets for their vast surpluses. The Dominions Office was very well aware of the constant seepage of resources (both human and financial) to the United States which resulted from this. Grasslands brought into production between 1914 and 1918 were now reverting to wastage so that between 1920 and 1927 there had been an overall decrease in homestead entries, something which had last happened in 1874.[88] A Dominions Office survey in 1929 concluded

> In any event it does not seem likely that the rapid growth of agriculture in the first twenty years of the present century will be continued. That period witnessed the construction of the transcontinental railway and the opening to settlement of the fertile and almost treeless prairies. The Peace River country is the last great agricultural frontier of . . . western Canada.[89]

It is against this background that the failure of each element in the Men, Money and Markets trinity must be seen. First of all, the optimistic belief that the 1922 Empire Settlement Act would inaugurate a process geared to balancing the Empire's resources of population, land and raw materials soon ran into difficulties. As we noted earlier,[90] that Act had emerged from the deflationary crisis of 1920–2. As the problem of unemployment moved to the centre of British politics during the rest of the decade, migration became a recurrent element in the formulation of economic strategies. The Treasury resisted this because it felt that settlement loans only increased the burden of Dominion indebtedness.[91] Otto Niemeyer[92] thus described Amery as a 'Mad Mullah Minister'[93] and Treasury officials generally distrusted the vulgar Keynsianism they perceived in both the Colonial and Dominions Offices. Treasury obstruction, however, could not stop the migration bandwagon once officials and politicians realised that unemployment would not simply disappear with the trade cycle. Ian Drummond identifies the Industrial Transference Board, which Baldwin set up in 1927 to study the 'distressed areas' of the UK, as the key institution which boosted the concept of exporting the unemployed.[94] In late 1927 Amery toured the Dominions propagandising the migration idea, and Lord Lovatt, Parliamentary Under-Secretary for the Dominions Office, did the same in the Canadian provinces in 1928.

But although migration had become part of the stock of economic ideas amongst British officials, the barriers to its implementation remained huge. South Africa presented minimal possibilities. The Pretoria bureaucracy discriminated against British settlers, South African agriculture required large initial capital expenditures, whilst the bourgeois social tone of that Dominion was not congenial to the masses of Britain's unemployed. In contrast, the federal and state governments in Australia were, it seemed, willing to cooperate. For them, settlement finance was a means of expanding amenities. The Treasury tried to counter this by ensuring that British monies were expended on the actual movement of people, but ultimately most of the cash involved in large-scale programmes such as the £34m Agreement was spent on capital projects such as forest clearance, irrigation and roads. This meant the acquisition of long-term assets for Australia, but it also made the per capita costs of settlement remarkably high. The personal resentments and even tragedies subsumed in this process were acute. Ex-Indian Army officers, lured to rural Victoria in the early 1920s by promises of productive land and plentiful subsidies, were by 1929 demanding compensated repatriation to the UK.[95] In volume terms the Australian land settlement schemes were a resounding failure. The Western Australia group scheme, for example, was intended to settle 75,000 migrants on 5 million acres, but by 1936 only 390 families remained on the site. The only restraint on these diseconomies lay in the negative fact that there were never enough projects to soak up the available money. By 1928 only £8.8m of the £34m had been allocated. After the peak year of 1926, indeed, assisted migration to Australia consistently fell in numbers.

Given the limited absorptive capacity of South Africa and Australia, the migration lobby had to effect Canadian cooperation if their objectives were to be obtained. Mackenzie King, determined to give the Conservatives in Canada no opportunity to depict him as anti-imperialist, kept these hopes alive by making encouraging noises on immigration. But in fact, both he and Skelton were convinced that the growth rate of Canada's manpower needs had slowed significantly.[96] They quite legitimately feared that Amery's schemes were simply a means of dumping British unemployed males whose industrial skills were redundant. Canadian provincial governments, moreover, became equally reticent on the settler issue, not least in the West as the international wheat crisis mounted. In 1930 only 8000 UK migrants reached Canada under the Empire Settlement Act proper, and thereafter the number dropped sharply.

This sequence of failure and frustration was underlain everywhere by political factors. Dominion trade unions opposed British immigration because they saw in it a conspiracy between their own capitalists and metropolitan financiers to create a pool of cheap labour. The expansion of a Labour politics in both Australia and New Zealand during the later 1920s appeared as a final blow to the vision of redistributed populations.

'It seems possible that so long as Labour holds the balance between Government and Opposition', Archer of the DO predicted on his return from the Pacific Dominions, 'the existence of unemployment might be used to keep in place the embargo on assisted migration long after it could reasonably have been removed.'[97]

But economic causes were even more dominant in structuring the situation. The higher cost-levels in the Dominions meant that the assistance required by UK settlers was high, and needed to continue over a longer period than most settlement schemes could permit. Drummond, however, in explaining the failure of the Empire Settlement Act, stresses fundamental contradictions in the whole approach to migration in the 1920s.[98] Invariably the idea was to transform Britain's industrial unemployed into Dominion farm-producers, a proletariat into sturdy agrarian freeholders. This perception of things arose from the notion of complementary exchange within the Empire, from the Dominions' refusal to increase the pressures on their own urban amenities and their fear of importing city-socialists, and from the agrarian romanticism so closely wedded to the imperial ideal. Yet it was at best negative, at worst destructive, to increase the numbers of rural producers in the Empire when primary produce prices were already falling. Although Drummond calculates that the world wheat glut was already too big to be seriously affected by production increases attributable to the Empire Settlement Act, he does argue that the overexpansion (largely through Australian 'closer settlement') of butter, dried fruit, mutton and lamb could be blamed on the Act. But was there any real alternative to a rural image of Empire migration? Drummond concludes that a balanced concept of primary–secondary development might have provided a better basis for the efficient transference of people. This obviously is an infinitely arguable point, but on the whole it does seem unlikely that this could have been so when the productivity of secondary employment was also falling everywhere.

This general description of Empire migration is not enough, however, if we are to grasp the political pressures building up within Commonwealth politics. It is necessary to delineate the personal frustrations of those involved both as officials and migrants. One sample episode may convey something of this. One group which Whitehall was especially keen to see replanted on distant farms was the British miner. In 1927, in the aftermath of the General Strike, the so-called 'Harvester Scheme' was put into operation whereby British mine-labour was transported to Canada at cut-rates to work for western farmers at harvest season. Those who wished to stay on and had evidence of stable employment could do so, whilst the rest were guaranteed a free passage home. It proved a disaster. Many miners found no work available for them when they arrived in the prairie provinces because the western farmers had overstated their labour requirements to ensure low wages;

others, used to moist underground conditions, could not endure the dry continental heat of Manitoba or Saskatchewan. Whatever their motives, groups of British workers (distinctly uncomfortable in a society far more conservative in its social and political style than Britain) left the scheme altogether, 'hoboed' their way back east and left a trail of unpaid bills, strained relations and a few cracked heads behind them. This strange episode reached a climax when a band of disillusioned migrants occupied Toronto Town Hall, daubed it with Socialist slogans and had to be forcefully evicted by a troop of Canadian Mounties.[99] Although the Dominions Office attempted to cover-up the 'Harvester' debacle, it was not repeated and very few of its participants decided to stay in their new habitat.[100] It was incidents such as this which pointed towards not only great economic differences between Britain and the Dominions, but a growing sociological differentiation.

The 'money' part of the 1923 formula is less easy to deal with if only because contemporaries themselves were unclear as to the character of monetary change. It was clear to all immediately after the War, however, that Britain's overseas investments had not only been reduced in quantity by something like one-quarter, but that the quality of what remained also signified a decline. This was because the liquidations of 1914–18 had concentrated on the UK's American holdings, which had represented such a sound basis for Britain's investment income since the mid-nineteenth century.[101] The 'orthodox' free traders (which meant most of the establishment) thus saw the chief task ahead as the renewal of overseas investment and its direction into sound channels. The Empire clearly represented quality in an investment portfolio, as safe if not as spectacularly profitable as pre-war America. During the 1920s, therefore, UK additions to her overseas holdings rose as a proportion of total new investment, with £872m going abroad and £1127m being invested in domestic plant, equipment and stocks; and a larger proportion of this overseas investment total went to the Empire, primarily the Dominions, than in the past.[102] This might be taken as evidence of increasing capital linkages between Britain and the Dominions, and there was certainly a trend to give Empire issues a distinct preference on the London money market. But in fact Britain's programme of external investment was only possible so long as the United States agreed to maintain international liquidity both directly by lending abroad and indirectly by importing goods. The fact that she did so obscured the underlying fact that the balance of financial influence had shifted from London to New York. Once American loan capital ceased to be easily available as the US stock market boom began in 1928, and even more so after the Great Crash of 1929, the scale of the revolution in international finance became only too plain. Already by 1928 the Australian government was having to look to the US banking community for emergency credit, and other Commonwealth governments, including the British, were soon to follow.[103]

Not only the underlying structures were changing. Attitudes were quickly affected, even if there was no satisfying definition of events available. The British Treasury was increasingly determined to retain as much capital as possible at home to maintain the Gold Standard, and it began to apply more selective criteria when reviewing overseas issues. This applied to both Empire and foreign loans, and in particular critical attention was paid to Australian indebtedness. 'Amery and his friends were impressed by the fact that the Dominions tended to spend in Britain what they borrowed in Britain', Drummond remarks. 'Niemeyer and the Bank of England were impressed by the fact that they did not spend *all* they borrowed.'[104] Thus the fact that Empire investment rose as a proportion of Britain's exported capital was only part of a general process of financial selectivity and a political evaluation of loan situations; and this process was as likely in the long run to prevent an impecunious Dominion government obtaining London credits as a foreign one. If by 1930 migration remained a bigger source of grievance than money in Anglo–Dominion relations, the position was very shortly to be reversed.

The main focus of Commonwealth economic cooperation between the wars, however, was on markets rather than manpower or finance. This reflects the fact that the heart of the post-war problem was a competition for markets induced by an excess of productive capacity over demand within the international economy. Many saw Commonwealth as an economic mechanism peculiarly adapted to solving the dilemmas which flowed from this situation. This view was based on the assumption of complementary specialisations among Commonwealth partners – wheat in Canada, wool and fruit in Australia and manufactured goods in the UK, for example. This idea of rigid specialisation, however, was already by the 1920s out of joint with economic reality. The Dominions had developed their own industrial structures, and the enlarged political influence which they aspired to in the future hinged on continuing this diversification. Fulfilling the 1923 preferential promises to UK exporters would have run counter to this, and they were consequently ignored. Already in early 1926, therefore, the UK Board of Trade was exploiting this to validate their central policy argument that the expansion of international, not imperial, trade must be Britain's chief economic priority. Thus it noted that Canadian anti-dumping duties were a barely concealed device to keep out UK goods, whilst the Australian Tariff Board operated with a blatant partiality towards domestic producers.[105] 'I feel it is a disappointing response', Cunliffe-Lister,[106] the President of the Board of Trade, remarked of Bruce's refusal to reform Australian customs practice, 'to our attempts to do something for Imperial Preference'.[107] The Dominion refusal to help British exporters, however, was in certain cases compounded with a manifest desire to extend their economic relationship with foreign interests. South Africa was prominent in this. In the same month, significantly, as Hertzog negotiated his agreement with the Portuguese Government,[108] a German trade delegation arrived in Pretoria, and a draft agreement soon emerged which made no provision whatsoever for Imperial Preference. This represented a fundamental break in Commonwealth orthodoxy because Imperial Preference had become the key method of economic cooperation. A tense episode followed in which Clifford, attempting to hold Beyers (the South African Commerce Minister) at the door of the room in which the German delegates were assembled for the final meeting, pressed on him that the draft as it stood was a major blow to the British connection. As Clifford later commented to Harding, it 'revealed the determination of the Union Government to go its own way regardless of the expostulations of the other parts of the Empire'.[109] And when Clifford tried to raise the possibility of the agreement's revision with Bodenstein, the External Affairs Secretary merely responded by side-tracking the conversation into a meaningless exchange on legal terminology.[110] Subsequently Clifford attributed the emergence of a 'separatist' trade diplomacy to the influence of Bruwer,[111] Bodenstein and Beyers within the South African bureaucracy rather than any overtly 'political' decision by Hertzog.[112] What was certainly clear, however, was that Imperial Preference had worn very thin as a basis for imperial economic cooperation.

The emphasis in this account so far has been on the economic forces within Dominions counteracting Empire cooperation and the British reaction to this. But the restraints on any cooperative 'advance' were as much to be found within the UK itself. The economic themes of the 1923 Imperial Conference and Baldwin's conversion to protectionism had been the product of deflation and an intense pessimism (confirmed by the Ruhr crisis) regarding the prospects for European stability. This setting had changed by 1925. The movement of the trade cycle (politically assisted by the Locarno agreements) primed the pump of European trade. Baldwin's surprise appointment of Winston Churchill as Chancellor of the Exchequer in his second administration, followed by Britain's return to the Gold Standard, meant that economic policy was once again moving along a European, not an imperial, axis. The pressures building up in Geneva for the UK to participate in a wheat preference for the farmers of the Danube Basin and so contribute to European economic reconstruction was just one example of how priorities had entered a state of flux.

The DO showed no more inclination to promote an 'imperial economy' than did the other Whitehall departments. A faint contempt, indeed, began to appear whenever a Dominion sought to offload its crop surpluses. When Canada, for example, petitioned in 1926 for a preferential tobacco duty in West African markets hitherto dominated by American producers, one official bluntly remarked

> If Canada wants to push the sale of Canadian tobacco there is one way to do it and one only. That is to get the West African merchants to take it up and sell it. If Canada can supply suitable tobacco at a better price than the U.S.A. the job ought to be easy.[113]

The fact that, without some 'rigging' of the market, Canadian producers had no chance of displacing their American counterparts did not concern the DO. By 1928 the Office was showing an even keener edge to the commercial importunities of the Dominions. When South Africa demanded that the UK reciprocate the preferences she received in the Union, the negative reply was made, not simply in traditional terms (that, for example, the UK already provided a huge subsidy in the form of Imperial Defence), but on new and more fundamental grounds: that, since the War, the British and Dominion economies had diverged on basic principles, the former moving towards a 'modified free trade' and the latter towards a complete protectionism, and between these two systems there could be no rational or fair calculation of reciprocity.[114]

These attitudes were, of course, antipathetic to those of Leopold Amery, their political head until May 1929. But, even more than in the early 1920s,[115] the officials had come to fear any political intervention to coerce Dominion economies into an imperial pattern. The *laissez-faire* responses of the DO, however, did not derive from the grip of nineteenth-century ideology (the Office personnel were the most unintellectual of civil servants) but because anything smacking of planned direction could only intensify internal Commonwealth pressures and make their particular task more difficult. Thus, as vested interests in Britain were stampeded by depression into protectionism during 1929 and 1930, the DO became commensurately more caustic. Batterbee dismissed Beaverbrook's Empire Free Trade crusade as a banal exercise in fantasy and deception. 'The general position is, of course', he briefed J. H. Thomas,[116] the new Secretary of State, 'that the economic policy of the Dominions is protective and that there is at present no likelihood whatever of getting them to abandon that policy.'[117] The facts supported this view. Eastern industrialists in Canada had accorded Beaverbrook's schemes a 'chilly reception' and subsequently had used the Anglo–Argentine agreement on wheat imports as a means of 'hammering sundry nails into the Beaverbrook coffin'.[118] The Australian government had carefully limited itself to the statement that public expenditure depended on high customs revenue – a polite way of saying that taxes on British goods could not be lifted.[119] It was therefore quite logical that the DO felt more at home with a Labour government after mid-1929 which showed no signs of seeking to solve economic problems through exaggerated notions of Empire development. The officials were careful not to state their party preferences, and there is no clear evidence that they rejoiced to see the back of Leopold Amery. Still, Wiseman, an Assistant Secretary, implied a lot when he stressed his department's agreement with the Labour view of Commonwealth economic cooperation and its limits:

> the present Government, like its predecessor, is a firm believer in the principle of imperial economic unity, but does not believe in attempts to achieve economic unity which would involve injuring its foreign trade or adding to the burdens of the people. There are other means of tightening the existing economic bonds between the various parts of the British Commonwealth than by proposing taxation . . . for the purpose of granting preferences. Among these methods may be mentioned the Empire Marketing Board, the Colonial Development Fund, and the numerous other Imperial organisations such as the Imperial Shipping Committee, the Imperial Economic Committee, the Imperial Agricultural Bureau, etc.[120]

Between these lines lay the DO's determination to keep the Commonwealth relationship clear of the party struggle. The Office was certainly eager to obtain such cooperation as was possible within the status quo, but no more than that. Above all, they feared a situation in which such cooperation – and with it the Commonwealth itself – became an issue in the Empire parliaments, preventing any rational evaluation of its benefits and exposing it to the manipulation of group interests.

Unfortunately for the DO, the impact of the Depression made it impossible to protect the Commonwealth from political events. The underlying clashes of interest between the British and Dominion economies were revealed with novel clarity; economic groups within the Commonwealth were pitted more directly against each other; and the imperial relationship as a whole was drawn into party politics. How did this happen? One of the key factors in the Depression was that the world price level of primary produce fell much more steeply than its industrial counterpart. This meant that agricultural countries simply could not afford to buy the usual quantities of goods from advanced industrial nations, and a substantial margin of world trade was automatically written off. These developments were vividly expressed within the Commonwealth where the relationship between agricultural and industrial economies was especially crucial. The terms of imperial trade moved decisively against Canada and Australia in their exchanges with the UK; and this, far from helping the UK, ultimately meant a reduction in her volume of exports, even if in the short term British consumers benefited from cheaper food. This economic sequence proved the falsity of Amery's assumption that the diversity of economic roles within the Empire, with primary satellites and an industrial metropolis, was a force for complementarity, integration and development. In fact this could only have been so where the terms and volume of trade were neatly balanced. Where these fell into disequilibrium, as they did after 1929, economic diversity made for competition and disunity because the Commonwealth was split down the middle between primary producers on the one hand and industrial producers on the other.

One major example of economic confrontation will suffice. This is the Anglo–Canadian struggle that occurred in the wheat market. Because Canada was the chief supplier and Britain the chief buyer of that commodity, there was a competitiveness inherent in the structure of their relationship. As long as the world wheat market remained buoyant and the Canadian farmers could find buyers elsewhere for such of their surplus as the UK did not consume, this competitiveness lay dormant. But in 1929 the world wheat price collapsed. This was broadly due to the delayed effect of over-production since the War, leading to stockpiles depressing the market. But the dumping of unrefrigerated Argentine supplies in that year, combined with a scare that Russia was about to re-enter world markets for the first time since 1914 and that the Bosphorus was crammed with her cargoes about to set out for Europe, were the immediate precipitants of a slump in that particular commodity. This inevitably led to a price battle between Canadian farmers and export interests on the one hand, and British millers and consumers on the other. This meshed dangerously with old Canadian images of a neglectful, self-interested Motherland. Hadow explained to Thomas

> The belief is engrained in Canadian minds that the last twelve months have seen a gigantic tug of war between the Canadian Wheat Pools and the Liverpool Grain Exchange for the control of the world's wheat prices. Superior strategy and knowledge of world stocks, as well as full use of 'cheap labour' Argentine or 'bounty fed' French and German wheat has won the day for Liverpool.[121]

If Canada had had some alternative to the British connection, such as a new trading alignment with the United States, this situation would have no doubt led to a politics of anti-imperialism. But the 1929 Hawley–Smoot tariff in America was decisive confirmation that Canadian producers could not hope to find outlets to the south. Hence the wheat crisis paradoxically created intense Canadian resentment of Britain's economic management and at the same time a tendency to 'look vaguely but expectantly to Great Britain for a solution to this vital problem'.[122] The political psychology of 'loyalism' and 'nationalism', therefore, were by no means easily differentiated. The one could very easily slide into the other, depending on changing conditions in international economic conditions. It was such volatility that the Dominions Office wished to skirt round, but the play of events was making this impossible. Bennett's victory over Mackenzie King in the 1930 general election on a platform of an imperial economic solution to Canada's dilemma meant that Commonwealth affairs had, in fact, become an issue in party politics. Clark warned Thomas in November 1930, on the eve of the Imperial Conference

> An unusual feature in the discussion [in Canada] – and one which represents an undesirable departure from the usual amity in such matters as between the member states of the Empire – is the frankness with which the possibility of a change of government in England is being canvassed in the Canadian press as bearing upon the prospects of Mr Bennett's claims.[123]

Anglo–Dominion relations had therefore moved into a politically volatile phase. In the relatively stable context of the 1920s the various Commonwealth leaderships had been able to build a relationship around the ambiguities of Imperial Preference, Balfour's Report and an 'Empire Foreign Policy'. But ambiguity always carries with it an area of risk and compromise for the parties involved; and conditions were making such agreements much more difficult. The 1930 Imperial Conference which followed showed that, although the scale of economic and diplomatic crisis had yet to be apprehended, there was a growing paranoia on all sides as to the benefits and direction of association.

7 The 1930 Imperial Conference

The accumulating tension described in the last chapter rose to the surface at the 1930 Imperial Conference. But before dealing with the course of that Conference, it is necessary, first of all, to set it in the context of changing international conditions, especially the failure of the Locarno system to stabilise permanently European relations. Clearly this latter point can only be dealt with very briefly here. It is enough to state that the continuance of Franco–German rivalry undermined the liberal regime in Weimar Germany and destroyed any possibility of replacing the security obsessions of France with a spirit of reconciliation. Consequently the increase in tariffs and arms expenditure and opposed alignments from 1928/29 onwards induced a psychology of crisis in European relations. In Britain this led to a reaction against the continued sacrifice of British interests for the sake of Europe. One example of this was the position taken up by Philip Snowden,[1] the Chancellor of the Exchequer, at the 1929 Hague reparations conference where he insisted that the UK's share of payments had been consistently whittled away without a comparable degree of restraint and compromise emerging from other countries, and that henceforth the Labour government would reject additional cuts. Although League enthusiasts condemned this as a lamentable recrudescence of power politics (alleging that the Chancellor was 'blocking the peace of Europe for a matter of £2½ millions a year',[2]) it did express the 'Britain First' sentiments which increasingly characterised domestic opinion. Indeed, MacDonald's defence of his colleague ('I believe we can get fair dealing without . . . breaking up . . . the Conference. Snowden is the man of the moment and I rejoice. The poor old country wants it badly and if he pulls it off, it will be a tremendous lift to our prestige.'[3]) reflects the sense of fatigue, barely repressed anger and self-pity which was now evident in British thinking.

It was the European situation, then, which determined the general atmosphere surrounding all other policy issues, including inter-imperial relations. Thus the same theme of reasserting 'British interests' can be seen in Whitehall's changing evaluation of Commonwealth. In the latter instance this took the form of the argument that 'freedom' had outbalanced 'unity' in Commonwealth affairs, and that mounting external pressures necessitated, and made practicable, a readjustment. This duality shows that the process at work was not a crude attempt to 'get out of Europe' or a 'return to Empire'. Rather it can be said that after 1930 all areas of British policy were affected by the desire to regain some unilateral influence over affairs, an influence which since the war had been mortgaged to the unlikely success of League Assemblies, the meetings of European statesmen and Imperial Conferences. The depth of this reaction was such that it affected the UK approach to constitutional reform, which of all the issues facing the 1930 Imperial Conference might have been taken as the least controversial. 'The current' Lord Sankey,[4] Lord Chancellor and chairman-designate of the Inter-Imperial Relations Committee, stated during his preparations 'is beginning to run against the disjunctive tendencies created unconsciously at the [1926] Imperial Conference.'[5] Amery was less optimistic. If he had supported legal devolution whilst in office, out of it he showed little faith in the ability of others to handle such a delicate process. He doubted whether a Labour government could discern where tactics ended and fundamentals began. In particular he doubted whether the new administration understood why the indivisible monarchy was so important. Amery appealed to Jowitt, the Attorney-General, to resist separatist pressures at the Conference in the same way as Selborne had appealed to him four years before.[6] After Amery had typically donated the Attorney-General four copies of his own collected speeches as inspiration, he exhorted

> As long as that principle [of the indivisible monarchy] is preserved there is nothing to prevent increasing unity in the future. If it ever goes we may soon break up entirely. We preserved it alright in 1926, though there were one or two phrases like 'freely associated' which Balfour let in, in spite of my objections, which may be held to imply a constitutional right of secession, as apart from a disclaiming of the idea of unity being maintained by coercion. The Report on Dominions Legislation preserves it, especially if all its recommendations are read in the constructive rather than the negative spirit.[7]

Hankey especially, however, felt that the Conference was likely to witness the final convulsions of the 'constructive spirit' so sedulously cultivated in the preceding years. He became acutely nervous that Hertzog would try and put the right of secession at the centre of all discussions, and he spent much of his time considering how this challenge could be met. Calculating that South Africa and the Irish Free State would meet with the determined opposition of the other Dominions, he advised the Prime Minister to imitate Asquith's conduct in 1911 and, by refusing to arbitrate, let both sides stalemate each other. 'The question is a trap', the Cabinet Secretary concluded, 'If we agree the right of secession de Valera will exercise it. If we refuse to admit it, we shall have no end of trouble. . . . I cannot see why we should discuss these abominations.'[8] This did not meet with Dominions Office approval. The idea of scrapping Conference management to let Dominion factions bring all their differences into the open seemed likely to destroy years of careful work. Instead Holmes[9] told MacDonald that the British should meet the Hertzog case on 'general grounds'.[10] This meant that the debate had to be gently escorted away from the ideological grounds selected by the South African leader.

> To consider what would be the position . . . of a Dominion which had decided to secede from the Commonwealth seems to me to be falling into the error which Balfour described in December 1926 in a debate on the 1926 Imperial Conference in the following terms: 'You might as well consider all the causes of divorce before you decide upon the problems of matrimony'. Indeed this remark seems most appropriate to any proposal for the discussion of secession at an Imperial Conference, the prime object of which might reasonably be supposed to be the discussion of modes of cooperation.[11]

This was just one occasion when the use of logic by the DO to clothe its narrow departmental purposes in the garments of 'general interest' broke down altogether: for if questions such as secession must give way to 'modes of cooperation' as the proper subject-matter for a Conference, it might be supposed that the agenda was full of schemes for military, economic or diplomatic partnership. In fact, if any such schemes did surface, they usually did so in the face of DO opposition. The Office had become the prisoner of a revolving conundrum whereby Dominions nationalism was always appeased in order to facilitate cooperation, whilst cooperative initiatives were always rejected for fear of stimulating Dominion nationalism. The real objective was to stifle any activity, be it of the secessionist or cooperative variety, and therefore protect a weak department from any criticisms it could not easily sustain. It was because Holmes recognised the weakness of his main contention, perhaps, that he added a further line of defence, one more explicitly aimed at the issues Hertzog was supposed to be preparing but which, Holmes stressed, should only be used as a final resort.

> Of course, there is a difficult problem as to whether it would be 'constitutional' for the Union of South Africa to secede; but this is a question which . . . would have to be argued on quite different grounds – for example, whether remaining within the Empire was not a part of the bargain made between the separate Provinces at the time the Union was set up – a bargain which could not, morally, be broken now.[12]

Moral arguments always had an irresistible appeal for MacDonald if they coincided with his own predilections. 'British connection was the assumption', he minuted approvingly, 'The connection cannot be made and then held to break itself.'[13] The ready reversion of both Holmes and MacDonald to 1910 indicates how historically superficial Balfour's 1926 Report was as a factor in imperial continuity. That Report had been a hasty improvisation to hold the constitutional lines, and at the slightest rumble of secession the British official mind rushed back to the deeper memories of Union-making. But Holmes's emphasis on the moral basis of Commonwealth is also noteworthy because it shows how Commonwealth was becoming an intensely ethical conception. On the one hand reference to concrete political themes of Empire had become impossible, because the likely effect was to polarise relations; and yet on the other, as international conditions worsened, leaders associated with Commonwealth affairs had a psychological need to assert that this potentially useful mechanism still existed, to prove, if only in words, that it was actually there. The reiteration of moral themes met this need whilst being within the limits of political acceptability. The theocratic overtones of the Commonwealth idea were not, as Corelli Barnett evocatively declared,[14] the product of minds besotted with the evangelicalism of the British public school system, but were a calculated response to the sort of relationship now subsisting among Commonwealth members and the ideology it was capable of supporting.

In fact it soon appeared that Hertzog was not going to press the constitutional question at all. Hertzog, indeed, had for some time previous sought to relegate the 'independence' issue to the background. Having been elected on a nationalist platform in 1924, he now wished to consolidate his power by dominating the centre ground in South African politics; and this meant appealing to both English and Afrikaner sections by stressing their common interests in the face of a 'black menace' rather than the historic Anglo–Dutch divisions. The Flag controversy especially had indicated that the recurrence of inter-white rivalries benefited Smuts rather than himself.[15] Thus in December 1928 Hertzog had told Clifford plainly that his days of 'Commonwealth-bashing' were over.[16] By 1930 events had moved on still further. The deepening economic recession had, by underlining the need for party cooperation in unstable conditions, opened the way towards a coalition of the Smuts and Hertzog factions. For this to take place Smuts had to cut loose from the 'jingo' Unionists whilst Hertzog had to reject his old relationship with Afrikaner extremists. In July 1930, therefore, Hertzog gave a major policy speech in Pretoria in which, whilst asserting the right of secession in a brief paragraph, it was made clear that the 'turbulent irresponsibility' of the Republican clique in Bloemfontein would no longer be tolerated.[17] Clifford had recognised this growing, if limited, acceptance of the imperial connection on Hertzog's part and argued that it should be carefully exploited as a basis for Anglo–South African understanding. He knew that the Commonwealth idea could only develop within the limits laid down by domestic Dominion politics, that in times of peace such an understanding would be much curtailed, but that it ensured broader cooperation in an international crisis.

But this political sensitivity was still largely absent in Whitehall. Although the Dominions Office had been moving towards a similar position, most other departments and leading politicians retained a false fundamentalism in which Dominion statesmen split crudely into those 'for' and 'against' the Empire. This fundamentalism sprang from a failure to appreciate the force of restraint which narrowed the options of even a nationalist leader in a Dominion. Obsessed with Dominion opposition to economic or military cooperation with Britain, the British mind frequently latched onto a series of external 'bonds' (the residual powers of Westminster, or the common monarchy, or the irreducible moral qualities of the basic constitution) as an assurance that the slide towards disintegration could be halted. Hankey therefore reacted with horror at the merest mention of 'secession' by Hertzog without noting the more subtle way in which the South African Prime Minister was trying to take the question off the nationalist agenda. Equally, on hearing with 'extraordinary relief' that Hertzog did not intend to push constitutional matters at the Conference, the Cabinet Secretary went to the other extreme and interpreted it as a conversion to the ideal of Commonwealth cooperation.[18] In short, in the early 1930s there was still no mature understanding of the Hertzog brand of Commonwealth membership.

Amidst all this uncertainty it was possible for different interests to attempt to impose their own pattern. Thus, whilst some UK officials sought to ensure a quiet Conference by taking secession off the agenda, others sought to add substance to the event by putting defence onto it. The Treasury saw an opportunity to press for a thorough reallocation of financial contributions to Imperial Defence.[19] It was ridiculous, they argued, that Australia and New Zealand would make only 'occasional gifts' of money towards the Singapore Base when it was their prime guarantee of survival, and they set out the demand that Empire defence costs should be redistributed on the basis of the 'commercial and other interests' of the various Commonwealth partners.[20] The DO saw in this not only a threat to the stability of Empire relations, but felt their own place as the cautious managers of the system to be under attack. Harding warned the Treasury that pressure on the Dominions would only lead to the destruction of such military cooperation as already existed – Canada would scrap the destroyer she had promised to build, whilst Australia and New Zealand would evade Singapore commitments altogether.[21] 'Who is to determine what are the commercial and other interests of the several parts of the Empire?' Batterbee questioned

'And what is the answer to Canada if she should claim (as she has claimed in the past) that she already protects Imperial communications over 3000 miles of land?'[22]

It was the DO's refusal to give short shrift to such transparently shallow arguments as this, and the way in which the Office actually redeployed them within Whitehall exchanges, that earned it the contempt of fellow-departments. The Chief of the Imperial General Staff, Sir George Milne,[23] tried to align Commonwealth management with what he saw as the inescapable realities of worsening international conditions. Mere repetition of the bland Defence Resolutions of 1926 would only confirm

> the inference, undoubtedly drawn by many of the Dominions . . . that the U.K. would automatically shoulder the bulk of the responsibility . . . in a major war . . . .The extent of the cooperation by the Dominion forces, even when it is assumed that the latter would be cooperating, cannot be gauged, and the Dominion forces would have to be regarded largely as an extra asset not to be taken into account.[24]

But these arguments failed to convince MacDonald. He was too committed to a policy of disarmament and could not afford to be seen by either German or American opinion to be concocting some new military system. During the Conference, Chiefs of Staff meetings were therefore held at which Dominion service personnel were present, and ornamental features such as a naval display off Portland, an army mechanical exhibition at Aldershot and the inevitable trip to Croydon Aerodrome were organised to show that imperial defence in some shape or form still existed, but that was all. Even Hankey's suggestion that common military planning should not be discussed at Conference sessions but at a more informal meeting of the Committee of Imperial Defence (to which the Dominion leaders could be conveniently invited) was rejected.[25] Hankey commiserated after the Conference with the Chief of Imperial General Staff:

> Like you I am bitterly disappointed that we failed at this Conference to get any progress in revising the Defence Resolutions or to discuss Defence adequately. My experience of the last stages of the Conference, however, unfortunately more than confirmed the impression I found earlier that we should meet with considerable difficulty . . . even the very brief and innocuous paragraphs of the published Report . . . had to be modified to meet the difficult internal situation of the Irish Free State ministers.[26]

Indeed, it was economics, not defence, which dominated the story of the Conference.[27] This had not been the intention of the UK Government. MacDonald's internationalist foreign policy was even more strongly linked to a commitment to free trade and the restoration of the European economy than its Conservative predecessor; whilst we have already noted the stringent Whitehall critique of Dominion protectionism. Originally, therefore, the British suggestion had been merely a general review of trade.[28] This, however, did not meet Dominion needs. With the collapse in primary product prices from 1929 onwards Dominion politicians were under enormous pressure to obtain a larger share of the UK market for their producers. The Australian bulk purchase proposal which Scullin[29] wished the Conference to consider, for example, implied, as Drummond remarks, that 'in effect, Britain should underwrite whatever standard of living the Australians thought their farmers and farm labourers should enjoy'.[30] R. B. Bennett, too, approached the Conference determined to 'deliver the goods' to the electors who had so recently elected him to power on a doctor's mandate. For this he required a quasi-monopoly (be it through tariffs, bulk purchase, import boards or any other convenient mechanism) on timber and, above all, wheat. Leo Amery saw in Bennett and Scullin's dilemma an opportunity finally to force through imperial economic reform. Indeed, his own thinking had undergone a turn around since 1926. Whereas then he had sought a constitutional agreement as a prelude to economic change, now he argued that economic change was essential to offset the constitutional rot. 'I needn't tell one like you who knows the constitutional position', he had told Jowitt, 'how urgent it is to make progress on the economic side.'[31]

The issues which Amery, Bennett and Scullin wished to raise, however, went to the heart of British politics, and posed a challenge which MacDonald as much as Baldwin was determined to evade. At no point did the British Cabinet address itself to the problem of the form which imperial economic cooperation could in the circumstances assume. To have done so would have triggered off both party and national controversy of a very delicate kind. How, for example, could a Labour government adopt a policy which raised living costs, especially food prices, at a time when unemployment was steadily rising? And yet to refuse some attempt at an inter-imperial response to trade depression jarred with the image of Commonwealth as an association geared to mutual cooperation and protection. The contradiction was plain, and the Labour government's approach was simply to wait and hope the problem would go away. The Cabinet's only conclusion before the Conference was to recognise that

> it would be as difficult for the Dominions to offer a secured market for the manufactures of the Mother Country without detriment to their world trade, as it would be for the United Kingdom to purchase from

the Dominions their requirements to the detriment of their trade with foreign countries, such as, for example, the Argentine.[32]

This situation suited the Chancellor of the Exchequer, Philip Snowden, because it left him complete freedom of action in the Conference. A rigidly orthodox free-trader who equated socialism with consumer rather than producer interests, Snowden was prepared to confront the Dominion protectionists with the same aggressiveness as he had faced his European colleagues at The Hague conference. Just as the Europeans had always expected the UK to transfer uncomplainingly her reparation payments to them, so the Dominions had always expected the UK to guarantee their trade balances at the expense of the British housewife – giving little or nothing in return. So that when Bennett, trying to capitalise on the growing weakness of the MacDonald administration, stormed the Conference with a proposal that all the Commonwealth governments should increase their tariffs 10 per cent 'all-round' (a proposal which would clearly cost the UK more than anybody else, because she was the largest international trader and therefore more vulnerable to retaliation) Snowden's response was unequivocal. According to the Free State delegate, Fitzgerald,[33] the Chancellor proceeded to 'wipe the floor with Bennett';[34] and when the Canadian Prime Minister responded by accusing the British Ministers of wilful blindness to imperial interests, Thomas dismissed his demagogic tactics with a phrase ('Humbug!') which was still rankling in Ottawa two years later. Not surprisingly, not even the barest framework of an agreement emerged from these exchanges. Beneath the abuse were the political facts that Bennett was not prepared to alienate industrial interests in Ontario by letting in more UK manufactures, whilst the UK was not prepared to offend British consumers and other international primary producers by letting in more Dominion foodstuffs. Although an attempt was made to disguise failure by declaring the economic agenda only 'adjourned' until a new meeting to be convened in Ottawa two years later, it was clear that imperial economic relations had moved into a new and disruptive phase.

The rancour of the economic debates certainly reacted on the constitutional discussions too. The Dominions Office had hoped originally to draw up a comprehensive legal description of Dominion status so that aspiring colonies, such as Malta and Southern Rhodesia, could be cordoned off from the 'club of 1926'. After numerous variants were put up and found to be wanting, the task had to be put aside. 'If we indulge in new-fangled definitions we shall be raising questions and doubts' it was concluded 'which we shall have no authority to answer or allay.'[35] The Office adopted the narrower Conference objective of securing agreement of British officials and Dominion politicians to the 1929 Report. In addition to this it was hoped that the Dominions might be manoeuvred into a recognition of the *inter se* principle (that is, that inter-imperial relations could not be legally regarded as being of the same character as relationships between separate foreign states) and that some movement could begin towards an inter-imperial tribunal to ensure that Commonwealth disputes could not be made subject to League arbitration.[36] These objectives reflected the overriding concern of the Dominions Office with the working of the Commonwealth as a unit in international diplomacy rather than with the Empire's internal constitutional structure.

The Conference sub-committee which dealt with constitutional issues, however, was headed not by the Dominions Secretary but by Lord Sankey. Sankey was, it could be mildly said, an unfortunate choice for this responsibility. His appointment as Lord Chancellor in 1929 can be explained as essentially the payment of an old political debt by MacDonald and because he was the only leading figure in the legal profession willing to serve in a Labour administration; but his political perceptions were limited both by his native naïvety and by a morbid and repressed personal life.[37] His mistake in 1930 was not to realise how much politics had to be a factor in constitutional change; and instead his attitudes were formed by a mixture of judicial pedantry, legal romanticism and a brisk reaction against the modernisms of the previous decade. He told Ramsay MacDonald before the Conference opened

The difficulty we are in is the most unfortunate Declaration made at the 1926 Conference by the Committee . . . presided over by Lord Balfour. I am far from saying that Declaration was a wrong one; the real cause for complaint against it is this: as it was couched in general and abstract terms in a rather hurried way, without considering the logical and legal effects it might have when translated from generalities into particulars. It is easy enough to gain a passing cheer, but the difficulty is when you begin to translate them into action. Logically pursued these phrases necessitate the examination of constitutional questions which are better left unexamined. The law with regard to them is obscure; the reasons for their enactment are not so plain nowadays as they were doubtless when they were made, but it is a mistake to think our forefathers were fools, and to repeal constitutional measures which have been useful and unquestioned for generations. As a result of the Declaration a Committee sat in 1929 to consider the Operation of Dominion Legislation and to produce a Report. This Report I personally do not like, and it has created amongst many people not only in England but throughout the Empire . . . something like amazement, if not consternation. Let me at once say that I think the 1929 Report is the legal and logical result of the 1926 Balfour Declaration, but life is not governed by logic and you can have too many laws. Not only has this Report got to be discussed at this Conference, but also . . . numerous other thorny topics arise as a result of the Balfour Declaration.[38]

To pronounce these feelings privately to MacDonald was one thing, to put them before Dominion leaders at a Conference quite another. They confirmed all the recurrent allegations that since 1926 the UK government had consistently tried to sabotage the effective political expression of the legal assumptions in Balfour's Report. Above all, Sankey was faced with a new radicalism on the part of the Irish Free State representatives. In 1926, barely recovered from the civil war and deep into difficult negotiations with the UK government over such matters as compensation for British ex-civil servants, Cosgrave's delegates had supported Hertzog from the sidelines rather than adopt any independent initiative themselves.[39] For the next few years British opinion as a whole basked in the happy delusion of Anglo–Irish reconciliation, and in 1930 Sankey was confident that the Free Staters could be controlled. Vain and inexperienced though they were, he was certain that they would bend to 'judicious handling'.[40] 'We must not forget', he noted with the simple paternalism which characterised his thinking on all Commonwealth matters, 'that young men and growing nations can be tiresome at times.'[41] But the political context of Anglo–Irish relations was changing rapidly. Already in 1929, Cosgrave's early nervousness gone, the Free State had begun to stake out a more independent position in the international sphere. By 1930, even more significantly, it was becoming apparent that Cosgrave's popularity was under intense pressure from de Valera, and this pushed the former into a pronounced anti-Commonwealth pose. Whilst Hertzog was moving 'right', therefore, Cosgrave was moving 'left', both for domestic political reasons rather than as a result of any re-evaluation of the imperial connection as such. From the start of the Conference sub-committee, therefore, the Free State delegates dominated proceedings. MacGilligan's intransigence culminated in his objection to the appellation 'British' before 'Commonwealth' in the title of the association of which, with obvious reluctance, he admitted himself to be a member.[42] Sankey's paternalism soon degenerated into economic threat. 'I put it to him [MacGilligan[43]] privately', the Lord Chancellor recorded, 'that as long as the Exports from Ireland to the UK were £40 millions and the exports from the UK to Ireland £39 millions, we had better not be foolish enough to create difficulties.'[44] Sankey had to learn what the British government would deduce under even more bitter circumstances later, that the Free State government could not be coerced by the level of economic pressure which it was politically possible for the UK to bring to bear. The Free State continued to oppose any dilution of the 1929 proposals, and personal rancour reached the point where Fitzgerald had to absent himself from Sankey's breakfast meetings for sub-committee personnel because, as he told his wife, '. . . he [Sankey] couldn't stand the sight of me'.[45]

Sankey, however, noticed that the Free State delegates got little verbal backing from the other Dominion leaders, and this led him to think that MacGilligan and Fitzgerald could be outmanoeuvred. 'They are . . . putting up the backs of every other Dominion . . . ', the Lord Chancellor noted, 'and therefore I am continuing these discussions really for the purpose of isolating the Irish.'[46] This was a misjudgement. Whereas the Free State had been happy for Hertzog to do their work for them in 1926, in 1930 Hertzog was happy for the Free State to do likewise; to hope to drive a wedge between them was delusory. Scullin, meanwhile, was too immersed in his private battle to force through the appointment of Sir Isaac Isaacs as Australian Governor-General against the King's wishes[47] to take any part in the other constitutional questions, but as a Labour prime minister he was not likely to let himself be implicated in Sankey's machinations. But what really tilted the balance was the Canadian attitude. Canada, occupying the centre-ground between Free State and South African radicalism on the one hand and the relative conservatism of Australia and New Zealand on the other, was always of critical importance in shaping the outcome of Commonwealth controversy. Sankey presumably anticipated that the Conservative–imperialist Bennett would support his cautious approach to constitutional change. Bennett, however, consistently voted with the Free State; and when MacGilligan questioned Guthrie,[48] the Canadian Minister of Justice, why this should be, he was told that if Bennett could not have his wheat monopoly the British could not have their constitution.[49] Sankey's only ally, indeed, turned out to be the New Zealand premier, Forbes,[50] and he was of little use because, as Sankey himself admitted, '[Forbes was] evidently dull and slow-witted' and during the Conference had 'shown no more knowledge than a sheep-farmer (which he is) of a difficult constitutional question'.[51]

Inevitably the 1929 Report had to be accepted *in toto*, and there was deadlock on the problem of the *inter se* doctrine, the Privy Council and the inter-imperial tribunal. This outcome led more than ever to a cynical attitude among British officials towards the Commonwealth relationship. Mounsey caught the general tone well when he wrote to Sankey shortly after the Conference delegates had disbanded.

I can well understand that it must be disappointing to you, as it is to me, to think that all this work of the last few months and weeks has not produced more immediately satisfactory results, but . . . the Empire still goes on, and we can only hope that as in the past, it may continue to thrive on the insolubility of the constitutional problems which attend its progressive development.[52]

The 1930 Imperial Conference was the first of its kind to break the conventions of harmony and gentlemanly compromise which had come to dominate its institutional image. These conventions had been able to survive because, even in wartime, the Conferences had been symbols of mutual interest rather than forums for hard political bargaining. The economic crisis, however, had given the imperial connection a political relevance it had not had before. The extent to which the Commonwealth shared compatible interests was therefore being put to the test; and the failure to establish any common economic approach was a warning that the habits of unity could snap if the Commonwealth were transported from its heavenly estate (unquestioned, untested and draped in rhetoric) into a real political world where its various partners competed against each other in a closed, poorer and probably insecure imperial system. If Amery saw the international depression, then, as an opportunity to re-open the case for imperial reform, it did in fact threaten to expose the unrealism of the values which lay behind his aspirations.

It should be stressed, however, that the uncertainties and tensions of the Imperial Conference had been indicative less of political change internally generated within the Commonwealth relationship than of a collapse in the wider international economic and political system established by the post-war settlement. Moreover, although the Conference had been another blow to any idea of a 'natural' Empire unity, it had nonetheless demonstrated that the Dominions could not afford to pull out of that association altogether. The constitutional discussions of 1930 (with their underlying threats and fears of Dominion secessionism) proved to be the tail-end of that 'legal politics' which had been such a prominent part of inter-imperial exchanges since 1926. It was not that the constitutional issues had been solved in any way but that for both the UK and the Dominions they lost their relevance in a world primarily concerned with unprecedented unemployment and heightened international insecurity.

8 The Commonwealth and the Economic Crisis 1931–1939

The economic and political crisis of the early 1930s effectively destroyed the internationalist consensus which had helped stabilise European affairs since the war. 'For the first time since the peace', Robert Vansittart noted in 1931 looking back on the preceding twelve months, 'people talked of war, foolishly no doubt, as a thing no longer unbelievable. It became once again a possibility in the mind of man.'[1] And because British diplomacy and prestige had been so clearly identified with the League's success it was inevitable that, in particular, doubts should now be felt as to the UK's capacity to maintain the Versailles system. The moral legitimacy of British power which for Austen Chamberlain had been symbolised by the achievement of Locarno was being destroyed, Vansittart remarked, by the idle chatter of British decline around the cafe tables of Paris, Berlin and Geneva.[2] In Whitehall, too, considerable effort went into analysing Britain's failure to keep a European concert in being. Social division at home, the sustained depression in the traditional export industries and the continuance of tense Anglo–American relations preventing cooperation among the Anglo–Saxon powers were all prominent as explanations. In January 1932, however, Vansittart added one further factor

> One reason for our loss of weight since 1926 has been that the 'foreigner' – we must be insular for a minute – has been secretly anticipating the gradual dissolution of the Empire, and some of the Commonwealth delegations have not at times exactly discouraged the idea. It is therefore essential that this hand should be played with the greatest possible measure of unity among the Commonwealth representatives . . . it is impossible to separate ourselves from, or to go against, the Dominions at this crisis. . . .[3]

Thus even a pronounced Europeanist like Vansittart was, by early 1932, thinking in terms of 'closing the Commonwealth ranks'. This isolationist reaction had been given a strong boost by the advent of the National Government and the rejection of the Gold Standard. This latter event was the most overtly isolationist act taken by a British government between the wars; it was, in effect, an assertion that the British economy could function independently of Europe and America. Sir John Simon,[4] the Foreign Secretary, had told the Cabinet in late 1931:

> Leaving the gold standard has placed a powerful weapon in our hands, and has released us from French and American domination; other Dominions and foreign countries already are following the £ sterling rather than the gold £, e.g. Australia, New Zealand, India, Canada, Rhodesia, Crown Colonies, Denmark, Norway, Sweden, Portugal, Finland, Egypt, Argentina, Brazil, Chile, Peru, Bolivia, Mexico. The sterling bloc is almost self-contained.[5]

The fact that this group of primary producers supplying the UK market included as many foreign as Commonwealth countries explains the structural problems involved in the establishment of a Commonwealth economic system. But at the time it was natural that the discarding of the gold standard should have put the aspiration for imperial autarky back in the political picture. The gold crisis, in fact, had seemed to confirm the assumption that in an emergency the Commonwealth links always tightened in exact proportion to the degree of external pressure. Thus, when the dramatic news reached Geneva that the pound was 'on the brink', there was an immediate drawing together of the Commonwealth delegations. Clutterbuck, the Dominions Office representative in the UK delegation at the League in 1931, reported the intense shock which had swept through the Dominion delegates, how all of them had dutifully attended an emergency meeting of Empire representatives (some, especially the Free State, having consistently boycotted them in the past) and how Cecil had glumly communicated what little information he had at his disposal.

> There was then a rather touching scene. After Wilford[6] had thanked Lord Cecil and declared the readiness of everyone to be called together, day or night, Collins[7] paid a handsome tribute to the courage and wisdom of His Majesty's Government in the United Kingdom in adopting the course they had taken. It was a special matter for congratulation . . . that this crisis had come upon them when steps had been taken to balance the budget; if it had come a month ago, when the budget was still unbalanced, the situation would have been very difficult to control. As it was, he ventured to prophesy that when the immediate panic had spent itself, the pound would be found to have depreciated very little below gold point. Guthrie agreed and said that Canada had such complete confidence in 'British' finance that he felt sure that they would have no alarm. In fact he had

been informed that the pound would open today on New York at 4.85 dollars. Not much more was said but there was a general air of readiness to stand by us which was very encouraging. Rather like the War in fact! The Irish in particular seem to be taking things very well. . . .[8]

If the politics of Commonwealth relations is to be properly understood, episodes such as these have to be emphasised alongside the evidence for growing Dominion independence. Even in those Dominions whose domestic politics could be defined in terms of nationalist aspirations a 'loyalist reflex' was easily touched off by external pressures. This was true even of the Free State. 'Here as there (i.e. Great Britain) the general public has no clear idea of what is meant by a gold standard', Peters reported from Dublin 'There is, however, a thorough realisation of the fact that the two countries stand or fall together under present circumstances.'[9] Ironically the economic 'maturity' of Dominion life which underlay their political and constitutional advance during and after the war meant a greater sensitivity to international conditions and, by the same token, an inability to exist apart from the imperial connection without a fundamental disruption to their social structures. The rhetoric of 'equality' and 'freedom' in the 1920s, then, have to be seen not so much as a process of legal and political separation but as a response by the Dominions to an extended interaction with the British, and more generally with the international, economy.

But if the UK's move away from the gold standard had in some respects provided an index of Commonwealth unity, it also underlined the doubts as to the UK's ultimate reliability as a source of wealth and protection. Thus the failure of the 1930 Imperial Conference to provide an imperial solution for Canada's economic problems boosted the arguments put forward by important groups in that Dominion for an alternative trade alignment with the United States.[10] It was only the United States's own commitment to protectionism (a commitment even more in evidence during the depression) which limited Canada's freedom of manoeuvre on economic questions. Yet if the US were not prepared to take in greatly enlarged quantities of Canadian goods, she had long been prepared to invest her capital in Canadian production, not least as a stratagem to 'get under' the system of Imperial Preference. Thus by 1931 the US provided 61 per cent of the total overseas investment in Canada whilst the UK share had sunk to 35 per cent.[11] This clearly meant that Canada had financial options apart from her relationship with Britain, and Bennett decided to exploit this situation. Although Canada therefore officially left the gold standard the pound sterling was fixed for purposes of duty assessment at the old parity of 4.86 dollars, and when the rate inevitably depreciated with sterling's fall on both the New York and London exchanges Bennett imposed a series of anti-dumping duties on British goods – all of which ensured that British exports received none of the advantages in Canadian markets which the new monetary policy was designed to achieve.

Bennett's intentions here were twofold and in some ways contradictory. The first was to extend Canada's range of options in her external relationships. Her surplus of primary produce, indeed, was such that even the UK market could not consume it all at a reasonable price level, so that Canada was searching for wider international opportunities. The second was to build up a strong bargaining position at the forthcoming Ottawa Conference which was to look specifically at the evolution of Commonwealth trading relationships. But as Whiskard,[12] Assistant Secretary in the Dominions Office, commented, Bennett's action made a fruitful outcome of the Ottawa negotiations even more unlikely because, from the Whitehall perspective, the key to economic recovery in the Empire lay in wider opportunities for UK manufactures in the Dominions rather than for Dominion primary products in the UK.[13] The long-standing British perception of Canadian economic policy as selfish and short-sighted was confirmed by Bennett's wrong-headed attempt to put the cart of Dominion prosperity before the horse of the metropolitan economy. Even some of Bennett's Ottawa associates shared this view. Colonel Vanier[14] characterised his actions as tantamount to ' . . . hitting a man when he is down'.[15] Inter-imperial relations were thus increasingly subject to conflicting forces and calculations as political leaders, confronted with disgruntled electorates demanding effective action to remedy depression, tried to steer a course towards secure ports of call wherever they might be found.

More of a shock that Bennett's attitude, however, was South Africa's attempt to stay on the formal gold standard. If a political rationale for this could easily be found in Hertzogite nationalism, a credible economic rationale could not. 'Devaluation meant Socialism', Havenga[16] had explained – 'that the strong must make way for the weak, the rich for the poor'.[17] But although this pointed accurately enough to the acute differentiation now evident between South African and British political culture, it was clearly not in itself a sufficient explanation. South Africa did not have, like Canada, access to a major source of funds apart from the London market, and it was inevitable that British capital would be repatriated to London as the South African economy, trying to maintain an unrealistic parity, came under competitive strain. Various suggestions were put forward. It was speculated in the Dominions Office that

One of the main considerations may be what they [the South Africans] apparently call the 'long view' – which apparently is that if South Africa joins the countries which have temporarily abandoned gold, this movement may be accelerated, and a position may eventually be reached where the monetary demand for gold may diminish seriously with disastrous effects for South Africa.[18]

The fact that the Pretoria administration could attach a higher priority to considerations of domestic economic structure than to their financial relationship with the UK indicates a crucial shift in their conception of self-interest.

Hertzog's decision, however, proved politically divisive. The mine managements gave it unwavering support and it soon appeared that one of the main motives had been the fear that a temporary devaluation followed by an irreversible stabilisation of higher wage rates would make the lower-grade mines permanently unprofitable.[19] On the other hand, financiers, wool-growers and fruit-producers abhorred a policy which led to a shortage of liquidity and which handed Australian competitors a 30 per cent advantage in the British market at a time when the American tariff ruled out any compensatory gains in the United States.[20] In addition, the fact that Nyasaland and the Rhodesias had automatically left the gold standard with the UK meant that South African exporters were losing out in their local markets to the north too.[21]

What was the British response to this strategy of financial independence? One option, of course, was to exert official pressure to ensure that British interests began to liquidate their South African investments. South African commerce and industry would very quickly grind to a halt for her domestic capital was insufficient to lubricate the large-scale economic enterprises which existed, and Hertzog would soon be forced to peg the South African currency at the same level as sterling. Predictably, it was precisely this sort of conspiratorial activity which the Nationalist press immediately attributed to the British government. *Die Burger*, for example, repeatedly accused the Bank of England of collaborating with both Barclays Bank and the Standard and Chartered Bank to precipitate a flight of capital from South Africa, and had also explained Hertzog's failure to raise a £5m loan from Morgan Guaranty of New York in terms of the insidious influence of the British government.[22] The British government, however, was not so crude. Political intervention might be immediately effective in forcing South Africa to follow sterling, but it would equally be effective in forcing the moderate Afrikaner community into the arms of right-wing Malanite extremism. The antennae of the Dominions Office were too finely turned for such an error to be committed. Officially, the wisest policy was to strike an attitude of resigned acceptance whilst tempting a reversal of South African fiscal policy by promising, firstly, that sterling would be stabilised at very near the old gold-point and, secondly, that the British government would never attempt to evade domestic economic pressures by an inflationary spiral.[23] This line was followed. Thomas was thus able to impress on te Water,[24] the South African High Commissioner, that the UK was not attempting to 'rig' the market,[25] whilst the Treasury assured the Dominions Office that this was, in fact, true.[26] Unofficially, however, the British attitude was by no means so detached; the Dominions Office and Treasury impatiently waited for the market forces to have their natural effect. Stanley,[27] Clifford's recent successor as UK High Commissioner in South Africa, told Harding that it could not be long before internal political pressures produced 'qualms conducive to wobbling' and he made no attempt to conceal his delight when reporting the debacle of the New York loan.

> Louw[28] [the Union Minister in America] was instructed by his Government, soon after the U.K. went off gold, to put out a very discreet feeler with a view to ascertaining whether, in the event of the Union requiring a loan to help her stay on gold, she could look to America. His enquiries were to be very tentative . . . . Louw (who has the reputation of being the soul of indiscretion) got hold of Professor Kaumann of Princeton – according to Totton anything but a leading light in the U.S. – and went off with him to Morgans who . . . promptly turned him down.[29]

In a liquidity crisis such as that of 1931/32 not even the US financial houses were likely to extend credit to South Africa, particularly credit likely to be wastefully consumed in financing a policy doomed to failure. By mid-1932 most South Africans saw Hertzog's decision as an unjustifiable economic sacrifice for political ends, and Smuts's initial allegations that South Africa was, under Nationalist impetus, 'heading straight for disaster' now reflected the general mood more accurately than the Nationalist Government.[30] The monetary controversy thus became entangled in what had emerged as the central issue in South African politics, that of a possible coalition between Hertzog and Smuts. If Hertzog wished to absorb the South Africa party within his governing arrangements, he had to make some concessions to the English section, and in the context of 1932 one of these would have to be a recognition of the necessary connection between sterling and the South African economy. This concession was, in fact, only marginal for by the end of the year South African reserves were almost depleted; and when Roos, who was a crucial negotiating link between the South Africa and Nationalist Parties, gave a speech in December calling for a dual policy of coalition and devaluation, an 'orgy of speculative transfer of money to England' ensued and Hertzog intervened to suspend the convertibility of rand into gold.[31]

The economic crisis of 1931/32 had thus produced a variety of responses within the Commonwealth relationship – a spontaneous expression of loyalism when it seemed that the pound might slide to dangerously low limits, an attempt by the two Dominions (Canada and South Africa) with the strongest and most diversified economies to protect their particular interests against the consequences of the British action, and finally the acceptance by Hertzog of a common financial policy which was itself part of a wider reorientation of South African politics towards a limited cooperation with her Commonwealth partners. The lesson seemed clear. Imperial unity was best left to work itself out as a natural product of insecurity rather than risk complications by frantic and ultimately counter-productive opposition to a Dominion which moved in an independent direction. But whilst in South Africa the limitations to Dominion separatism were being defined almost simultaneously the structural flaws in any strategy of imperial economic cooperation were being equally exposed at the Ottawa Conference.

The origins, course and consequences of the Ottawa Conference is a complicated subject, but even a brief treatment such as this can only make sense of it by trying to define the exact context. The fundamental fact was that the British economy had failed, despite the re-imposition of gold standard disciplines in 1925, to adjust itself to world competition. Such an adjustment in the early 1930s would have required much more than a reduction in wages commensurate with the price deflation which had occurred, although many industrialists did see the situation in this crude light. It could have necessitated the renewed willingness of labour, capitalists and managers to leave traditional activities and move into new sectors of production. The cotton age had ended and the motor age had begun but institutional factors, such as the growth of trade union influence, and social factors, such as the bedding down of industrial wealth in the comfortable grooves of nineteenth-century technologies, had weakened the UK's sensitivity to this transformation. Nor were the political parties prepared to risk losing votes by revealing unpleasant truths. As all the various groups concerned with economic management (the politicians, the industrial proprietors, the union leaderships) sought to avoid reform of a system in which they, in their various degrees, predominated, an effective consensus emerged based implicitly on the acceptance of reduced growth. As British industry found it increasingly difficult to survive in the international market-place, section after section opted for protectionism in the acceptable guise of Empire trade agreements. Industrial experts knew this to be an evasion of the structural problems inherent in Britain's economic system, so that the Federation of British Industries (rapidly emerging as the mouthpiece of industrial management) distanced itself from the protectionist campaign,[32] but the FBI's sense of institutional self-preservation soon made it surrender on this when protectionist interests, assured of massive industrial support after mid-1930, established a rival body, the National Chamber for Commerce and Industry.[33] The labour government continued to resist this trend for a while but the sterling crisis of

September 1931 led shortly to a National administration whose ideology and constituency made it more vulnerable to protectionist pressures. Industrialists feared that the new Cabinet would seek to take the pressure off itself by promoting tariffs as an economic cure-all. Instead many leading manufacturers demanded a more radical strategy in which tariffs played only a part and which attacked the problem of high industrial costs.[34] But there was little chance of this approach being adopted. MacDonald, still hoping to keep his support among worker organisations, would not tolerate any reduction of social services;[35] Baldwin was bound to support the traditional and uncompetitive industrial interests which looked to him for protection. These political forces paralysed economic policy. Meanwhile a floating pound, the only positive decision that had been taken as funds had left London, could not of itself counteract the decline in trade. For one thing, other countries could quickly eradicate its export-boosting effects, as Canada had done with its exchange duty; for another, Neville Chamberlain and the Treasury soon began to worry over the inflationary effects of rising import costs.[36] The Ottawa strategy was in part, then, an expedient which emerged from a set of political and social constraints taking shape in the Britain of the early 1930s.

Imperial protectionism, however, must also be related to what was happening in the international economy. World trade in manufactures had continued to fall. This was partly because primary-producing countries had less to spend as the value of their own product fell, but it was also due to the action of European nations who, for a mixture of strategic and monetary reasons, formed themselves into regional groups and retreated from multilateral trading. But whilst industrial trade was falling, the incidence and pace of industrialisation was accelerating in many areas. Rural economies faced with unemployment in the country-side had sought to create jobs by factory development, the import substitution effects of which also helped their balance of payments. These events brought about a massive overhang of excess industrial capacity liable to glut world markets for years to come. Inevitably such international movements had their expression within the Commonwealth; indeed, the economic intimacy between its members led to an intensification of certain facets of depression. The chief example of this was the problem of indebtedness. The financial links between the London money market and producers in the Commonwealth might in normal times make for stable and harmonious relations; in periods of economic disturbance they pitted one system against another. Thus in Australia one of the key problems of recovery was the servicing of London debt as export income fell, and the natural solution was a ruthless reduction of sterling imports.[37] Import substitution industries emerged, and the possibilities of these new plants shutting down once prosperity returned were small to say the least. The net effect of all these trends was the final destruction of the pre-1914 balance between agricultural and industrial production. Britain, like all the other major industrial producers, was faced with the task of setting limits to the resulting disequilibrium. In the Empire, it was felt, there lay to hand a mechanism which could provide a trading unit in which the traditional specialisations of function between 'old' and 'new' countries remained reasonably intact. Imperial protectionism, therefore, held out the possibility that Britain could escape the disruptions which rapid economic change had caused on the international scene.

Such was the general context surrounding Ottawa. But, because the decision-makers involved had a very imperfect understanding of the problems confronting them, the Conference events were not precisely tailored to the situation described. Officials and politicians were to disagree bitterly on the objectives and desirability of the agreements. Perhaps the most significant point here, at any rate for the purposes of this study, is that the DO was not happy with the prospects of Commonwealth trade talks from the start; initial unease quickly developed into outright opposition to British government policy. This may seem to conflict with what has hitherto appeared as the main theme of DO practice, the consistent appeasement of Dominion leaderships. With the Dominions, at long last, enthusiastic for common action on the trade and monetary fronts, the DO might have been expected to promote agreement at whatever price (a wheat quota, meat duties or restrictions on foreign dairy products) was necessary. It was noted earlier, however, that even in the early 1920s the Dominion experts of the Colonial Office were sceptical about the whole development thesis. By the early 1930s this scepticism was subsumed into a much more hard-headed, interest-oriented conception of Commonwealth. The Dominions Office was determined to ensure that the British delegation went to Ottawa prepared for a tough round of bargaining. Thomas, still Dominions Secretary in the new National Government, warned the Cabinet:

> In all the economic discussions which have hitherto taken place between the U.K. and the Dominions, the U.K. has allowed itself, rightly or wrongly, to be placed on the defensive, and any concessions have been apt to be regarded as the overdue payment of a debt of economic gratitude owed by us to the rest of the Empire . . . . I feel strongly that we should make it perfectly clear at Ottawa that insofar as any concessions which we might be prepared to offer are designed primarily to benefit the overseas Empire Producer and not for our own benefit we expect to receive real concessions. . . .[38]

This attitude reflects the essentially 'political' view of Commonwealth emerging within Whitehall. Increasingly Commonwealth was not perceived as an absolute 'value' worth preserving at almost any price (as the rhetoric of World War I had projected it) but a political relationship the utility of which depended on the terms of its operation. It was, in short, negotiable.

The Dominions Office attitude to the Conference was shaped by this changing psychology of Empire, but it was also influenced by more specific considerations. The Office was keen to satisfy Bennett's economic demands, providing certain limits could be kept. Thus Thomas supported a wheat quota and the establishment of imperial economic machinery to provide continuity of discussion between Conferences. But what set the limits beyond which the Dominions Office felt it unsafe to go? The answer was the inflationary effects that inter-imperial agreements would have on UK food prices. Thomas and his officials felt able to accept a wheat quota because they knew this would not drive British bread prices above world levels. The Empire produced much more wheat than Britain consumed, so that reserved quotas for the Dominions would only succeed in diverting foreign wheat to third markets where it would itself displace the Dominion producer: a case of gaining on the swings of imperial preference only to lose on the roundabouts of international markets. It was because the Australians realised this that they essentially ignored the wheat problem before and during the Ottawa negotiations. Bennett, in contrast, wanted a wheat quota for political rather than economic reasons, because he could claim afterwards to have obtained continuity of income for the western farmer, however hollow such a claim was. Here the Dominions Office was only too happy to close with Bennett, because it cost nothing. The problem lay not with a major commodity like wheat, but with what in volume terms were the lesser products of meat, fruit, dairy produce and wines. Here Empire output did not outstrip British consumption so that quotas or duties would have discernible price effects; and what little pre-Conference contacts took place (there were few, because Bennett tried to keep control of the agenda in his own hands) indicated that these commodities, particularly meat, were to be the heart of the matter.

But why should the Dominions Office apparently be more concerned than the British government for the UK consumer? Surely the former was less sensitive to the pressures of democratic politics than the latter? The Dominions Office's governing consideration was that a pro-tectionist Conference would revive and intensify the old antipathies of metropolitan masses towards programmes of imperial cooperation involving higher living costs. An anti-Commonwealth reaction might spread across all sections of British opinion. Indeed, by aiming at the impracticable objective of a Commonwealth trade system it was possible that the basis for more realistic forms of cooperation, achieved through intelligently and moderately structured preferences, would be jeopar-dised. The Dominions Office officials tried to drive this point home when the UK delegation arrived in Ottawa. Whiskard, who was the Office representative at the Conference, wrote home to Harding:

> The real danger which I have stressed to J.H. [Thomas] is that, if the people at home find the result of the Ottawa Conference is that food-prices rise stiffly while there is no immediate increase in employment, they may say 'If this is what Imperial Preference means, we have had enough of it', and that if the principle of Imperial Preference goes now, it will have gone for ever.[39]

The slump had confirmed the Dominions Office view that Commonwealth trade expansion could only occur within, and was limited by, the international economy. Whiskard, Batterbee and Harding were well aware that since the war the Dominions had extended their commercial exchanges with foreign countries. They knew after 1929 that the various Commonwealth economies were as much competitive with, as complementary to, each other, and that a closed imperial system would set each at the other's throat; far better for their interactions to be absorbed within a wider, more disparate set of economic relationships. The mechanism which Whiskard therefore promoted amongst his British colleagues was a 'domestic competitor' formula; that is, a limitation of duty to the equalisation of industrial costs among Commonwealth partners. This would be, Whiskard contended, 'a first step towards the return of economic sanity'.[40] By this he meant a return to specialisation whereby producers, Empire or foreign, made what conditions best fitted them for, and afterwards traded on a multilateral and open basis. For the Dominions Office, Commonwealth was only a fragment of this international system; and anything which broke that system would inevitably go on to destroy the balance of interests within the Commonwealth and disconnect its component economies. Thus the tactics of Commonwealth manage-ment drove the Office to take up internationalist positions in economics as well as diplomacy.

Most of the National Government leaders, however, could not allow themselves the luxury of such detached analysis. Elected on a platform of economic recovery, they were unable politically to adopt the internal measures (such as a reorganisation of industrial plant on a more efficient basis) which might have produced some steady improvement. Equally, for a complex set of reasons (namely American refusal to reduce its trade surpluses, French refusal to disgorge its gold stocks and German refusal to contribute towards political stabilisation) international economic solutions did not appear to be available to them. A Commonwealth trade agreement was the only policy the National Government had left to justify their possession of power; that policy had, therefore, to be pushed beyond the limits of realism. If in the end imperial protectionism would take money out of British pockets by raising the total import bill, in the short term it might (if the Dominions lived up to their promises of tariff reductions on UK goods) protect employment. The politics of jobs distorted the National Government's consideration of the economy as a whole and of the stabilisation of Empire relations.

If these were the general forces pushing the National Government towards Ottawa, individual members of the UK delegation arrived in the Canadian capital subject to particular pressures. Baldwin, for example, was now having to fight to retain the Conservative leadership and 'imperial agreements' would clearly reinstate his ideological appeal to Tory backwoodsmen. Meanwhile, perhaps more critically, Neville Chamberlain, Chancellor of the Exchequer, showed signs at Ottawa of an almost pathological need to finally achieve his father's dream of an economically united Empire. He thus brushed aside the bargaining attitude of the Dominions Office as mercenary and unimaginative. Fearing that Baldwin might in the end make some rational calculations about the imperial economy, the Chancellor urged his party leader towards a contemplation of almost spiritual horizons

> I said I thought we had made a mistake in attempting to value [Dominion] concessions in terms of money. It was bound to lead to counter-estimates and they were in any case of no real importance. With this view Baldwin declared himself in full agreement . . . . I concluded . . . that if we were to carry our people with us we must show them something that would touch their imagination. We must open up the vision of a great Imperial policy having within itself the mainspring which would continually move us on closer unity. Again Baldwin expressed his wholehearted approval.[41]

The Ottawa Conference was the only occasion in British economic history when a Chancellor of the Exchequer conceived his objectives in a distinctly imperial framework. Even so, Chamberlain's approach differed significantly from other Dominion leaders. The Australians and Canadians, for example, wanted a substantive discussion of monetary policy; the combination of high levels of public debt and low levels of commodity prices led them to think in monetary terms. Chamberlain and his Treasury advisors were scared of the currency devaluation implied in this. They looked to the Conference to strengthen, not weaken, sterling. The Chancellor had, however, his own solution to what everyone recognised was the key to recovery, the raising of commodity values. This was a strict system of production control within the Empire. The British market would be divided up among Empire suppliers and the production quotas would, by taking up the slack left after restrictions on foreign imports, allow for some increases on 1932 levels; but any producers who failed to keep their UK shipments within the quota limits should be heavily penalised by their governments. This greatly antagonised both Bennett and Bruce who jibbed at the idea of returning home to tell their electorates to moderate their productivity drive just when they were pushing it forward to offset falls in income. But it also horrified the Dominions Office who saw in the process of quota-allocation an intensification of Commonwealth polarities. 'This scares me stiff', as Whiskard tersely put it to Harding.[42]

Whiskard and Malcolm MacDonald (the Dominions Office Parliamentary Under-Secretary also in Ottawa) found that they were not the only British officials to be disturbed about the direction of their political leaders. They quickly found firm allies in the Foreign Office advisers present. If the DO and FO had frequently been divided on the proper tactics for handling Dominion nationalism, they were united in their opposition to schemes of imperial economic integration. The FO's overriding concern was that Commonwealth trade treaties which reduced the UK's scope of operations within international markets would lead to an immediate reduction in her influence on diplomatic affairs generally. More specifically, Britain's relations with the Argentine, the Scandinavian countries and certain European nations, from all of whom the UK imported considerable quantities of primary produce, were likely to be deeply affected by whatever was decided in Ottawa. But perhaps the main problem here was Russia. From 1930 onwards, as Drummond emphasises, Dominion leaders had been concerned about the revival of Russian exports to the West.[43] Indeed, their anxiety was especially intense because they misunderstood the fundamentals of the Russian situation. No doubt influenced by the propagandist reports on the achievements of Stalin's Five Year Plan, they lived in daily expectation of massive Russian intervention in world markets. In fact Russian export management aimed only at the acquisition of such foreign exchange needs as the essentially insulated 'socialist' economy of the Bolshevik regime required.[44] Canadian wheat and timber interests were the chief sufferers from this persistent sense of insecurity in the early 1930s. Chamberlain admitted in Ottawa that Bennett 'evidently wants prohibition of Russian trade all through the Empire'.[45] 'Another anti-Soviet bloc is being formed', Ashton-Gwatkin,[46] one of the FO economic advisers, contemptuously reported to Vansittart, and he continued

> Mr Bennett has just scored a local triumph in the signature of the St Lawrence Waterway Treaty with the United States . . . . He now appears to be in the mood to double up on his winnings, and to pull off something Big as a World Statesman. He now dominates this little town . . . with something of Mussolini's gesture. He looks as if he might dominate the Conference also. . . .[47]

Ashton-Gwatkin's contempt was partly patrician disdain for the provincial egoism of Bennett. But it had deeper roots in the FO conviction that the chief UK interest was peace, and that the problem of peace had a primarily European focus. The Ottawa strategy, by reducing the UK's involvement in plans for European economic recovery, was therefore in direct opposition to the national good. It is at this point that we meet the dichotomy between Britain's European and Imperial interests which at critical points intrudes into the policy debate during the inter-war years. As long as this dualism was absorbed within a commitment to international stability as a whole, based on the relatively free movement of goods and capital, no crude choices (such as Empire or Europe, isolationism or involvement) were forced on British policy-makers. But once political factors caused resources, such as exports and imports, to be abstracted from general market influences and concentrated on one side of the line, a dichotomy (the sort, indeed, that Amery had long advocated) was created. The Dominions and Foreign Offices, although their departmental objectives were distinct, both sought to avoid what they saw as the posing of an unnecessary 'choice', and consequently their mutual rapport was much greater in the 1930s than during the calmer days of the previous decade.

The opening rhetoric of the Ottawa Conference gave no hint of these subterranean dilemmas. All the leading delegates pronounced that their common objective was to 'clear out the channels of trade' among themselves by reducing tariff levels within the Empire, and thereby open the way towards a liberalisation of world trade.[48] Repeated *ad nauseam*, this assertion created the necessary picture of 'British' nations once again leading the entire democratic world back to stability. The tariff-reducing image of Conference aims did, in fact, represent the optimal desires of the UK. Chamberlain and his colleagues obviously hoped to obtain increased preferences in Dominion markets for UK manufacturers, but even this could be squared with overall tariff reduction if it could be achived by reducing existing duties on UK goods rather than raising them on foreign goods. The UK personnel tried hard subsequently to keep the original principles alive, and the 'domestic competitor' formula which came to be the heart of the UK's case reflected not only the specific interests of her industrial producers but also her ideological view of the Conference's proper role: the freeing of Empire trade as one necessary element in the rehabilitation of international commerce.

In the end, however, the pattern of the Empire's political economy meant that the only way to clear the channels of inter-imperial trade was to dam the flow of the Empire's exchanges with other countries. Why was this? Firstly, the Dominions refused to narrow the band of protectionist duties between their domestic industries and those of Britain. This was predictable, for how could they be expected to increase urban unemployment at such a time of social and political uncertainty? Or increase their industrial imports when their sterling reserves were so depleted? Whatever the reasons, the Dominions' attitude meant that British preference could only be increased by imposing extra tariffs against the foreigner; and from this point on the dynamic of imperial cooperation raced off in protectionist directions. Secondly, the Dominions could only afford to increase British preference at all if they sold more primary products on the UK market. It was Britain's unwillingness to accept the argument that any restructuring of primary trade was an essential precondition of revival, and her belief that the stimulation of metropolitan prosperity would soon multiply benefits in all directions, which allowed her delegation to unblushingly describe themselves as tariff reductionists. But the Dominions not surprisingly felt that the strategy of recovery had from the start to distribute benefits equally between British and Dominion producers; and ultimately the British delegates accepted the taxation of foreign food imports in order to buy Dominion cooperation on the industrial front.

The actual events in what, luckily for the participants, turned out to be a relatively mild August in Ottawa must be treated briefly. Whiskard's view was that the British Ministers 'wholly failed to accept the challenge of Dominion protectionism'.[49] Exhausted and angry after continuous meetings in which he saw his political superiors consistently outmanoeuvred, he told Harding that Baldwin 'had no backbone', whilst Runciman[50] (President of the Board of Trade) proved to be 'a very tired man' totally lacking the political will and courage of Philip Snowden.[51] The only prominent UK delegate who seemed likely to question the Conference direction was the Dominions Secretary. Thomas bluntly told his colleagues that

> He declined any longer to be blackmailed . . . the U.K. delegation had been giving way to the Dominions in every possible direction, and the point had been reached when it was only possible to defend the concessions which we had made by an appeal to sentiment.[52]

Thomas's famous irascibility, indeed, was roused by his Dominion antagonists and Whiskard had great difficulty in keeping his Minister's temper under control. Once, when Whiskard had advised Thomas to avoid attacking Bruce (who had still further reduced Australian concessions to British manufacturers) at a formal Conference committee, the Dominions Secretary 'jumped down my throat and said in effect he would have a row with whom he pleased and when he pleased'.[53] But privately Whiskard was no less disgusted by what he too saw as the crudity of the Dominion negotiators. The New Zealanders were 'both weak and stupid'. Bennett had 'the manners of a Chicago policeman and the temperament of a Hollywood film star', and Bruce was little better.[54]

But what had the UK been blackmailed into conceding? Very quickly the Conference had broken up into a series of bilateral meetings, the great majority of which involved the UK and another Dominion. In this context tariff reducing principles rapidly got lost. During the Anglo–Canadian talks, for example, Bennett went back on his original promise of free entry for such categories of British goods not yet made in the Dominion.[55] Under intense pressure from a well-organised Ontario lobby, Bennett's list of articles not yet in Canadian production became ludicrously short; he even tried to make his agreement to the steel arrangements already concluded at a Montreal cartel conference into a bargaining counter.[56] The same process took place in the Anglo–Australian talks, even though Bruce was not quite so evidently swayed by the lobby groups. The Australian leader had begun by saying that his country was prepared to 'give anything which seemed possible, within reason . . . short of wiping out her own industries'.[57] But in return for this he demanded very large concessions, and in particular a tax on foreign meat; and he actually threatened to *reduce* British preferences if these were not given. The polarising effects of the Ottawa negotiations, then, ended up by undermining those areas of common interest (however limited) developed since the early 1900s, and the British delegation had to bargain to retain the existing preferential system. 'The Anglo–Canadian Agreement and the Anglo–Australian', Drummond remarks, 'should be seen as defensive measures – attempts to prevent the two large Dominions from behaving in even more inconvenient and uncomfortable ways.'[58] Although Thomas, with some halting support from Runciman, managed to dissuade Chamberlain from agreeing to a meat-tax, they failed to prevent a consensus emerging around the concept of quotas. Chamberlain had swept aside the arguments of his officials as 'anti-Canadian propaganda'.[59] Meanwhile Bennett and Bruce, realising that the British politicians had got themselves into a position where they could not go home without 'imperial agreements' to wave enthusiastically at the electorate, exploited their tactical advantage to the full. They even scrapped previously agreed terms at the very end of the Conference and levelled new demands

> . . . brutally and as if they were dictating terms to a beaten enemy, as indeed they were – and all were at once conceded: 14/– instead of 13/– on butter, 15 % instead of 10 % on something else . . . and a new Russian clause.[60]

The Ottawa Agreements were finally signed on 19–20 August 1932. As the tension lifted, the British representatives began to feel more approvingly about what had been achieved. Even Whiskard, after two days of 'utter peace' on the homeward cruise, felt able to say that 'they [the Agreements] are not too bad'.[61] Briefly, Britain had agreed to restrict a variety of foreign meat imports over a five-year period. In return, the Dominions were to restrict voluntarily their meat shipments to current levels throughout 1933 and so avoid any dramatic effects on the export revenues of Britain's other suppliers, especially the Argentine. From the beginning, however, there was little chance of the Dominion governments concerned actually holding their producers to this commitment. On wheat, the UK gave a duty, although a saving clause was added outlawing any Canadian–Australian attempt to form a 'ring' with price-raising objectives. Although Bennett failed to extract any public agreement on the reduction of Anglo–Russian trade, Chamberlain and Runciman sanctioned a private formula whereby countervailing duties would be levied if Russian exports appeared to undermine the Ottawa arrangements. On dairy goods and fruit, too, the UK gave sufficient concessions to get the Antipodean politicians 'off the hook', because they could then go home and claim to have opened the way towards increased producvitity.

What did Britain obtain in exchange? Actual extensions of British preference amounted to very little. It was estimated, for example, that even after the UK had surrendered on wheat and meat the Canadian offer to British producers was worth no more than £4m.[62] In fact, from early on the British negotiatiors had accepted that the cash benefits of Ottawa would be negligible. What they aimed at, therefore, was to create mechanisms and a general climate of opinion likely, in the long term, to liberalise Empire trade and scale down Dominion protectionism. The Agreements did include elements of this kind. Customs procedure was to be less arbitrary, Tariff Boards were to police the Canadian and Australian schedules and give audience to British complaints, whilst the Dominion governments gave vague promises that they would only encourage such industries as were justified on grounds of economic competitiveness. Thus, from a UK vantage-point, the real economic effects of Ottawa could not be measured in the short term.

Politically, however, Ottawa had one immediate repercussion: it split the Cabinet and caused the resignation of Liberal Ministers. This was not a simple matter of free trade representatives finally breaking with a tariff Government. Factional tactics were equally involved. The Samuelite Liberals saw Ottawa as a last desperate attempt by MacDonald and Baldwin to control the economic situation, and that both were essentially 'finished'.[63] They felt, therefore, that the opportune moment had arrived to re-unite the historic Liberal Party on the basis of opposition. But not unnaturally, though their motives were those of political tactics, the Liberal rump chose to explain their resignations in terms of economic principle, and they castigated the absurdity of seeing British problems through an imperial lens. 'There are differences of economic interest between the parts of the Empire which arise inevitably from their differing conditions', Samuel[64] and his colleagues remarked in an open letter to the Prime Minister 'To bring these into the forefront of the political field is to invite disagreements between the Empire governments which are likely sooner or later to become acute. Tighter bonds might mean greater friction. The policy is most dangerous to the whole future of the Commonwealth.'[65] This was precisely the view the Dominions Office had circulated in the privacy of Whitehall one year before. Now that Office could only look on as Commonwealth affairs was shaped into a political football and the whole institution of the Imperial Conference virtually destroyed as an effective instrument for the future. The DO's anxiety that the imperial relationship would become the focus of popular criticism seemed to be foreshadowed when Snowden sent his final recriminatory letter to MacDonald, and saw fit to add the Dominions to his extensive demonology.

> They [the British delegation] have come back, after weeks of acrimonious disputes, and sordid struggles with vested interests, with agreements wrenched from them to avert a breakdown of the Conference and an exposure to the world of the hollowness of the talk of Imperial sentiment in economic affairs. . . . The Dominions are to dictate to us where we shall buy and where we shall not buy. The agreements have surrendered our fiscal autonomy, and have handed to the Dominions the control of British trade policy, reducing this country below the status of a Dominion. You cannot expect Free Traders, even passively, to acquiesce in such a policy of national humiliation.[66]

The effect of the Conference was to reduce the emotional force of Commonwealth within Whitehall. It is not too much to say that it brutalised Anglo–Dominion relations in the sense that future negotiations showed few signs of that genteel enthusiasm for compromise so obvious before 1929. It ensured that in future the protectionist argument had to be couched in terms other than the old imperial ones. But for these critical changes to be clearly seen it is important to jump ahead of our story (for at this time the Irish and European crises were also having dramatic effects on the Commonwealth situation) and deal somewhat briefly with the economic events that occurred between 1932 and 1939.

The National Government's optimistic presentation of the Agreements as a 'solution' to domestic problems proved predictably false. Between 1932 and 1935 the UK's declining share of the Dominions' imported manufactures was indeed halted, but the effect on the UK economy as a whole and specifically on job-creation was minimal: Drummond calculates that the Agreements increased UK output by £26 millions in 1933 and £56m in 1937 – no more than 0.5 per cent and 1.0 per cent respectively of total British output in those years.[67] It was clear very early too that the economic improvement of 1933/34 had as much to do with the competitive advantage accruing from sterling's depreciation as with the trade diversion or stimulation resulting from Ottawa. What, of course, rescued the National Government from the mid-1930s on was not any growth in Empire trade but the institution of a rearmament economy.

The fact that in 1933 and 1934 the UK was able to make trade agreements with a number of foreign countries (especially Denmark and the Argentine) does show that Ottawa had not destroyed Britain's ability to negotiate internationally. But these additional treaties meant that across a wide range of commodities – above all on meat and dairy products – the British Government was now committed to policing the surpluses of bitterly competing exporters. This competition divided not only the foreign from the Empire supplier, but led to commercial hostility between Dominions. On lamb, for instance, New Zealand resented what she saw as Australia's devious evasion of production control. The fact that meanwhile UK agriculturalists, firmly supported in Cabinet by their relevant Minister, Walter Elliot, were pushing for reduction in *all* overseas food imports only made an inflamed situation more vicious.[68] The British officials tried various ways of controlling market pressures. They tried to bludgeon the Dominions into an International Meat Council which might have achieved a degree of self-regulation; they attempted quotas, only to find that the Australians paid scant attention; and they toyed with the idea of a levy–subsidy, paid for out of a duty on imports, to raise the incomes of domestic producers. None of these worked, and essentially the British government had to incur the odium of limiting deliveries. This task was fortunately eased by general economic recovery after 1933 which increased consumption and therefore the scope for deliveries, and stockpiling for war in 1939 began to create a totally new situation. But by then not only had the political fabric of Commonwealth been very badly stretched, but part of its underpinning – the critical significance of the British market for commodities – had been brought into question. As early as 1934 the Dairy Industry Commission in New Zealand had seen this. 'We must', it said, 'abandon our traditional view of the United Kingdom as a bottomless market.'[69] This represented, as Hancock stresses, a breaking-point in the economic psychology of Empire.[70] It made every Dominion acutely conscious of its role as a world, not merely an imperial, trader. If this reduced the forces making for imperial unity, it also, as we shall shortly see, fitted neatly with Britain's changing perception of her own economic role.

The industrial aspects of post-1932 developments were just as important as the commodity situation. The chief point here is that the Dominions did not, in fact, restructure their tariff schedules. The most conspicuous culprit was Australia. By May 1934 UK manufacturers were losing patience with the Australian failure to implement a new preferential scheme. Crutchely, the UK Trade Commissioner, sadly reported that Canberra's procrastination

> proves what I have repeatedly said about the political impossibility of the present Government carrying out the Ottawa obligations unless they were prepared to commit suicide for conscientious reasons, which frankly they are not.[71]

Admittedly the Lyons Government, elected in December 1931, moved away from Australia's historic attachment to ideological protectionism. Australia's stringent programme of 'bilateral balancing' in 1936, aimed at eradicating the payments deficits with Japan and the US, also appeared likely to help British exports. By 1938 British industrial opinion had largely concluded that the Australian Tariff Board had probably made as many concessions as the political situation around it permitted.[72] But if as time went on less antagonism was felt towards the Australian default on her Ottawa promises, this was only because in general the expectations revolving around Empire trade had been severely cut down in size. It was recognised that the level of Dominion industrial activity was likely to grow and British exports to fall proportionately. Providing that this process of adaptation within Anglo–Australian economic relations could be staggered, British opinion could digest it without excessive concern. It was when Australian interests, frequently with American financial backing, penetrated sensitive areas of production that the UK sought a means to block change. Thus the UK's opposition to setting up military aviation plant in Australia was really due to fear that the technology would soon be exploited to stimulate Australian motor-car manufacture.[73] It was episodes such as these which gave 'imperial economic cooperation' a distinctly dated ring.

It was, however, the Canadian case which best reflects how the Commonwealth economic context had changed by the late 1930s. As early as 1933 Bennett was looking to the US to provide the vent for Canadian produce he had failed to obtain from the UK. Because the idea of North American reciprocity was traditionally a Liberal strategy, the Conservative leader had to be careful in presenting this turnabout to his public. But, as Clark impressed on Thomas, the position had totally changed since the issue had last exploded in the 1911 'annexation crisis'.[74] Even within the Canadian Conservative Party the bulk of opinion now looked towards American reciprocity, and nobody thought of the Ottawa Agreements as a sufficient consideration to obstruct progress.[75] There were clear signs, moreover, that Canada, far from being merely an observer of the New Deal system emerging under Roosevelt's guiding hand in America, was actually being absorbed within it; the ramifications of the National Industry Recovery Administration were too complex and far-reaching to be avoided.[76] What was the British response to these trends? Clark's view was that the experience of the early 1930s had shown clearly what little room for manoeuvre even a tariff government had when it came to commercial negotiations, because at every turn some sectional interest was likely to protest about schedule reform; thus the Canadians would not really be able to offer the Americans very much. This comforting attitude became so widespread that the UK at no point risked crude interventions to protect the few benefits she had gained at Ottawa. The Board of Trade, indeed, was much more concerned after 1932 to preserve the UK's freedom to negotiate with foreign countries than it was to maintain imperial preferences;[77] whilst the Board also felt that Canada benefited so much from Ottawa that they would not readily scrap its operation completely.[78] This proved accurate. Even when Bennett was defeated by Mackenzie King in the 1935 election, the experienced Liberal leader did not move against the Agreements he had criticised so much at their inception. In fact Mackenzie King, at the end of his negotiations with Roosevelt, had resisted pressure to reject the *principle* of imperial preference on the grounds that it was a 'family matter' not open to barter.[79] Certain aspects of the final Canadian–American Agreement in 1935 had a substantial appeal to British interests. If Canada's surplus of natural products could find American outlets instead of being dumped in the UK, for example, considerable pressure would be taken off the commodity gluts we have already described.[80] Where UK producers had been badly affected was in the reduction of Canadian duties on US manufactures and the resulting evasion of preferences. When the British High Commissioner tried to get the margin of preference re-established, Dunning[81] (the new Minister of Finance) refused, pointing out that the whole context of Anglo–Canadian economic relations had been transformed since he had left office in 1930

At the present time the situation was quite different. He [Dunning] would not be dealing with the same Great Britain and he had never before had to talk to a tariff Government in the U.K. He was not criticising the change of policy by the British Government, but he had to recognise a different atmosphere and . . . he was very conscious of what he called the tariff virus in the U.K. and also the resentment which was widely felt at the tactics adopted by Mr Bennett at the Ottawa Conference.[82]

Dunning was right in his implicit assertion that the British and Canadian economies could no longer be matched along 'imperial' lines. It was not a simple matter of the US displacing Britain as the predominant external influence in Canadian affairs. The process of economic change meant that in many areas of production, agricultural and industrial, British and Canadian interests did not fit together in any precise way. The Board of Trade had by 1936 effectively absorbed this and sought only to stabilise the preferential position on key items within a general, internationally-oriented programme of tariff reduction. This left Commonwealth partners a wide area of flexibility in their search for new trading partners elsewhere. With this, the ideological shadow of Joe Chamberlain, Milner and Amery had dwindled to almost nothing.

This account of post-Ottawa economics has so far concentrated on what happened in the Dominions, and how the British perceived events. But, in pointing out that the UK had itself become a different kind of economic animal, Dunning was absolutely right. At the heart of this change was a basic reassessment of Britain's relationship to international economic exchange. This deeply affected industrial management, the trade unions (the TUC, as Partha Gupta notes, had 'woken up from its imperial economic dreams'[83]) and the Whitehall policy-makers. An Economic Advisory Council report in May 1935 perhaps best sums up what had taken place.

An outstanding feature of the crisis of the years 1929–33 was unfortunately the need . . . for a fundamental readjustment. In the years 1927–9 this country was in the habit of investing £100 millions annually abroad. The events of the last few years have made it abundantly clear that this rate of investment cannot be sustained indefinitely; for in the last analysis its soundness depended on an indefinite expansion of the demand on the part of industrial Europe for foodstuffs and raw materials produced in the under-developed countries of the remaining continents; and it is no longer possible to count on such an expansion.

In future, though it may still be possible to find some profitable fields for investment abroad, we can no longer hope to achieve a favourable balance of payments of the size to which we were accustomed before the depression. Thus, one of the conditions of maintaining an adequate purchasing power in this country since the depression has been the transference of demand from the export industries, which benefit from foreign investment, and to investment in industries generally catering for home consumption.[84]

Probably the most critical factor lurking in the background of this Report was demographic. British and European population growth had, by the mid-1930s, come to a standstill. It was this which made it almost impossible for industrial Europe to generate, through its consumer capacity, economic development elsewhere in the world at the old breakneck pace. The implications of this for Britain, who had for so long used up its assets in maintaining political and economic connections with the extra-European world, were much greater than for any of the Continental nations. Britain, indeed, had already become a capital importer and was in no position to restock its investments in the Dominions as old debts matured and were paid off by governments which, after the Depression trauma, were determined never again to become so burdened with external liabilities. During the 1930s, then, all the Dominions reduced their dependence on London money markets.[85] This was by no means unwelcome in Whitehall, for it took at least some of the strain off sterling. In fact it was the London authorities who encouraged the growth of central banking institutions in the Dominions so as to share out the burden of managing currency and credit, forcing the nationalist factions back on the argument that now the Bank of England, not Westminster, was to be the mechanism by which England maintained her rapacious predominance.[86] Not surprisingly, this lack of surplus population and capital together removed Empire migration from the agenda. In August 1934 the Inter-Departmental Report on Migration Policy concluded that most of the migration planning since the Empire Settlement Act of 1922 had been unsound.[87] It emphasised that British economic problems could no longer be viewed in terms of excess population, or the simple equation between chronic unemployment in one part of the Empire and vast unoccupied spaces in another. 'The history of migration in modern times', the Report concluded, 'proves that migration is a symptom of prosperity and not a cure for depression.'[88] Moreover, the problem of ensuring adequate food supplies for the UK population began to be seen less in terms of an industrial metropolis interacting with primary producing satellites, and somewhat more in terms of stimulating domestic agricultural production and achieving a greater balance between the rural and urban sectors of the internal economy. This made considerable strategic sense, too, as British naval mastery could no longer be relied upon to keep open the food lanes in wartime. There were limits to this agrarian protectionism because the Government soon recognised that new technology reduced the employment-creating effects of rural development, whilst by 1936 British industrialists were beginning to fight what they saw as a threat to their operating costs and their exports.[89] But it had a distinctly reorientating effect on British economic perspectives.

It was the last factor of rising agricultural output at home which most concerned the Dominions Office, because it threatened Dominion prosperity and with it the whole Commonwealth relationship. The fact that British farmers and Ministry of Agriculture officials saw their future in terms of increased meat and dairy production rather than arable crops only sharpened this anxiety, because these were the critical growth areas in Dominion agriculture too. If the DO had therefore attempted to restrain Neville Chamberlain's overblown imperial economic strategy at Ottawa, the Office had now to turn round and protect the current levels of Anglo–Dominion commerce.[90] Thomas impressed on the Cabinet:

> We have to remember that the U.K. is still, in fact, if no longer in form, the centre and mainstay of the British Commonwealth. Taking the long view, surely we stand to gain by retaining the confidence and goodwill of the rest of the Empire, and particularly the Dominions, in relation to our economic policy, even at the expense of some immediate sacrifice of commercial advantage.[91]

It was in order to 'pick up the pieces' of economic cooperation that Thomas pressed for an Imperial Conference in 1935.[92] The purpose of this would have been to 'review' Ottawa, by which Thomas meant the unscrambling of the quota arrangements which were exposing the imperial preferential system to more political pressure than it could bear.[93] But, as usual, the DO could never make its voice heard unless other departments joined in the chorus, which in this case they did not. The general consensus, indeed, was that the UK must never again make the mistake of convening a Commonwealth conference to discuss economic matters in detail because in such situations it inevitably became the victim of 'smash and grab' tactics from every side. An Imperial conference did not meet until 1937, and by that time the situation had been metamorphosed by Anglo–American trade talks. It was these talks, and the Treaty which emerged from them, that signified the end of that economic nationalism which had governed world events since at least the late 1920s. They represented a recognition by the two greatest international traders (both of whom, Britain with her sterling alliances and the US with her New Deal experiment, had tried to cut an independent route through the commercial jungle of the 1930s) that recovery could only be permanently stabilised on the basis of freer exchange. But the logic of Anglo–American agreement necessitated a weakening of 'Empire trade'. Thus, if the US was to permit the UK to sell more goods in its home markets, Britain had to be prepared to pay for this by absorbing much larger quantities of American natural products. Only by intense British lobbying of the Dominions at the 1937 Imperial Conference, with an emphasis on the opportunities that the Dominions would also possess once the American market was opened to them, were the other Commonwealth leaders both bludgeoned and persuaded towards an acceptance of the Treaty.[94] The Anglo–American Agreement, of course, must be set in the context of a deepening diplomatic crisis if its full significance is to be appreciated. But even in purely economic terms it represented the fag-end of an era in which Britain had formed a Commonwealth–sterling bloc as a way of staunching the effects of Depression, but had finally admitted that such a trading unit was neither of a type nor a size which could generate long term growth.

And so the imperial economic idea expired. Its death was largely obscured by the immediate pressures of a new world war; it was, indeed, to enjoy a brief but glorious resurrection during the epic dollar shortages after 1945; and even in the early 1970s obscure parliamentarians were to be heard muttering in the background of the Common Market debate about the enormous potential of Anglo–New Zealand trade. These latter situations, however, related to specific monetary or political crises rather than representing a continuing *perspective* of British economy and politics as it had been originally presented by the Chamberlainite school and diffused, in attenuated form, throughout the UK establishment. This imperial perspective, itself arising out of the accelerating struggle for markets and raw material supply in the early 1900s, had never really challenged the liberal–internationalist orthodoxy until the 1920s; and even then only a slump of such unprecedented proportions that it seemed to threaten the survival of capitalism had been sufficient to push the UK into a course of 'economic imperialism' in any planned sense. It was, in effect, a refugee imperialism brought about by the impracticality of other preferred options, by the political impasse into which the National Government had moved and by the panic of the times. Ultimately the same impulse of economic contraction which had forced Ministerial thinking into a contemplation of a closed Commonwealth system ensured that the attempt itself failed because the participating Governments could not in these depressed conditions afford to offer each other the concessions necessary for its success. By thus exposing the imperial relationship to political pressures which it was not accustomed to bearing the Commonwealth was permanently fractured; or, to be more precise, the myths involved in its conceptualisation were for once measured against reality, found wanting and subsequently discarded. These economic developments were part of a wider deplomatic story in which British power could, it was found, only be maintained within an international framework. But for the moment it is necessary to turn to another confrontation in which inter-imperial relations were engaged during 1932. For whilst most of the Dominions were squabbling in Ottawa over such matters as wheat, meat and processed milk, the Irish grandly continued to conduct their politics along the righteous paths of justice and freedom. The election of Eamonn de Valera as Prime Minister of the Irish Free State in February 1932 had marked a new stage in the Anglo–Gaelic struggle.

9 The Irish Impact

The constitutional conclusions of the 1930 Imperial Conference were given parliamentary expression in the 1931 Statute of Westminster.[1] The departmental discussions which accompanied the drafting of this legislation did not touch at all on the larger constitutional implications involved and concentrated on tangential points such as the UK's right to extend Commonwealth membership to India at some later date[2] and the existence of military discipline under Imperial regulations over British troops in the Dominions.[3] If the Bill enjoyed an undisturbed passage through the Whitehall bureaucracy, however, Winston Churchill welded together considerable opposition in the House of Commons.[4] This opposition has to be seen in the light, not of any systematic interpretation of the 'imperial constitution', but of the growing right-wing opposition to Baldwin's leadership of the Conservative party. Although this movement was only to gain real momentum three years later over the reform of Indian government, the Statute of Westminster provided an early focus for rebel sentiments within the National administration. But Churchill's filibustering during the 1931 legislation did not represent the dominant reaction either within or outside Westminster. Sankey, whose native banality frequently made him an accurate barometer of mass feelings, caught the national mood well when he noted in his diary for 3 November 1931, 'A turning point in the British Empire. Personally I am rather sorry . . . but we had no choice. England must keep her word.'[5]

For most Dominions, however, the Statute of Westminster put an end to the constitutional issues which had played such a large part in their domestic policies since the War. Particular problems, such as the law of nationality, continued to cause friction between the UK and South Africa, for example, but they no longer held the old political significance. The reasons for this are twofold. First, the constitutional separatism of the Statute of Westminster was about as far as a Dominion leader could go without losing his place in the 'centre' of his electorate. 'Constitutionally the limits of centrifuge had been reached', Casey remarked five years later, 'if any Dominion takes a further step this can only consist of secession.'[6] Secession was too radical an act for such essentially moderate politicians as Mackenzie King and Hertzog. Second, in the context of economic and military insecurity after 1931 the politics of inter-imperial equality was replaced by a politics of international survival. A discreet search for limited but effective cooperation dominated the attention of Empire statesmen. But from this pattern there was one spectacular exception – the Irish Free State.

Anglo–Free State relations between the wars still awaits a comprehensive study. Here it is only touched upon: the present theme is that it was the impact of de Valera's quasi-republicanism in 1936–7 which finally broke the ideology of the Empire-state. In this sense de Valera's External Relations Bill, which expunged the monarchy completely from the Free State's internal government, was more of a landmark than the Statute of Westminster. Little, however, has been written on these events. This is in part a reflection of the larger failure of British historians to work on Anglo–Irish history, preferring the more distant complexities of the Nigerian Hausa or caste politics in Bihar; the Right has been ill at ease dealing with Britain's greatest failure, whilst the Left has found tropical climes more suited for the cultivation of its moral superiority. The best accounts of the Irish Free State remains those of W. K. Hancock[7] and, more particularly, P. N. S. Mansergh.[8] More recently D. Harkness has written on the 1921–31 period, although this work is concerned with constitutional matters rather than economic or political developments;[9] whilst Lord Longford's biography of de Valera is marred by an excessive admiration for his subject's puritanical zeal.[10] Clearly work on this subject remains to be done, and the current chapter, focusing on the response within Whitehall, can only be a minor contribution.

To put the later period in perspective a few remarks need to be made on the 1920s. Harkness argues that the Free State was a disruptive and radical force in Commonwealth politics from its inception as a Dominion.[11] This is not substantiated by the British records, which more than anything else reveal a general contentment that the Cosgrave group had been forced into the Commonwealth camp. Problems such as the pension payments of British civil servants who had served in the old south were relatively minor obstacles to a smooth transition. The Dublin leadership indulged occasionally in anti-imperial rhetoric, but they avoided consistently adopting anti-British positions since to do so was to concede that the Republicans had been right all along about the unworkability of the 1921 settlement. In fact the Free State government tried very hard to keep the British connection out of politics, and to project an image, not of revolutionaries enjoying the vicarious experience of power, but of good liberals implementing a programme of efficient government.[12] This passivity and concern with domestic matters meant that the Free State had minimal influence in the Commonwealth setting. It also lulled UK opinion into believing that the Free State had been permanently put under the terms of 1921. This optimism soon waxed into a romantic conviction that Anglo–Irish history had been reversed. Lionel Curtis, predictably, was the most eloquent exponent of this. In 1928 he wrote to Churchill that the new harmony between London and Dublin could only be explained by 'the intervention of a special providence. One gets the feeling that the curse which had bedevilled Anglo–Irish relations for 700 years had been deliberately lifted,' and he praised the Conservative Chancellor for treating the Free State 'as a Dominion Government . . . until through the force of sheer example you brought them to play the game'.[13] These sentiments also prevailed in the Dominions Office so that Batterbee was always expressing his conviction that the Free Staters had 'come through' to a proper understanding of the liberties implicit in Commonwealth membership.[14]

The recurring linkage between Empire and the morality of 'fair play' was always more pronounced in the Irish context than any other. Curtis's words, however, implied that he, no more than other makers of Britain's Irish policy ever since Strafford, was able to understand the mechanics of Southern politics. Did he understand how great were the risks the Cosgraveites took in spurning a revolutionary legitimacy? Did he appreciate that in the long term a treaty-government was bound to be seen as a government of limits and impositions? Certainly in 1928 Curtis could not have predicted how agricultural crisis was to explode any attempt to focus Free State politics on internal issues, and threw into sharp relief the sharp edge of Anglo–Irish relations. As early as 1930, however, Peters (the UK Trade Commissioner in Dublin) began to warn Batterbee that de Valera was making rapid headway at constituency level

> This is not to my mind so much because of a change of colour of political opinion but because many voters of the more moderate type who sympathised with a good many points in the Fianna Fail programme used to abstain from voting . . . simply because they were afraid that the advent of de Valera meant a 'second round with England'. These voters are now beginning to feel more confidence that a change of Government is possible without a violent conflict.[15]

Noting especially the growing support for the Irish Republican Army in the countryside, Peters recommended that the only way to undermine secessionist politics in the Free State was an outright declaration that any Dominion government could, if it wished, unilaterally withdraw from the Commonwealth.[16] This suggestively coincided with precisely the same ideas which Clifford and Houston-Boswall were concurrently sending back from South Africa. The failure of the Dominions Office, despite its own flexible predilections, to put this suggestion to the politicians at home indicates its weakness within Whitehall. Anti-Irish feelings were so widespread, and not only on the Conservative benches in Parliament, that the department refrained from advocating a concession with explosive political implications. Indeed, the Dominions Office did not even see fit to transmit to the UK Cabinet the vital information that the basis of their calculations regarding the Free State was disappearing. 'We ought not', Malcolm MacDonald concluded, 'to scare Ministers unnecessarily.'[17] This was a costly error since the confrontation of 1932–7 might have been avoided if the political mythology of the 1920s had been questioned within Whitehall before de Valera came to power in Dublin.

After his election in February 1932, de Valera executed his two chief platform pledges – the cancellation of annuity payments due to UK landlords whose Irish estates had been appropriated under the old land reforms, and the formulation of a Bill to remove the oath of allegiance to the King. Narrowing his attack to the oath had, ever since 1927, when he had begun to operate within the institutions of the Free State polity, been de Valera's way of constitutionalising himself. Such a strategy allowed him to appear as an opponent of British imperialism whilst functioning within the status quo. It would have been logical, then, for informed British observers to see de Valera's concentration on the oath as a concession, an implied statement that he wished to delete the symbols of Commonwealth rather than its operation. But we have already seen that in the 1920s all the Dominions had collaborated in emphasising monarchy as the residual source of unity; it was this consensus which had lubricated an easy process of compromise in other areas of policy; and so the oath represented a political emotion which could not be displaced without affecting the guarantees, stability and sense of 'fair play' which had encrusted themselves around the kingship. Significantly it was not only the UK who were concerned about the new situation. Every other Dominion leader, including Hertzog, personally appealed to de Valera not to rush unthinkingly into a Republic. The South African government, no more than the British, wished to see de Valera pumping life into great constitutional issues they had all been at such pains to asphyxiate gently. Equally pertinent, too, was the desire of all Commonwealth politicians not to complicate matters so close to the Ottawa Conference. But de Valera was unmoved. As he explained to Hertzog with unrepressed anger, Fianna Fail had never accepted Dominion status and could not therefore be brought to heel now by appeals to the shibboleths of 'freedom', 'equality' or 'moderation' which attached to it.[18] After the failure of this concerted Commonwealth attempt to absorb de Valera within the comfortable ambiguities of the 1926 compromise, then, the UK government was left facing a Free State regime whose clear intention was to breach the 1921 Treaty.

To understand the reaction which followed it is necessary to stress the sea-change in British opinion in the early 1930s. By mid-1932 the 1921 settlement was usually seen as the price Lloyd George had paid for

American friendship. But neither this, nor the ending of the Japanese alliance, nor the payment of Britain's war debt to the US at high interest rates had succeeded in eliciting American cooperation on world problems. The mood of intransigence which de Valera was soon to come up against in British circles was thus not least a ripple effect of an anti-American spasm marking the period 1931–5. But it was also at this time that British policy-makers, following the Indian Round Table Conferences, first glimpsed the real strength and complexity of mass colonial nationalism, a political movement which could not be quelled by a rapid fusillade of the Amritsar sort. This nationalism had, unlike the Dominion variety, nothing 'British' about it at all; it was, apparently, irrational and therefore incompatible with a liberal order; negotiations with it were doomed to futility. The new Free State regime was subsumed into these apocalyptic anxieties. 'De Valera an impossible fanatic', Sankey scribbled in his diary,[19] whilst Curtis, a major advocate of concession in 1921, urged Thomas that now the Devil had come into the open he had to be tackled.[20] Curtis impressed on the Dominions Secretary that the UK was in a much better position to stand up to the Irish than she had been in the early 1920s.

> When people talk of the failure of the Irish settlement they ignore the utter difference between the situation now and that which existed from 1921–24. The Irish settlement was then one which might easily have involved a sanguinary struggle which would not have been confined to Ireland, but which would have reacted throughout the whole Anglo-Saxon world. It might interest you to know that in 1914 the military organisation in Ulster was largely financed by a millionaire sheep-farmer in Australia. In those days conflict with Ireland not only affected our imperial but our foreign relations. Today we have the whole Empire behind us . . . and our foreign relations remain quite unaffected by de Valera's antics.[21]

Curtis's assumptions here were extremely questionable. Because other Commonwealth leaders had found de Valera's moves embarrassing did not mean that they could be anything other than hostile to UK coercion of a fellow-Dominion. It seemed possible, moreover, that the international situation made the UK less, rather than more, able to risk an open breach with the Free State. Did not the deteriorating security problem in Europe make it even more imperative to buy Free State cooperation at the going price, be it the annuities, the oath or even the Crown itself? This was precisely the calculation taking shape in de Valera's mind. When Thomas and Lord Hailsham,[22] the Minister for War, visited Dublin in June, de Valera presented them with the stark choice between an independent and cooperative ally or a coerced but obstructive Dominion. 'A free Ireland would come to the support of

England', de Valera enticingly predicted, 'in the same way as England was compelled to go to the assistance of France and Belgium in 1914.'[23] But the British government was not yet sufficiently disturbed by European pressures to purchase cooperation at the expense of that indivisible monarchy which continued to symbolise in Whitehall the guarantee of imperial unity. A Special Duties Bill designed to reduce Free State imports into the UK was rushed through Parliament in July, and at the same time it was announced that, if de Valera did not drop his legislative proposals, the British Ministers at the Ottawa Conference would refuse to negotiate any agreements with their Free State colleagues.[24] Thus, when a Dominion had eventually taken a radical constitutional step, the UK had not been slow in reacting with what can accurately be described as nervous paranoia.

The Dominions Office, however, from the beginning of de Valera's administration, recognised the necessity of maintaining a 'negotiable' attitude. This did not mean that already in 1932 the Department was willing to tolerate fundamental changes in the overall conception of Commonwealth (as it came to do within five years) but that it felt patience and moderation could wean the Free State leader from extremist policies. For example, Harding commented in August 1932:

> Perhaps it may be suggested that Mr de Valera's policy during the first few months of office was directed to having as little as possible to do with the British Commonwealth. It seems clear that Mr de Valera is beginning to change that attitude (the fact that he has just made his first formal submission to the King and there described himself as His Majesty's obedient servant is an illustration) but that the change must necessarily be slow. Historically the position has a parallel in the attitude of Mr Cosgrave . . . immediately after the Treaty settlement came into force, and in the attitude of General Hertzog on coming into office in 1924. In both these cases there has been a very marked movement in the direction of accepting the principle of cooperation within the British Commonwealth.[25]

This reflects the DO's consistent view of Dominion nationalism as a scheme designed by a particular group as a means to power and which, given democratic pressures, had to be consummated in some decisive act once control of the state had been achieved; but it was never long, the DO believed, before the facts of power led to a reversing movement in which British help (money, or guns, or diplomatic assistance) was required. But quite apart from promoting this model of Commonwealth politics, the DO hoped that by painting an optimistic picture they could restrain the UK Cabinet from drastic action which would push the Free State leader over the edge of secession. The DO was therefore adamant that the Oath Bill, whilst indisputably a breach of the 1921 Treaty, was not a *de facto* secession.[26] This bought time to explore a *modus vivendi*. At the same time the Office argued that Britain could only exert pressure on the Free State by forming a solid Commonwealth front, and that Hertzog's participation in this could only be obtained if the anti-secessionist case abjured all constitutional dogma and rested 'simply on considerations of public morality and good faith';[27] here again we see the tactical roots of the Commonwealth's moral persona. Even so, some legal formula would be required whereby the Fianna Fail legislation could be squared with the British Cabinet's determination that the Treaty should not be breached. The Dominions Office now argued, therefore, that, since in the 1921 treaty the Irish Free State position had been analogically compared to that of Canada, the status of the Irish Free State must be considered to have advanced in line with that of British North America.[28] This concept of legal mobility allowed the Free State to have left the Treaty position behind without having actually 'breached' its provisions.

Having put together the essentials of an argument, the Dominions Office found in the Ottawa Conference a perfect forum for an attempt at Anglo–Irish reconciliation. Harding worked out a plan whereby, at the final Conference session, the UK should formally offer de Valera's representatives, led by O'Kelly, a judicial enquiry into the annuity issue conducted by the Chief Justices of South Africa and Canada.[29] By starting with the lesser financial issue, Harding was confident that a common approach could be worked out on the larger constitutional question; whilst, by initiating a solution in a formal Commonwealth setting, with all the attendant rhetoric and where the UK was plainly only an equal among others, it would, he felt, make it very difficult for the Free Staters to maintain their intransigence. The Dominions Office had been encouraged to push this plan among their Whitehall colleagues since an important ally had emerged in the form of Hankey and the Cabinet Secretariat. Hankey had urged the Harding suggestion on Ramsay MacDonald

A time will be reached, perhaps in the autumn, when the economic pressure on Ireland may become so severe as to produce serious reactions. These might take the form of attacks on our forts, of some aggression against Northern Ireland, or even a general election fought on the issue of a Republic . . . . Whatever form these take there is the gravest danger of their reacting in the U.S.A., to the jeopardy of your World Policy. . . . From this point of view it is important not to leave the matter until too late . . . at Ottawa we have a valuable line of communication with the Irish Free State.[30]

Hankey had grasped de Valera's point that the UK's international dilemma had become too acute to allow itself the luxury of inter-imperial confrontation. But both Hankey and Harding were civil servants able to make dispassionate judgments on the Free State problem without needing to take account of party political factors. Ramsay MacDonald, above all preoccupied with preserving the National Government and his own tenuous leadership, could not afford to alienate the anti-Irish right-wing in the Conservative ranks who were demanding the continuance of economic sanctions. He therefore tried to stop Harding and the Dominions Office in their tracks. He told the former on the 'phone from Lossiemouth, his Scottish retreat, that the special duties could not be repealed until de Valera had completely backed down. 'It was clear that it would be impossible to resort to that pressure once it had been taken off,' MacDonald said. 'The critics of the Government would certainly say their trade had been upset for nothing. He [the Prime Minister] would get the blame.'[31] The Dominions Office, in fact, was so suspect of being 'soft' on the Free State by this time that there was an attempt to shut the department out of discussions on the matter.[32]

Harding's ploy, however, already had too much momentum behind it to be stopped quite so readily. This was not least because of the tremendous confusion in Whitehall during the Ottawa Conference, when half the Cabinet were absent. Moreover, Thomas, with his usual proclivity towards the unexpected, had formed a closer personal friendship with the Free Staters in the Canadian capital than with any of the other Dominion officials, a friendship facilitated by a mutual dedication to poker-dice.[33] Sankey[34] and Ramsay MacDonald[35] were therefore horrifed to find that the Dominions Secretary had already broached Harding's plan with O'Kelly. They need not have worried. Harding had miscalculated that de Valera would prove sensitive to the atmosphere of an Imperial Conference. On the contrary, the last context in which the Fianna Fail leader would allow himself to be seen negotiating with the UK was at such a conspicuous gathering – even one so symbolic of Commonwealth disunity as Ottawa. The idea of a judicial enquiry had therefore to be dismissed, and by late 1932 the situation had moved into a state of deadlock. Moreover, the general deterioration in Anglo–Dominion relations caused by the debacle of the Imperial Economic Conference gave extra edge to the bitterness felt towards the Free State regime. Ramsay MacDonald was soon likening de Valera to Ghandi – a man of such devious cunning that even his handshake should be avoided.[36] When the Archbishop of York urged the Prime Minister that an economic war among Commonwealth members was incompatible with the values which that association was meant to embody, the latter curtly replied that an agreement was out of the question

He [de Valera] would have another election in Ireland before you could say 'Jack Robinson' . . . he would increase his majority, no doubt partly by fair means but certainly with the assistance of pretty foul ones, and then would proclaim himself Pope.[37]

Meanwhile Curtis was warning Thomas that to negotiate with de Valera on the basis of amendments to the Oath meant legitimating secession and 'rubber-stamping' his authority.[38] Thomas, never a man to stick for long to any policy disliked by the rest of his Cabinet colleagues, was himself soon espousing the need to 'stand fast to our guns'.[39] Hankey, too, fell silent on the issue. The permanent officials in the Dominions Office were left, therefore, helpless in the face of Anglo– Free State confrontation.

It was, as we shall see, the intensification of European insecurity in 1935/36 which was to force the Dominions Office views on other parts of Whitehall. Again, the course of inter-imperial relations can only be explained as a response to the UK's changing international position. It is important to show, however, how an altered approach to the Free State was rationalised in the UK because this reveals the shifting character of the Commonwealth idea in British thinking. As early as 1933 (by which time the Removal of Oath Bill has passed into Free State statute) the Dominions Office had moved beyond any analysis of the rights and wrongs of the Treaty and was facing up to the real challenge of outright republicanism which de Valera posed. Its mind had been jogged in this direction by Reginald Coupland,[40] Beit Professor of Colonial History at Oxford, who had submitted a lengthy memorandum in which he pleaded for an immediate negotiated settlement with de Valera. He had stated,

If we assume (as all these reflections assume) that a Republic is probably coming and that we will not prevent it by force, let us face the fact of defeat. However strong our case and weak de Valera's, the institution of a Republic against our known wishes will be a blow to our prestige – a final proof of our inability to solve the Irish Problem. But surely the effect of this will be lessened if we declare beforehand that we will not oppose it and give our reasons. For our reasons do us credit. Why do we refuse to prevent the Republic by force, when we certainly possess the strength to do it? There are doubtless several minor reasons, but the major reason is that our Ministers and the mass of the people are convinced that in an issue of this kind the use of force achieves no permanent solution and is wrong . . . . If we take our stand on practical post-War idealism, on the principles of the new world-order of peace and international cooperation, we put the Irish Republicans on the moral defensive. If they proceed to their Republic in the face of such a declaration, the fact that they are putting nationalism before internationalism will be more manifest to the world . . . . My last impression . . . is the need, both for Ireland's sake and our own, to eliminate what Cecil Rhodes used to call the 'imperial factor'.[41]

Coupland's arguments fitted neatly with the internationalist assumptions now dominant in the Dominions Office. Moreover, his contention that the only way to locate a new equilibrium between the UK and the Free State was within the limits set by the latter's domestic politics found an echo in the Department's own political pragmatism. The advice which Clifford and Peters had been giving for the previous three years (i.e. that clinging to rigid orthodoxies only succeeded in fuelling a politics of irrationality in the Dominions) was by this point clearly seen by Harding and his colleagues to be valid. But Coupland also introduced a new element into the debate. If, by accepting a Republic in the Free State, de Valera could be kept within the British Commonwealth, it would be much easier to persuade nationalist leaders in places such as Egypt and India later on that real autonomy could exist without a complete rejection of the British connection.[42] As the Anglo–Irish division deepened, therefore, it became clear that large questions were being raised across the whole spectrum of imperial relations.

Harding, although he agreed with the essential thrust of Coupland's analysis,[43] had to recognise two sets of limitations on effective action. The first was that the UK Cabinet was still antagonistic to any appeasement of Free State radicalism. The second was more complicated and indicates the crisis of political calculation which had taken shape: if the UK did indeed negotiate an agreement with de Valera, was there any guarantee that the latter could make it stick? As Harding explained to Smuts at a London dinner, there was a very real danger that de Valera, should he appear to trifle with a new form of 'Commonwealth republicanism', might be outflanked by his own extremists and particularly by the IRA.[44] The UK would then be left holding an agreement with even less promise of stability attached to it than the old Treaty had possessed. But during 1933 and 1934 the Dominions Office became convinced that, although this danger remained real, a compromise with de Valera was the one chance of keeping the Free State within the Commonwealth orbit. In addition information was not lacking that de Valera was the only Free State politician capable of averting a renewal of civil war,[45] whilst Peters stridently advised that as de Valera 'holds the stage . . . we should not waste time on a search for a possible alternative'.[46] Peters's estimation of the rest of the Fianna Fail leadership, indeed, had risen appreciably over the course of the preceding year. Thus Lemass[47] was now 'able and adaptable'; Ryan[48] was 'honest'; Derrig[49] had 'a lot of horse-sense'; whilst even O'Kelly was 'a reasonable mortal until he got up to make a speech'.[50] There was also a widespread belief that the deteriorating international situation was making the Free State more pliable. 'Ottawa, Geneva and the present conference', one visitor told Malcolm MacDonald at the World Economic Conference in 1933, 'had undoubtedly had a considerable influence on their [the Free State] Ministers'.[51] In 1934 de Valera had gratified the UK delegates at the League when he spoke on the sensitive issue of minorities, and his comments proved to be on 'much more moderate lines than might have been anticipated'.[52] By the time that the diplomatic crises of Abyssinia and the Rhineland changed the context of British policy, there was thus already a battery of arguments pointing towards a conciliatory approach to the Free State.

De Valera properly calculated that by October 1935, with the UK facing a possible war in the Mediterranean, the time had arrived to test how 'rattled' the British Cabinet had become and how ready to swap a constitutional compromise for limited cooperation on defence. Walsh, the Free State representative in Geneva, therefore, put out a feeler to Anthony Eden,[53] the League Secretary. De Valera, he pointedly remarked, had hoped to see Eden on his way to a Lausanne oculist and had only been prevented by an untimely cold.[54] Eden promptly responded by inviting Walsh for talks on the Anglo–Irish impasse.[55] The probing conversation which followed on 14 October by-passed all the constitutional difficulties which had hitherto preoccupied the UK Cabinet. Instead Eden remarked favourably on the common stance between the Free State and the UK during the Abyssinian debates at the Geneva Assembly. 'Mr Walsh said certainly this was so', Eden reported, 'and . . . would always be so. There was no reason for any divergence of view between us in foreign politics, since our interests were the same.'[56] Walsh went on to stress the Free State's willingness to provide expenditure for the maintenance of port defences and the construction of destroyers.[57] Here was a fairly clear offer – a friendly, cooperative and, in certain crucial areas, coordinated ally in return for a 'blind eye' to constitutional reformation. In the new perspective of 1935, an agreement along these lines seemed much more attractive than three years earlier. Hankey, having maintained silence on the topic over that period, was now determined, for example, to integrate the Free State into the UK's 'War Book' arrangements, and he was willing to pay the necessary price. Batterbee told Malcolm MacDonald

> Hankey . . . thinks that the time has come when the special question of the Free State Government requires consideration. Discussions which have been going on this week show that in such matters as censorship the full cooperation of the Irish Free State would be practically essential if our measures are to be effective. Sir Maurice Hankey thinks that the best plan would be to open up with de Valera in Geneva with a view to . . . cooperation in all these matters.[58]

The Dominions Office now faced a difficult choice. A belated initiative might merely be taken by de Valera as a sign that the British will had finally broken and that he could push on with his secessionist plans without risk of retribution. On the other hand an immediate approach might be the last chance of forestalling Republican legislation. Malcolm MacDonald, the new Dominions Secretary, opted for the latter and he told Dulanty,[59] the Free State High Commissioner, that he was working on proposals 'over the whole field' of Anglo–Irish relations, a broad hint that the constitutional as well as the financial, question was regarded now as 'negotiable'.[60] In February 1936, Hacking,[61] the Parliamentary Under-Secretary in the Dominions Office, was despatched to Dublin to sound out de Valera's position. De Valera left him in no doubt that the only choice before the UK was between a semi-republicanised Free State (with a King whose legal competence lay only in the sphere of external relations) and outright secession.[62] But he also implied that if the UK accepted that a Dominion could declare itself a Republic, he would be prepared to continue to act as a Commonwealth member and would even welcome a royal visit to Dublin as a token of good intent on each side.[63] Hacking returned to London convinced of de Valera's logic and captivated at the prospect of a British King once again in the Irish South.

It would in effect be a re-conquest of Ireland by King Edward VIII. To attain this result it is worth-while to exercise the greatest patience with the Irish people and give them the utmost latitude compatible with their retention within the orbit of the Commonwealth. . . . The actual position of the Free State at this moment is little removed from that of external association . . . . Recognition of the status of External Association would in fact be little more than recognition of what already exists.[64]

Hacking's favourable report persuaded Malcolm MacDonald to take the plunge and invite de Valera to London. The meeting took place in April with the Rhineland crisis still in motion. The Dominions Secretary made it clear that the UK now wanted a 'comprehensive settlement', and when de Valera replied that such a settlement had to cover the essential issue of the Crown, MacDonald agreed that 'if discussions were started, no proposals were ruled out'.[65] This was tantamount to admitting that the Crown had become an 'open question'. It soon became clear, however, that not even this concession was enough to restrain de Valera from unilateral action, and in June the Free State leader signified his intention to proceed with an External Relations Bill which rooted out all references to the King from the internal constitution, created the office of President, abolished the Governor-General and left the King constitutionally alive only in respect of relations with foreign countries.[66] The Abdication crisis which followed in December was singularly fortuitous for de Valera for it allowed him to push this legislation through with the least amount of publicity as the UK was so immersed in the drama of the King's American romance. All that was left for the Dominions Office was to debate whether the Free State legislation had indeed finally broken the Commonwealth connection.

The comprehensive character of the External Relations Bill meant that a fundamental readjustment in the concept of Commonwealth was necessary if the Free State was not to be thought of as having seceded. The Dominions Office thus set out to frame a definition which included the essential elements in Commonwealth membership without ruling out the existence of a Dominion–Republic.

> The essence of the Commonwealth . . . is that it is an association of free and equal nations between whom war is ruled out as a means of settling differences, and which are able to solve all their own problems not by any form of coercion . . . but by discussion and mutual arrangement . . . and to cooperate together to solve the problems of the world. Hence the real value of the Commonwealth is that it may well save the world, not only by its exertions (the effect of which must exceed the sum total of those of its members taken individually) but by its example of the proper method of conducting relations between different states . . . . Can Mr de Valera's idea be said to offend against this? On the other hand would not acceptance of the idea, by indicating the flexibility of the British Commonwealth, be a demonstration of wise statesmanship and of the value attached to membership of the Commonwealth which would add enormously to its international influence?[67]

Although this diluted conception of Commonwealth was all that de Valera's *fait accompli* now permitted, it is noticeable that the Dominions Office found it by no means uncongenial. After all, Harding, Batterbee and their departmental colleagues had been stressing the international, rather than the imperial, setting of the Anglo–Dominion relationship ever since the late 1920s. By taking the 'imperial factor' out of Commonwealth, as Coupland had earlier suggested, much of the old political friction could be left behind and practical problems of cooperation approached in a narrower but more effective manner. The Department thus noted the various objections to accepting the Free State Republic as a Commonwealth member but rejected them one by one. The argument, for example, that a Republic could hardly be bound to fight for the indivisible Crown (and hence for the UK) was not considered very strong because even those Dominions such as Canada which retained the monarchical link were themselves now claiming the right of neutrality. 'An assurance of voluntary cooperation', it was concluded, 'might be of more value than any expectation based on the

idea of allegiance.'[68] Another projected line of reasoning was that by
granting de Valera a Republic the UK would earn Hertzog's resentment
for it would highlight just how moderate the Nationalist leader had been
since 1924, a revelation the Malanites could certainly exploit. But the
DO was now convinced that the guarantee of a Dominion staying under
the Crown lay in the balances of its internal politics, so that, whatever
Hertzog might privately feel, he would not take any retaliatory action
for fear of undermining the coalition with Smuts. Finally, the possibility
was considered that a Dominion–Republic might be taken as proof that
the Commonwealth had ceased to be an entity in international affairs.
The departmental response on this point was that all the old arguments
for and against the existence of a Commonwealth-state were left
unaffected by the new dispensation.[69] But beneath this brevity lay the
recognition that those arguments no longer possessed any political
relevance. Commonwealth cooperation in another war was seen now as
a matter for careful political negotiation (as we shall see in the next
chapter) in which constitutional arguments based on the Crown played
no part.

In fact the UK Cabinet was not to authorise a final agreement with de
Valera until January 1938,[70] but from the point of view of British
attitudes to the Commonwealth relationship, the break with much of the
old Empire ideology had taken place by early 1937. A new tone was
apparent in the statements of UK officials. Clive Wigram, for example,
King George V's old Secretary, had written to Batterbee in late 1936 to
prophesy that de Valera, once appeased, 'may quite possibly feel that
there is no further need of emancipation, and that the next phase is to
develop ties with the Commonwealth. His Left wing would not like that,
but he is less afraid of them than he used to be.'[71] Wigram's cold
calculation implied the dissolution of ideas (loyalty to a single monarch,
automatic unity in war and so on) which had been compressed into a
political emotion by the events of 1914–18 and which in the following
years had acted as a guarantee that the British alliance was still intact
and capable of mitigating the collapse of international stability. By
bringing the Irish problem within the Commonwealth it was always
possible that the coherence of that association would be deeply tested.
The crises of the 1930s, by rekindling the dissident forces in Southern
politics, revealed the underlying contradictions. But the period of
Cosgrave's leadership had so integrated the Irish Free State with the
institutions and politics of Commonwealth that any subsequent attempt
at withdrawal was bound to have repercussive effects on the wider
character of Anglo–Dominion relations. The Dominions Office was
therefore correct to evaluate de Valera's 1936–7 legislation in terms of a
transformation of the Commonwealth conception as a whole. The result
was that 'ties', to use Wigram's word, had replaced an ideology. For
those actually concerned with the management of affairs this rep-

resented a change of ideas and style. If cooperation was to be achieved, it was not through an intimate knowledge of group-interest, but rather the product of confused bilateral barter. To paint this picture clearly, however, it is necessary to see just how Commonwealth politics interacted with European instability. This study will therefore conclude with an analysis of the Commonwealth and the diplomatic crises of the 1930s.

10 Commonwealth Cooperation and the International Crisis 1931–1939

The approach that has usually been taken to the relationship between the Commonwealth and British foreign policy has consisted of an analysis of the Dominions as an 'influence' or pressure group, and an investigation to see whether any twist or turn of policy can be attributed to them. But this is much too specific a question to have value, for the Dominions did not possess any such precise or determinative functions. Thorne, struck by this in his study of the Manchuria affair, concluded

> While the Dominions were kept informed of Britain's general policy, they contributed almost nothing in the way of advice or even demands for discussion at government level. They *existed* as a defence, that was all.[1]

The Dominions, either individually or collectively, never developed approaches on major international issues outside British policy. They did, however, possess a set of ill-defined preferences and instinctive responses (such as antagonism to European guarantees and a minimalist interpretation of League obligations) which amounted to a more pronounced isolationism than Whitehall could entertain. But where these Dominion preferences clashed with the predilections of the Foreign Office they were silently ignored, as over Locarno, or 'bulldozed' as in the case of Australian opposition to unqualified signature of the Optional Clause. Occasionally the UK used the wishes of other Empire governments as a reason for adopting a certain position, but this was only where other factors had prescribed the course of action in question. This is Ovendale's conclusion on the Dominion role in the policy of appeasement between 1937 and 1939,[2] and it is also true of the period between 1926 and 1937.

But this apparently passionless role is deceptive. For, if the Dominion governments could have little direct influence over UK decision-making, the fact of the Commonwealth connection nonetheless affected the general assumptions with which British policy-makers approached the decisions that they had to make. Thus the Commonwealth existed not only as a defence problem, but as a factor underpinning those isolationist aspirations which formed a significant, but never dominating, part of British diplomatic psychology after 1918. Any estimate of the Dominion influence on British policy, then, has to go beyond specific instances where Dominion pressure either failed or succeeded to dissuade the UK from a certain action, and look at the relationship between the Commonwealth idea and British isolationism as a whole. But this thesis is less concerned with the changing shape of British foreign policy than with the Commonwealth relationship itself. The more relevant question to ask, then, is to turn things on their head and to consider what effect changes in international politics had on Anglo–Dominion affairs. The answer is that it was the international crisis from late 1935 onwards which, by destroying the old assumptions of immutable obligations to each other, took the imperial dimension out of Commonwealth relations. This erosion of old assumptions, however, was offset by a common sense of vulnerability which provided a political focus for more functional, if more limited, understandings as the prospect of war grew larger. Thus, if Hitler's impact destroyed the imperial ideology previously implicit in Anglo–Dominion relations, it also ensured that those relations remained tightly bound together.

The first major diplomatic crisis of the 1930s was the Japanese invasion of Manchuria. We have already noted Thorne's observation that the Dominions showed no inclination to influence or participate in Britain's Eastern policy. But this indicates not disinterest but rather the assumed consensus that Japan should satiate her ambitions in Manchuria rather than in China or South–East Asia. 'She [Japan] must ere long expand *somewhere*,' Birdwood,[3] the old Anzac commander at Gallipoli, pleaded with Simon. 'For goodness sake let (or rather encourage) her to do so there rather than Australia's way.'[4] This consensus provided such a comfortable rallying point for Commonwealth opinion that a light-hearted jollity appeared at times to tinge the periodic discussions on the matter. 'Mr de Valera dined with Sir John Simon and Lord Lytton[5] on Monday evening', Price, a Dominions Office observer in Geneva, reported, 'and I gather that the party went off very successfully, Manchuria of course being the *pièce de résistance*.'[6]

The existence of such a consensus is hardly surprising because almost all the Commonwealth governments, including the UK, perceived themselves to have a vital interest in the continuance of the Eastern status quo and were prepared to 'buy off' Pacific revisionism. Thus Australia was no more eager than Britain to see collectivist action against Japanese 'aggression' which risked the spread of regional instability in the Pacific. Runciman, for example, warned the Cabinet

that, because of the very close connections between textile industrialisation in Japan and the Australian woollen industry, it was most unlikely
that Australia would participate in any trade war between Japan and the
Empire;[7] whilst Latham's[8] visit to Tokyo in May 1935 was sure proof
that Australia wished to see a Pacific *modus vivendi* which took account
of Japanese interests.[9]

But this general agreement at the level of official policy should not
blind us to more subterranean differences of interest and perspective.
Thus a consensus on Manchuria could not completely conceal the fact
that Britain was prepared to go much further to appease Japanese
resentments of the status quo than some Dominions were willing to
tolerate. After 1932, for example, a strong pressure group emerged in
Whitehall which wished to renew the Anglo–Japanese alliance discon-
tinued as a result of Canadian and American entreaties in 1921. The
roots of this reassessment lay in a vehement critique of British
concessions to the US since the War which, it was felt, had yielded no
benefits in terms of diplomatic support. Indeed, Britain had almost
mortgaged her foreign and military policies to American agreement and
many contended that the time had come to reassert the capacity to act
unilaterally. Thus Clive, the British Ambassador in Tokyo, told Simon
that Washington saw its Eastern interests as purely commercial, and
that therefore her support of the status quo was 'never likely to go
beyond the writing of notes to defend the integrity of China'.[10] This
trend, however, clashed with the assumption held by all the Dominions
(but especially those directly involved in Pacific affairs) that Empire
policy should never run counter to close Anglo–American relations.
The Dominions Office was very conscious that if such underlying
divergences ever became expressed at the policy level, the thinly founded
edifice of 'Empire Foreign Policy' would crack. Thomas now argued,
therefore, that Britain's non-renewal of the Japanese alliance in 1921
had been an irreversible promise to the Dominions that British policy
would never run counter to American wishes, and he warned that any
new initiative by the UK in Tokyo, unless it took a tripartite form and
included the US, would invite public condemnation from both Canada
and Australia.[11]

Simon and Neville Chamberlain, however, were no more prepared in
Asia than in Europe to allow the Dominion factor to veto consideration
of a move which might otherwise be in Britain's interests. The Foreign
Secretary responded that the non-renewal of 1921 had been merely a sop
to Canada, a reading which made resurrection of the alliance easier to
contemplate in 1934; and he added that the very rationale of an initiative
at this point was to 'shock' the State Department in Washington and
make it more pliant for the future.[12] Meanwhile, however, the
Dominions were reacting suspiciously to the UK tendency to sacrifice
the military aspects of Empire defence on the pyre of political

appeasement. Thus Robert Menzies[13] stressed at the 1935 meeting of the Commonwealth Prime Ministers that Australian–Japanese relations had worsened visibly over the preceding six months, and attempted to strengthen British resolve against Japanese pressure by reporting that a delegation from Tokyo had arrived in Canberra with 'a bag full of astonishing demands' – one of which was that Australia should renege on the whole of her obligations under the Ottawa agreement.[14] The cynic, either then or in retrospect, might be forgiven for reflecting that the Australians were likely to renege on their Ottawa commitments even without Japanese encouragement. The underlying concern of the Australian government, of course, was with the military rather than the economic aspects of Japanese expansion. The ultimate calculation that had to be made was whether Britain would in future fulfil her traditional role as the Empire's protector, or whether the Dominions should seek their strategic insurance elsewhere. Smuts made this point clear at the 1935 London Naval Conference:

> If the British Empire made concessions to Japan which went too far, then she would become a second rate Power and go the way that the Roman Empire had gone. Therefore, if Japan persists in her present attitude, the British Empire must not fall behind in the race and she must build as Japan builds. The major issue was either a first rate Power at sea or a second rate Power and ultimate extinction. Summing up, he . . . advocated the maintenance by the British Empire of her position . . . and . . . the maintenance of good relations with the United States of America.[15]

These implicit differences, however, never became sufficiently defined to be politically dangerous. Whatever instinctive anti-Americanism prevailed in Whitehall during the early 1930s, the Foreign Office was not finally prepared to alienate the US administration, whilst the Dominions were not prepared to publicise the fact that the Royal Navy had ceased to be a reliable guarantee against aggression. These mutual restraints ensured that the Commonwealth could turn a reasonably united face to the world; but it was (looked at in longer perspective) the intrusion of such doubts and half-formed reassessments as Smuts hinted at which partly explains the fragmenting experience of the 1930s.

It was differences on European rather than Pacific diplomacy, however, which determined the primary fracture between the UK and her fellow Dominions. It was clear that a Pacific war would only break out if European conflict triggered a more general destabilisation, so that all Commonwealth governments concentrated their attention on the Rhine rather than the Yangtse. But the controlling factor was that, whereas in the Pacific almost all Commonwealth governments recognised their direct interests to be at stake, only one – namely the UK –

accepted that it had an irrevocable role in European security, although that Government was the one which prescribed the contents of 'Empire policy'. If Britain was therefore drawn to guarantee the Dominions in the East, the Dominions were not similarly compelled to guarantee the UK in the West. A debilitating tension within Commonwealth relations arose from this fact.

The permanence of Anglo–Dominion differences on Europe only became apparent after 1933. Immediately after the War it was assumed that the Dominions had once and for all accepted that their interests could not be separated from those of Britain, and that this carried with it a willingness to assume at least some responsibility for European stability. The Chanak and Locarno episodes cast doubt on this, but it was felt in Whitehall that the new consultative apparatus subsequently introduced and the general logic of events would force imperial unity. As long as the European remained calm the British did not attempt to pressure the Dominions into precise obligations; when a Mediterranean Locarno was under discussion in 1930 the Dominions Office did not even discuss the adherence of the other Empire Governments.[16] But after 1932, and as the prospects of actual conflict became more real, the feeling grew that the UK should not take up any positions unless the Commonwealth nations had already been dragged in the British wake. Thus in 1933, when it became clear that a guarantee for French security was the price that had to be paid for her cooperation in disarmament, there was an attempt to coax the Dominions into line. Price informed the Foreign Office from Geneva,

> It is most important that we should not enter into any undertakings of this nature without the Dominions, and I have put forward to Riddell[17] and Mr Desy[18] the general considerations at the back of our proposals, e.g. the necessity of giving some satisfaction to France, the fact that we should naturally work in close touch with the Dominions and most important, the fact that we were making the agreement with the U.S. essential to the plan. But we are up against something of an *idée fixe* on the part of Canada. . . .[19]

Price accurately detected a hardening Canadian attitude against 'involvements', for the same factors which made the UK reluctant to make diplomatic moves without the Dominions simultaneously confirmed the Dominions in their isolationist prejudices. Thus, in May 1933, te Water bluntly told Thomas that the time had come to 'look West' and construct an Anglo-Saxon bloc which could abandon Europe to its tribal hatreds.[20] Such Dominion views were grist to the mill of British isolationists who, more forcefully than ever, wove the theme of 'imperial unity' into their anti-European tirades. Hankey used this tactic against the plan for an 'Air Locarno'

At the very moment when the Locarno 'sanction' is breaking down owing to the overwhelming pressure of public opinion, it seems extraordinary that we should be entering on a new and much more onerous commitment of the same kind, which points and sharpens all those aspects of Locarno that are most unpopular. . . . Broadly my impression is that no Dominion *Government* will go so far as to criticise any decision His Majesty's Government may take on a matter concerning our own security, but that popular opinion everywhere [in the Empire] . . . will, in the long run, reject anything that is regarded as a new commitment . . . the tendency, therefore, will be the weakening of those intangible bonds that provide the real Imperial link.[21]

Where did the Dominions Office stand in this debate on European commitments? If the Continental connection was such a geological flaw in inter-imperial understanding, it might logically have been ultra-isolationist, whatever the cost in terms of international trade and influence. In fact, the Dominions Office never criticised the UK's European obligations except where they showed signs of straying into areas east of the Rhine. To begin with, Harding and his colleagues lacked the departmental weight, unlike Hankey and the Cabinet Secretariat for example, to oppose established policies. Amery had, it is true, shown some dissatisfaction with the Locarno negotiations, but he had been reticent in doing so and had not taken the matter to the Cabinet. In addition none of Amery's successors as Dominions Secretary had the same general weight within the respective administrations which they served. Passfield and, even more, Thomas were in personal decline during their periods of office, whilst Malcolm MacDonald, despite his own ability, had the worst of both worlds – too young in his own right, and too closely connected to his father's falling star, to exercise real influence. The splitting of the 'personal union' of the Dominions and Colonial Offices after Passfield's tenure also meant that his successors had minimal leverage on broad questions. Given this weakness within the bureaucracy, the Dominions Office met with patronising contempt from other departments and politicians. 'I must say I didn't find the Dominions Office very well organised,' Sankey confided to his diary in December 1932, 'but no doubt they have their difficulties' – which, considering the simultaneity of the Ottawa Conference and the crisis of de Valera's election, was something of an understatement.[22]

The Dominions Office, then, never developed the political muscle to affect British policy-making generally, as Amery had intended in 1925, and had perforce to concentrate on tactics rather than strategy. The attitude of the department to Europe, however, was not merely a matter of limited bargaining power within the Whitehall system. The departmental atmosphere was consistently and positively internationalist in its predilections. Its fear of economic protectionism on an imperial basis has already been sufficiently stressed. But the department's internationalist stance also reflected its conviction that the regional differences within the Commonwealth had to be accepted as a reality. Thus Canada could have a special relationship with the United States, and similarly the UK with Europe, without being accused of anti-imperial tendencies. Such flexibility, the Dominions Office argued, was critical to the tactics of Commonwealth relations. This explains the significance always ascribed to the League by the department. Regional differentiation could be kept within limits by the countervailing force of Geneva's universalism. The misty rhetoric of the League with its emphasis on 'peoples' and 'world opinion' rather than obligatory sanctions appealed to the DO strongly, because it kept actual commitments to a minimum whilst holding out the hope that in a crisis the Dominions might be carried along in the wake of an anti-fascist coalition. Through a recurring linkage of League and Commonwealth the DO attempted to reconstruct the latter on a basis of liberal internationalism. Once this was done its own bureaucratic task would be much easier, because the burden of forging effective cooperation could be shifted to those concerned with the success of the League. Thus Batterbee, in supporting a voluntary interpretation of international sanctions, stated generally that

> the great value of the British Commonwealth (which is in effect a League within a League) is that all members of the Commonwealth are in such close touch with regard to all important international matters that it may be hoped that, when an emergency arises, they will all be able to declare simultaneously and at once that they are determined to impose every practicable sanction if a certain power is guilty of some unlawful act of aggression. . . . It is world opinion and world opinion only which is likely to prevent wars in future and the members of the Commonwealth can play an invaluable part in helping by their own unanimity to mobilise that opinion quickly.[23]

The folk memory of 1914, when the British nations had reacted to the outbreak of war with an instantaneous unity, underlay this belief that a crisis would define a common imperial interest. But did the conditions of 1914 persist? Had not Dominion economic and political development displaced the insecurity which had then stampeded them into colonial submissiveness? When te Water bluntly informed Thomas that 'He [te Water] was personally convinced that, if there were another war, there would be no repetition of the events of 1914. None of the Dominions would follow the United Kingdom, and the British Commonwealth as at present constituted would disappear,'[24] he was only voicing a widely expressed opinion.

Certainly Dominion reactions to international tension after 1931–2 did indicate that a structural change had taken place in inter-imperial politics since 1914. Above all, the strategic inadequacies arising from British disarmament since 1918 were now transparently clear, and the Dominions were forced to re-examine traditional calculations. During the preparations for the Geneva Disarmament Conference, for example, they exhibited a deep seated reluctance to be associated with the UK's limitation of armament levels. The Dominions Office noted

> The reduction of our naval forces made it increasingly impossible for them to depend to the same extent as in the past on assistance from the U.K. in their defence. This is almost certainly a contributory reason for their desire not to commit themselves to restricting their defence requirements to existing levels.[25]

Just as the British connection, then, was ceasing to provide easy access to long-term finance, it was also failing to function as a guaranteed source of military security. Commonwealth membership was thus no longer of such comprehensive relevance to the economic and political problems of the Dominions, even if on balance it remained a necessary asset. The sense of vulnerability which sprang from this bred volatile and sometimes contradictory responses. Crutchely caught this moody metamorphosis in a memorandum which Batterbee promptly forwarded to Hankey.

> There has been noticeable lately a growing realisation in Australia of her position and possible responsibilities in the Pacific. At first it was just a case of nerves – rumours of designs by Japan, first on the North, then on Australia's manufacturing industries and her sacred standard of living.
> This feeling . . . is undergoing a subtle change – becoming more dignified and 'grown up'. The revelations about England's decline of defensive power has had an effect both sobering and inspiring. . . . In this new atmosphere . . . I detect a growing tenderness for England – a reviving realisation of what after all Australia owes to her in the essentials of national life – an increasing regard for the Empire link. Australians are rather shocked that England is now only the fifth in air strength among Great Powers; the fact has caused them to think and has certainly stimulated their desire to strengthen their defences.[26]

Australian opinion, like that of most Dominions, was thus tugged in two different directions – on the one hand driven to re-emphasise the necessities of imperial cooperation, and on the other drawn towards a new definition of regional self-sufficiency. It is this almost schizoid nature of Dominion thinking which explains the equivocal character of Commonwealth discussions on economic and military cooperation as the crisis of the 1930s developed. But if the Dominions were revising their estimates as to the strategic capacity of the UK, the attitude of the UK Service departments was changing towards the Dominions. Thus in 1930 the Admiralty regarded the preservation of a single Empire quota as a vital factor at the London Naval Conference, whereas by 1933 they had become suspicious of building such an indeterminate variable as Dominion cooperation into the planning of UK defence requirements.[27] In fact the British authorities continued to advocate the single quota simply because the Americans, fearing multiple quotas as a way of expanding Empire totals in disarmament calculations, insisted on it. It seemed, in this instance at least, that Empire unity was an index of outside pressure bearing down rather than any autonomous movement towards cooperation among Commonwealth members.

It was the international situation, therefore, rather than internal political change, which undermined the old Commonwealth orthodoxies. It is difficult to speak in generalities of this process because the context of each Dominion was so different, and any attempt to define the local characteristics of every Dominion in its relations with Britain would be confusing rather than illustrative. A brief treatment, however, of how the factor of insecurity affected Anglo–South African relations will help isolate the general trend. South Africa, indeed, was always a more sensitive part of the imperial tradition than Australia or even Canada; for, if the First World War had apparently validated the Commonwealth as a state-entity, the roots of that association's political romanticism are to be located not least in the politics of 'reconciliation' after the Vereeniging Peace. Any break between the Union and the UK would have been a fatal blow to the values taken to be implicit in Commonwealth – above all, the belief that cultural and historic differences could be swept aside by the natural beneficence of British liberalism, British justice and British monarchy. By the early 1930s, however, the liberal assumptions which had long prevailed in Whitehall as to the future of South African politics had largely disappeared. This disillusionment took even deeper root after the formation of the Smuts–Hertzog Coalition in 1932 in which the former was clearly the junior partner. Stanley, the UK High Commissioner, reported to Harding in June 1933 that

> The nature of this year's Union budget shows pretty clearly that in the present Government, Nationalism is the predominant factor, and that the South Africa Party Ministers, including Duncan, are meekly following at the tail of the Hertzog and Havenga chariot. . . . It is

conceivable that the ultimate outcome of the Coalition may prove to be the permanent reunion and solidarity of the Afrikaner Community and the departure of the English-speaking section into the political wilderness.[28]

This, to Hertzog's annoyance, made transfer of the Protectorate Territories an impossibility because the UK could not allow itself to be seen handing over native populations to Afrikaner racialism. Differences over native policy, then, rather than Anglo–Dutch rivalry once again became the chief stumbling block between the UK and South Africa. Nonetheless, despite these problems, the international crisis at first seemed to point towards enhanced imperial cooperation. South Africa, apprehending that Britain might not now be in a position to ensure stability in colonial Africa if a European war broke out, was determined to seek a larger role in regional affairs. This role could only be extended by persuading the British government to permit South African personnel to participate in colonial defence planning north of the Limpopo. A number of cooperative gestures were therefore made. Thus Geddes,[29] recently returned from South Africa in an attempt to extend Imperial Airways activities in the Union, saw Batterbee and with elated surprise explained that he had met with genuine assistance 'quite as much from the Boers as from the British'.[30] This encouraged British officials who increasingly appreciated the need for South African help in naval operations, particularly in the Indian Ocean. Here, then, was the basis for a mutually beneficial 'swap'–South African participation in the defence arrangements of British colonial Africa in return for South African naval assistance in the Indian Ocean.

Hankey was quick to see the possibilities of this and he impressed on the Dominions Office a long and carefully argued memorandum by Naval Intelligence.[31] This paper argued that the passage of the South African Status Act marked the expiration of the 'racialist phase' of antagonism between Boer and Briton; that Hertzog's intention henceforth was 'to turn to the next phase – that of Empire Cooperation and Coordination'; that Hertzog would never fall into the error of secessionism, because he knew this to mean civil war; that although Pirow, the Defence Minister, was stressing local operations in his attempt to outflank domestic opposition to military expenditure, he did in fact intend to build up forces for external (and, by implication, Imperial) service; and that the great need in the UK, therefore, was to eradicate suspicion of South African motives and recognise the virtues of Smuts's 'Pan-African and Imperial idea for a greater South Africa'.[32] These views were counterbalanced in Whitehall, however, by a deeply entrenched suspicion that South Africa would only use the imperial connection for ends that ultimately clashed with British interests. Stanley, for example, pointed out that Pirow intended to use air development as a method to mortgage British colonial authority further north to South Africa and that he planned to run South African air services into Rhodesia for the express purpose of smashing Rhodesia and Nyasaland Airways, a subsidiary of Imperial Airways.[33] In short, he saw the UK and South Africa in direct, if partly concealed, competition for aviation and ultimately political dominance in the sub-continent. The 'swap', moreover, lacked any reality until Pirow,[34] the South African Defence Minister, showed that he was prepared to make some solid proposals on the naval side of the equation, which he appeared more than reluctant to do – it had so far proved impossible to even squeeze a trawler for volunteer training purposes out of Pretoria.[35] But whatever assistance in this field Pirow might have been willing to dangle before the UK, one overwhelming factor militated against the recommendations of Naval Intelligence – the UK's determination to avoid at all costs racial instability in colonial areas, particularly Kenya. The Colonial Office rigidly upheld this priority.

If South Africa will cooperate reasonably over Defence it should be all to the good but if, in pursuance to that end, Mr Pirow starts beating the 'White Africa' drum – as he appears to be doing – incalculable harm may result. Such a policy, and a few unthinking references would be enough, would create racial feeling in Kenya thereby causing much trouble and leading to suspicion that the Union wants to take over Kenya – 'Carry the Vierkleur to the Nile' in fact. That would raise much trouble here and excite suspicion of the Union – already rife enough. So it is essentially a case of 'softly, softly'. . . .[36]

It was the opposition of the Colonial, rather than the Dominions Office, therefore, which was the chief obstacle to Hankey's suggestion. 'The present system of native regiments with British officers who appreciated British native administration works admirably,' Cunliffe-Lister, the Colonial Secretary asserted, '[and] it would be impossible to introduce into this force either Union officers or a Union contingent.'[37] But it is important to stress that both Floud and Cunliffe-Lister based their opposition on the assumed continuance of peace. Both realised that a war situation would see these priorities reversed. Thus Thomas was quite willing for the question of South African wartime cooperation in Central and East Africa to be discussed at the Committee of Imperial Defence,[38] whilst Cunliffe-Lister admitted with equal realism that during hostilities South African assistance would be required – presumably at a price.[39]

Whilst discussions on Anglo–South African defence cooperation was deadlocked, however, the Hertzog Government was forging a new political relationship with Hitler's Germany. Pretoria's motive in this was plain. Dr Gie, Hertzog's representative in Berlin, was quite blunt with one of his UK colleagues: 'South Africa', he said, 'needed the aid and support of a virile country in a future war against the natives,' and there seemed little doubt as to who was virile in the Europe of the 1930s.[40] German native policies, it was felt, had never fallen into such degradations as the French practice of arming natives or into the effete errors of British liberalism. Pirow was equally to the point when he declared that the connection between South Africa and Germany

> has nothing at all to do with our being German-minded or not. . . . On the contrary, it is a desire which lies at the foundation of our determination here in South Africa to maintain ourselves as the youthful off-shoot of Western civilisation, which gave us what we have and has made us what we are. In the unforgettable words of General Smuts, we are determined not to be drawn down, like older civilisations on our Continent, into the quicksand of African native blood. But for that we need allies on this great continent to help us against that fatal cowardice which wishes to pamper the native at the expense of the white man, and also against that delusion of others who play with the ridiculous idea of race mixture.[41]

Pro-Germanism in southern Africa took most overt form in the Nazi movement of the South-West African mandate. 'The Nazi organisation had grown in numbers and in insolence,' Stanley reported in August 1934: 'uniforms, parades and demonstrations, with the avowed intention of "keeping South-West Africa warm for Germany", had now become the order of the day'.[42] This, indeed, had not gone unnoticed in Berlin, because the decision of the Nazi *Kolonialabteilung* to concentrate its propaganda on the restoration of South-West Africa, rather than Tanganyika or Samoa, was due to the conviction that a deal was possible between a 'friendly Cape Government' and Hitler.[43] Pirow had certainly made hints in this direction,[44] whilst Stanley developed considerable anxiety over the close relationship between Bodenstein and the German Consul, Herr Wiehl – he particularly disliked their weekend rambles in the *veldt* where seditious conversations could go on unobserved.[45] Bodenstein also tried to unofficially censor press criticisms of the European fascist regimes, and ill-feeling on this reached a climax when two intoxicated officials from the German and Italian Embassies assaulted the offices of the *Cape Times* in 'truculent fashion' and wrecked part of the files.[46]

UK officials had to evaluate the seriousness of these facts. Was Hertzog just using Germany as a mallet to bludgeon British policy into a shape acceptable to himself? Did Germanophilia go much beyond Pirow, Bodenstein and their narrow caucus of Nationalist extremists? Was it not likely that if any new presence (German or otherwise) appeared on African soil, Hertzog would very quickly take up the cudgels of 'Imperial Defence'? On the whole, British officials were optimistic on these points, considering that the South African government had much less room to manoeuvre than Hertzog or Pirow led their public to believe. The possibility of Pretoria restoring the South–West Africa Mandate to Germany was not regarded as substantial. As Cunliffe-Lister observed, their real objective was 'a kind of Monroe Doctrine in Southern Africa' for themselves.[47] It was, after all, Hertzog's government, not Pirow's, and the estimation that Hertzog, despite occasional lapses, was not really anti-British still prevailed. Stanley reassured Thomas that Smuts and Hertzog were only divided on 'fine juridical points'[48] whilst the Dominions Office refused to be stampeded by Union Opposition claims that the 1934 Status Act had finally destroyed the 'state' concept of the British Commonwealth and fundamentally transformed South Africa's relations with the UK. 'The contrary view has . . . been expressed by Union Ministers (including General Smuts) in the Union Parliament and by Mr Duncan in a private letter,' Dixon concluded in May 1935, 'and we must take the Union at their word and assume that the Acts in question will be interpreted in a reasonable spirit'.[49] Such mild tolerance seemed well-founded when Hertzog instinctively turned to the UK for help after rumours circulated of Japanese ambitions in Portuguese East Africa.[50] By May 1934 the South African government was claiming solid information of a colonisation scheme by which 400 Japanese families were to be settled in Angola, and of Japanese plans to flood the whole of southern Africa with cheap goods – and wanted to know what the UK were going to do about it.[51] The Foreign Office were unconcerned because they considered the British commercial monopoly in the area to be unassailable.[52] Nothing was done and the settlers never arrived (presumably they went to Manchuria instead) but the episode indicated that, once threatened by international competition, South Africa quickly began to see her security through an imperial lens. One Pretoria official, indeed, comforted Stanley with the judgement that Pirow himself was too able a man to think in terms of breaking with British interests, and that his pro-Germanism would always be restricted to the occasional 'good turn' such as employing Junker models on South Africa's internal air-routes.[53] Reporting Nationalist attacks on Hankey's visit to South Africa in mid-1934, Liesching dismissed them as unrepresentative of broad opinion and summed up the situation:

South Africans know enough of the international situation to be frightened on the merits of the case. When they have Malan on one wing talking . . . of an impending war, and Smuts on the other wing speaking . . . of the 'dangerous era into which we are moving', and when both mining and agriculture know, as they do, that if war means the loss of the U.K. market, they are finished, the Malanites are in poor position to panic any noticeable section of the community into an isolationist policy.[54]

But if South African opinion was mature enough to recognise that they could not be immune to international developments, the corollary was that they would only cooperate with the British to the extent that those developments affected their own regional situation. It was the DO's belief that the South African leadership should be left to make its own choice as to where the balance lay that made it lukewarm towards Hankey's Empire tour of 1934, which was designed to force open the whole defence question in the light of the British government's recent White Paper on rearmament. Certainly Hankey quickly learned that political currents in all the Dominions continued to thwart any forward movement. Even in Australia his talks had to be 'veiled in secrecy' lest the Government were tainted with collusion in British militarism,[55] and the Cabinet Secretary had to conclude that Prime Minister Lyons (whom he considered a 'charming old boy' and nothing more) lacked both the ruthlessness and the Ministers to reform such stagnant institutions as the Militia.[56] In South Africa particularly, Hankey was educated in the gap that separated Britain and her Commonwealth partners on European policy. Instead of restricting himself to immediate issues such as local defence arrangements, Hankey brought up in his interview with Hertzog the inviolability of the Belgian frontier.

I read trouble in his [Hertzog's] eyes. . . . I reassured him by reminding him that I was not talking of any immediate danger; that no new commitment was contemplated; that it was not a question of whether we should intervene, but whether we should be capable of intervention.[57]

Hankey's attempt to 'cover his tracks' failed to stem a typical Hertzog attack on French obstinacy in Europe, the premature nature of the British decision in 1914 to help France and the fundamental dichotomy between European and Imperial interests.[58] They parted on this chasm of misunderstanding – and Roskill's judgement that Hankey's activities in 1934 helped bring South Africa into war in 1939 can at best be dismissed as partial history.[59]

It was the Anglo–Dominion divergence on Europe which dominated the Commonwealth talks during the London Jubilee celebrations of April 1935. By then pressure had mounted for a general settlement of Continental questions. But the form of such a settlement accentuated those cleavages because, in the British view, an *extension* of her commitment to western Europe was a necessary means of persuading France to accept any revision of Versailles. The Stresa Front, between

Britain, France and Italy was, from the UK's angle, primarily an attempt to assure France that revision would not prejudice her security. To the Dominions, however, Stresa appeared as a revival of diplomatic and military alliance-making aimed at preventing Germany from exercising her natural predominance in Europe. For them, a general settlement meant an immediate recognition of German claims for 'justice'. Simon strove in the London discussions to re-establish the even-handed, mediatorial image of British policy in Dominion eyes. He explained that the Stresa talks had been offset by a Ministerial visit to Berlin, and it was implicit in his statement that the UK accepted the principle of revision.[60] But he made it equally clear that such revision had to carry with it French agreement, and that German intransigence had made this very difficult to obtain. What Simon presented as 'balance', however, appeared to Dominion leaders as a continued pampering of the French. Hertzog retorted

> There was only one thing that would put Germany . . . in a position to negotiate freely, and that was if she was put in a position of complete equality; that is to say, in a position of standing, prestige, and so on, equal to other nations. . . . In South Africa he felt that the events of 1926 had brought about a changed mentality. How far had any attempt been made to tackle Germany from that point of view? How far were the victors, and especially France, prepared to look the facts in the face and to say 'This point and that point are a cause of humiliation to Germany'? South Africans could feel this in a way which perhaps was not possible here owing to their experiences.[61]

Hertzog's argument goes some way towards indicating the character of the dispute between the Commonwealth partners. Most Dominion leaders saw the 'German problem' in terms of status rather than power. They perceived not a 'struggle for mastery' in Europe but a demand on the part of an oppressed nationality for equality and respect. What Europe needed was what the Empire, however belatedly, had already achieved – an end to inferiority and imposition. There was a failure to realise that European neighbours did not share a sense of common interests which (although they would rarely admit it in public) did bind the Commonwealth together; as such, its divisions could not be healed or even ambiguously glossed over by a piece of rhetorical whimsy like the Balfour Report.

With basic assumptions so far apart no consensus could be expected to emerge. MacDonald had to fall back on the hollow procedural argument that 'Insofar as the progress of foreign affairs was reported to Dominion Governments and no objection was taken, agreement generally on the part of the Dominions would be assumed.'[62] But this was a precarious assumption on which to base British calculations because Dominion silence usually indicated a desire to distance themselves from imperial commitments rather than approbation. Bennett conveyed the real atmosphere of doubt and anxious questioning which pervaded the discussions when he commented to the departing Prime Ministers that

> he had never left this country with a greater sense of fear for the safety of the heart of the Empire. He could not help feeling that, with the European situation as it was today, the U.K. was unprepared. With all the magnificent outpouring of loyalty which had so impressed them in the last few days, he felt a genuine foreboding as to the future and deep sympathy for those responsible for the government of the U.K. He could not ignore the accounts which were abroad about the aircraft of other nations. . . .[63]

The British dilemma was plain. For years she had disarmed as the price for that European peace which obviously favoured both herself and her Dominions. Indeed, it was the fact that British policy was so clearly a 'peace policy' which had limited the range of inter-imperial divergence on international matters. But such British sacrifices for peace were diplomatically useless unless matched by the French, which they were not; so when the threat of war resumed, the UK seemed incapable of performing the basic function of Empire defence which the situation demanded. There could be little certainty of Dominion reactions in such a novel context. The DO was driven to revise an earlier estimate of South African attitudes.

> it will be seen that General Hertzog has made a number of statements of recent years to the effect that this [neutrality] is an academic question, but it will be noted that his view is based to a considerable extent upon the belief that the Covenant of the League of Nations and the Kellogg Pact have ruled out the possibility of war for a considerable period. If there occurs any breakdown in the League system of preserving peace, he might speak differently.[64]

This was, in many ways, the heart of the problem. The Dominions had emerged from the war with an awareness of their regional identities and a determination not to be dragged into another European debacle. This might have broken the structure of imperial unity in the 1920s if the League and the internationalist consensus had not provided a set of general objectives – collective security, arbitration, peace – which obscured differences on specifics. As long as British policy and its commitment to France could be filtered through the universalism of Geneva, the fundamental differences on Europe were prevented from becoming too sharply defined. But as the authority of the League declined, the crude fact of the Anglo–French connection became only too evident. The Abyssinia crisis which followed gave sharper point to this dilemma.

Some Dominions had very real interests at stake in the Abyssinia incident. Australia was determined to avoid any war across her naval path to her largest market, the UK, whilst South Africa was determined to avoid any military confrontation on African soil which took the form of whites versus blacks, and particularly a confrontation which threatened to produce a Negro victory – another Adowa might substantiate the growing expectations of race war in Southern Africa. In both cases, the conclusion was that Mussolini should be given what he wanted without more ado. Cockram,[65] a Dominions Office representative reporting the Commonwealth discussions at Geneva, noted

> Mr te Water and Mr Bruce, particularly the former, took the somewhat unexpected line that the only course was to have a week's enquiry at Geneva, declare Abyssinia an uncivilised country, eject her from the League and give Italy a mandate and military occupation. . . . Both Mr Eden and Sir Samuel Hoare[66] were rather taken aback by these suggestions.[67]

The effect that such a move might have on the League was of little moment to te Water or Bruce. For the Dominions, Geneva was a symbol rather than a substantive interest, and symbolism could not stand in the way of practical needs. But for the UK, the League was the only instrument which seemed capable of stabilising European relations and as such was a priority in itself. For Hoare and Eden it seemed that the League's credibility – badly damaged when confronted with previous challenges from Japan and Germany – could now be rehabilitated when faced with the lesser danger of Italy. The Foreign Secretary remonstrated with the two Dominion representatives that the obligations of 'collective security' could not so easily be shuffled off,[68] and the following day Hoare gave his famous speech in the Assembly in which he affirmed that 'the League stands, and my country stands with it, for collective maintenance of the Covenant in its entirety and in particular for steady and collective resistance to all acts of unprovoked aggression'.[69]

It is difficult to recreate the electric effect this had on the Assembly. Hoare having provided the protection others needed, almost all delegations, including the Dominions, jumped on the coercive bandwagon. By 24 September, Hankey was reporting that the Dominions appeared 'ready to play up'.[70] Eden held three Commonwealth meetings in forty-eight hours to ensure a common approach. He succeeded almost too well. On 26 September, Sir John Parr[71] of New Zealand was telling his Commonwealth colleagues that he 'would have liked to see the Suez Canal closed to the Italians tomorrow',[72] whilst de Valera, according to Walsh, was prepared to go even further and had 'expressed himself in somewhat violent language as to what he would do if he had the British Navy . . . he expressed himself in favour of closing the Suez Canal within five minutes'.[73] South Africa, as we shall see, was moving even further down the sanctionist path, and te Water's calls for effective action against Mussolini were hardly outdone even by Emperor Haile Selassie himself. The UK, unable to move faster than the French permitted, were now embarrassingly behind their Commonwealth partners in their fervour for League assertion.

The reason for this Dominion 'turn round' is instructive. South Africa's attitude, for example, did not hinge on any evaluation of the European situation *per se*, or even on whether Mussolini should be in or out of Addis Abbaba. Her only priority was to avert a mobilisation of black troops on either side. 'The last thing that Mr Pirow wanted was a military success for the Abyssinians,' a South African official subsequently explained to Wiseman, 'On the other hand, he did not trust the Italians . . . not to arm the native population.'[74] Once it became clear that Hoare would oppose Mussolini and that the Abyssinians would fight, Pretoria became desperate to thwart Mussolini by Mediterranean sanctions before he got defeated by native arms in North-East Africa. The British Foreign Office encouraged South Africa to approach the problem from this racial perspective. 'If Italian military measures should encounter serious difficulties, or still more if the Italian armies should meet with a reverse,' the High Commissioners had been told, 'the effect can hardly be other than to create or encourage among native races a spirit which may assume unfortunate forms.'[75] This tactic succeeded to the amazing degree that cinema audiences in the Union, responding to Hertzog's new found enthusiasm for the League in a way the Nationalist leader had certainly not intended, were soon ecstatically applauding newsreel of Abyssinian successes against the new white intruders on the African continent. 'Speaking of these things', Wallinger,[76] Political Secretary to the UK High Commissioner in Pretoria, wrote home, 'a Hertzogite Nationalist friend of mind remarked: Man! You don't begin to understand what it means for us Afrikaners to cheer when white men are being slaughtered by blacks!'[77]

The point which must be emphasised here is how a major diplomatic problem could be approached by Commonwealth partners from very different standpoints. For the UK, Abyssinia was a problem in European stability; for Australia and New Zealand, a problem in the maintenance of naval communications; for South Africa, a problem in African race relations. The UK was thus forced into a pincers, having to assure Commonwealth delegates that the French would eventually cooperate in sanctions whilst attempting to bludgeon France into meeting the challenge of collective security.

Whilst the French prevaricated, however, the coercive nerve of League members inevitably frayed and broke; and Canada played a not insignificant part in this pricking of the sanctionist bubble. The Abyssinia crisis had coincided with a general election in Canada which Mackenzie King clearly stood a chance of winning. Skelton, deeply worried that King would then dismiss him 'since it might be felt that he [Skelton] had become an imperialist during the Bennett regime',[78] had tried to re-establish his nationalist credentials by securing the appointment of Loring Christie, a staunch isolationist, to the Department of External Affairs. Christie was a bitter critic of Canadian participation in British-led sanctions. 'Skelton and the rest of the Department of External Affairs have . . . mellowed a lot in recent years', Archer reported, 'but in the presence of Christie's strong and experienced personality, they tend to revert to earlier views.'[79] But, whilst Ottawa officials were thus braced to draw in their sanctionist horns, the Canadian representative in Geneva, Riddell, had already gone beyond British proposals and suggested an oil embargo. Predictably Riddell was lambasted in separatist quarters as a front for the British Foreign Office,[80] although ironically it seems more likely that he had come under te Water's influence rather than Hoare's.[81] When Mackenzie King was duly elected, therefore, he faced an awkward choice of giving Riddell his head or disassociating the Canadian government from the oil idea. In fact he hovered between an enjoyment of sudden prominence in Geneva and his fear of Quebec before surrendering to the latter on 30 November when an official statement laid down that military obligations to the League could not be considered compulsory. Floud, Clark's successor as British High Commissioner to Canada, wrote in annoyance to the new Dominions Secretary, Malcolm MacDonald,

The fact remains . . . that for a month, during which the suggestion for the inclusion of oil sanctions against Italy was repeatedly referred to in the press as a suggestion backed by the authority of the Dominion Government, no steps were taken to correct this impression. Only when it was thought that Signor Mussolini would regard sanctions as a cause for war, did the Canadian Government show that they realised the possible implications of Dr Riddell's suggestion.[82]

Thus the impact of crisis, by bringing war closer than at any point since 1918, had defined Canadian isolationism more clearly than ever. The same process occurred in Australia. In parliamentary debate the Australian government made it plain that they reserved the right to determine the nature of Australian obligations arising from any dispute before the League.[83] This was not least a response to pressure from the Left, for Lang, the Labour leader in New South Wales, had been converted from being a League activist to a proponent of the argument that Geneva was an 'imperialist tool'.[84] And when the cry came from old Billy Hughes on the right that the League was a farce unless backed by military options he rapidly found himself dismissed from the Cabinet.[85]

These retreats from the Assembly rhetoric of September were not, of course, distinctive of the Dominions; they were paralleled in all those countries affected by Mediterranean strategy. Together they had the result of convincing the French that they could bank on little League assistance if Mussolini were pushed into aggression. And because Britain could not act without France, the only alternative was an agreement with the Italian dictator. The Hoare–Laval Plan, which granted the latter most of his demands, thus emerged. This plan, by breaking the spell of British commitment to League idealism, also broke the spell of a Commonwealth policy bound together by a set of common values. Subsequently it was to be much easier for Dominion governments to criticise British actions in Europe or elsewhere. Te Water thus conveyed to MacDonald South Africa's sense of betrayal.[86] Even those Dominions whose advocacy of sanctions had, unlike South Africa, wavered during the crisis, attacked the Anglo–French action in similar terms. Unwilling to face the war which a strong League policy appeared to entail, they nonetheless saw fit to react with indignant shock if the UK were forced to put that policy aside. 'He could not exaggerate the disastrous effect which the sudden springing of the Hoare–Laval proposals on New Zealand and the world generally . . . had had', Berendsen told Cockram from Wellington. 'They had come as an absolute bombshell.'[87] Bennett lamented to Archer in Ottawa that the incident had considerably damaged British 'face' in both Canada and the US and provided invaluable ammunition for the King–Skelton–Christie faction.[88] The fact that British public opinion forced the National Government to drop both the proposals and the Minister concerned in them did not alter the fact that henceforth British policy in Europe was much more exposed to Dominion accusations of being motivated by the secular interests of the UK. It was against this critical background that the Rhineland crisis now intervened.

In March 1936 German troops re-entered the East Bank zone of the Rhineland which had been demilitarised under the Versailles Treaty. If France were to decide to act against this infraction of international obligations, the UK (both as a guarantor of the Paris Treaty and a signatory of Locarno) was bound to assist her. The crisis meetings between British officials and the Dominion High Commissioners in London were therefore a perfect opportunity for the latter to press their critique of French intransigence, a critique given edge and bitterness by the events of the preceding months. Indeed, Massey,[89] the Canadian High Commissioner, and te Water, with sporadic support from their Irish Free State Colleague, Dulanty, sought to use the situation to 'bounce' the UK out of Locarno commitments altogether by characterising it as typical of the dangers implicit in European alliances;[90] whilst South Africa went even further down the revisionist path, stating that the 'psychological moment' had arrived to 'face the tension' and impose a settlement on Europe – meaning France.[91] If over Abyssinia, therefore, the UK had been pincered between a reluctant France and the initially sanctionist Dominions, over the Rhineland it had to balance between an assertive France and Dominions bent on passive acceptance. Duplicity was the only way to hold this position together. Malcolm MacDonald, therefore, throughout gave the impression to his Commonwealth colleagues that the UK would not fight alongside the French. Thus when te Water used the contention that the UK's signature of the Kellogg Pact cancelled her obligation to go to war under the Locarno contract, the Dominions Secretary agreed that 'we could not afford to overlook any argument'.[92]

Meanwhile, however, the UK had to coax the French into 'reasonableness' by assuring them that the UK would always guarantee their West Bank frontier. Te Water's request that the High Commissioners attend the meetings of the Locarno guarantors as 'observers' (a request which might earlier have been enthusiastically welcomed as a sign of encouraging Dominion 'involvement') had therefore to be rejected because it would make plain the extent to which British policy remained the creature of French fears. For the same reasons the High Commissioners' meetings had to be suspended when the Anglo–French talks got to the stage of solid quid pro quos, for to have kept the Dominions even minimally informed of the contents would have provoked a concerted attempt to stall the proceedings. Finally, France was persuaded to accept Hitler's *fait accompli* in return for a UK commitment to carry out the Locarno obligations irrespective of any 'backing-down' by others and a promise that this would be given immediate substance by staff discussions between the two countries. This clashed with the general assumptions which had governed the Anglo–Dominion talks. MacDonald struggled to retain some isolationist credibility by explaining that the military conversations

> would be strictly limited to the question of military requirements in the event of an actual German invasion of France or Belgian territory and . . . they did not commit the U.K. from the political point of view . . . the conversations were intended to have a psychological value, 'to help the French be helpful'.[93]

Dominion leaders, however, knew only too well that similar arguments had been used at the time of the Anglo–French staff talks of 1904. In short, the Abyssinia and Rhineland crises had shattered the League framework which had made it especially difficult for the Dominions to separate themselves from British policy, and created a more sharply defined Anglo–French alliance which the Dominions had traditionally opposed. But the Rhineland incident affected the Commonwealth relations in another related aspect. Mussolini, with League sanctions operating against him, had not surprisingly refused to add his name to the UK's reinsurance of France. Effectively, therefore, the Locarno front had been broken. From the Australian viewpoint the old likelihood of a war in which Italy would assist Britain against Germany, or at least be neutral, had not threatened her communications lifeline. But by shunting Italy into the revisionist camp, British policy had potentially isolated Australia from her markets and her source of protection. Page, the Australian Deputy Premier, stressed at the meeting of the High Commissioners on 2 April that Australian support must henceforth be regarded as uncertain. He said,

> the U.K. had taken isolated action which had committed the U.K. He felt it would inevitably have a bad effect on Empire opinion. The Commonwealth [of Australia] would have backed the U.K. and all the Locarno powers except Germany but now the united front of the other Locarno Powers had been broken.[94]

The obvious response to this dilemma was to restore good relations with Italy. Indeed, quite apart from problems of imperial defence, neither the UK nor France were prepared to face the twin burdens of Mediterranean instability and the now permanent state of tension along the Rhine. But having bundled the Dominions into sanctions how could they be bundled out again? Hertzog had already tried to 'head off' any such reversal by a major policy speech on 2 May in which he spoke with great fervour of the League idealism which underlay British policy – a piece of loyalist rhetoric the tactical objective of which was to keep British policy along lines desired by South Africa.[95] *The Rand Daily Mail* eulogised the South African leader for rising 'to the greatest heights of constructive statesmanship',[96] whilst the *Cape Argus* disparagingly compared Eden's prevarications to Hertzog's internationalist convictions.[97] But such attitudes were out of touch with any reality since Abyssinian resistance had all but collapsed. When the question arose in the Dominions Office of whether Hertzog should be informed of this crucial development, it was decided to let him stew in the juice of his own hyperbole. 'They [the South Africans] will learn the facts more suitably through Geneva', Wiseman observed, 'when the appropriate time comes.'[98] Neville Chamberlain indicated that the time had almost arrived in a speech to the 1900 Club on 10 June, in which he denounced the continuation of sanctions as 'the very midsummer of madness',[99] and although Baldwin disassociated himself from these words, it was clear that the inevitable decision was approaching. The South African press of all shades launched attacks on the British government hardly equalled since the Boer War. The Malanite *Die Burger*, which had always opposed Hertzog's sanctionism, was able to record gleefully that Hertzog had been 'left in the lurch' – a fate awaiting all those who were foolish or devious enough to collaborate with the imperialists,[100] whilst the *Natal Mercury*, which had supported League action throughout, blamed failure on British cowardice.

Mr Neville Chamberlain's speech in public preparation of a day of national humiliation at the feet of Italy is a . . . grave . . . act of political apostasy. Its plain meaning . . . is that the British Government is on the eve of acknowledging the bitterest diplomatic defeat in modern history and of reconciling itself to the final disruption of the present League of Nations system.[101]

South African reactions, however, could not stand against the overwhelming considerations which now obsessed the Foreign Office: that the success of sanctions could only mean the collapse of Italy as a counter-weight to German penetration in South-East and Central Europe.[102] Significantly, the Dominions Office made no attempt to oppose the termination of sanctions even though Australia was the only Dominion known to favour such a course. They complained about the lack of adequate notice to 'prepare' the Commonwealth governments and they opposed the idea of offsetting termination by guarantees to Greece or Yugoslavia since the extension of such Locarno-type commitments threatened to establish a wholesale structure of British obligations unconnected with the Dominions.[103] But that was all. The Cabinet discussions, too, reflected this scale of priorities. There was an easy confidence that most of the Dominions would 'fall into line', whilst te Water's threat to attack the move in the Assembly was 'not to be taken too tragically'.[104] Indeed, the suggestion that Italy should be induced by an offer of British financial assistance to satisfy South Africa's fears with a pledge not to raise a native army was summarily rejected.[105] Imperial unity, it seemed, was not even worth an injection of cash. This came out more plainly in the conclusion, which Eden was later to use in Geneva, that 'it was rather an advantage that from time to time a Dominion should take an independent line so as to show foreign nations that there was no "united front" between the UK and the Dominions'.[106]

Analysis of this last idea brings out some of the more general themes which this study seeks to elucidate. It was partly, of course, a response to the need to sweep the South African difficulty under the carpet. But it also points to a recognition that the rigid conception of 'Empire Foreign Policy' which, despite Chanak and Locarno, had still prevailed in the 1920s and early 1930s, could not be squared any longer with the new regime of involvements and obligations in the European order. As such, the attempt to maintain this conception only produced friction and embarrassment rather than influence or prestige. But on top of this there was a feeling that Britain's European allies always expected too much of her because they had a false idea of her capacity. This overestimation arose from the myth that the UK was the centre of a world-wide British alliance which she could tap for economic and military support whenever required. If this could be dispelled a more healthy realism would prevail in Continental affairs. The French, for example, might realise that the UK could not on its own guarantee the 1918 settlement and that this realisation would make her amenable to moderate revision of Versailles. At bottom this thinking represents an acceptance that Britain's fundamental role was European, not imperial, and that her political capacity even within that orbit had definite limitations.

But if official thinking in Whitehall was taking on a more pronounced European orientation, separatist ideas in the Dominions were also in process of solidification. The break up of the League's authority was a catalyst in this process. There was, it should be noted, a brief flurry of 'League reform' enthusiasm in mid-1936 which sought to keep Geneva at the centre of a European strategy – a campaign in which the Dominions Secretary played a significant part – but it was soon clear that internationalism was dead. We need only note one way in which this affected Commonwealth relations. Since the Versailles settlement the imperial obligations of Commonwealth members to fight for each other when attacked had been meshed into the commitments of League members to guarantee each other's security. Indeed, the League and the Commonwealth had invariably been spoken of in the same breath as symbolising the values of peace, cooperation and justice which they both represented. The fact that League obligations had obscured imperial ones had not mattered because it was always assumed that the UK. would be the victim, not the perpetrator, of aggression so that the Dominions would be bound to assist under League auspices. But now League members scrambled to emphasise that League commitments were not compulsory, and some Dominions took the opportunity at the same time to denounce automatic commitments arising from the Commonwealth association too. The baby was emptied out with the bathwater. Thus Mackenzie King stressed in his speech at the Geneva Assembly in September that both the League and the Commonwealth were mechanisms for conciliation and that neither could have a rigid claim on Canada's resources in a war

> The Canadian Parliament reserves to itself the right to declare in the light of the circumstances existing at the time, to what extent, if at all, Canada will participate in conflicts in which other members of the Commonwealth may be engaged.[107]

But because the imperial dimension was fading from the British mind, it is hardly surprising that this public statement did not produce the resentment and paranoia which it would have done a decade before. Garner,[108] a Dominions Office observer reporting Mackenzie King's speech, admitted that the neutrality claim had been 'unfortunate' and 'went further than any previous Canadian utterance on the question', but he concluded that 'politically his remarks were designed to be helpful to us'.[109] This mildness was rooted in the fact that behind the scenes MacDonald and Mackenzie King were evolving a subtler, more informal approach to Anglo–Canadian cooperation than the old structure of ideas (and the antagonism they generated) had permitted. In a long exchange King had convinced MacDonald that the preservation of Canadian unity and the impact of American isolationism necessitated that he disengage himself from any automatic connection with European affairs. But, given acceptance of this by the UK, he was prepared to appreciate the needs of Britain's own situation. 'Throughout the talk he showed every sign of a genuine anxiety to help us', MacDonald stated, 'and a readiness to be influenced by our opinions.'[110] The way was open for a more flexible, if more submerged, relationship. British officials gave up their nightmares of neutrality and secession when Mackenzie King felt compelled to make the occasional 'nationalist' statement, whilst Mackenzie King refused to be stampeded by isolationist pressure when it came to hard decisions. Thus the UK forbore to support the Canadian military establishment when they sought help against Mackenzie King's severance of direct correspondence between British and Canadian staffs,[111] whilst Mackenzie King ignored the separatist demand for a denunciation of Sam Hoare when he made a speech calling for a Commonwealth-wide approach to rearmament.[112]

It is the rearmament process, in fact, which illustrates how Anglo–Dominion cooperation crystallised after 1935 despite the fragmentation of imperial foreign policy. The shock of Abyssinia, for example, prompted the Australian government to embark on a public campaign of defence propaganda which the Dominions Office hailed as 'sound and useful doctrine based on Imperial Conference resolutions'.[113] This yielded some substance in December 1935 when Parkhill, the Australian Defence Minister, introduced a £20m Three Year Plan for military reorganisation. The extent to which the Dominions still relied on the UK as their source of heavy industrial supplies ensured that such military programmes were coordinated with British production. South Africa was thus dependent on the UK for the aviation models which she saw as vital for regional security. Because British firms, however, were already at full stretch in meeting domestic requirements, the allocation of supply became a critical issue. Pirow had become so desperate by October 1935 that he despatched one of his closest aides, Colonel

Holthouse, to Hawker Siddeley in Bristol to expedite deliveries.[114] Holthouse reported on his return that Hawker Siddeley bore no comparison to the efficient Junker factories with their disciplined Labour Corps in Germany and that South African needs were being ignored – the delivery in question had been found hidden away in a corner covered with dust.[115] Such allegations were rife, and Wallinger warned Batterbee that unless the supply situation improved, Pirow would be pushed even further towards the pro-German faction.[116] But whatever the ill-feelings may have been on this, it is evidence of how closely dependent the Dominions were on British assistance once security had surfaced as a dominant priority.

The South African government, indeed, was so anxious for British help in aviation matters that it was willing at last to trade off maritime cooperation. By January 1936 Pirow was pronouncing himself ready 'to face any internal political difficulties' to collaborate on such items as Naval Control Services. But such cooperation had to be carefully shielded from public view. Antrobus, Stanley's assistant in South Africa, explained that a compromise was therefore negotiated

> by which regular naval officers working in mufti would start the various services required, working from the offices of one of the big insurance offices. . . . We believe, however, that once war broke out Pirow would have no objecction to the calling-up of ex-naval officers resident in the Union. In fact, the above arrangement, which was required for internal political reasons, can be considered as a stop-gap which would only apply during any preliminary stage of emergency.[117]

More controversial, however, was the plan, championed by both Smuts and Pirow, for the construction of fifteen-inch gun emplacements at Cape Town. For this they wished to obtain UK subsidies and equipment, and presented their plan as a generous offer by South Africa to defend the Cape route for imperial shipping purposes. Ironically, however, it was opposed, not only by the extreme nationalist Right in South Africa, but also by the British military authorities because the latter were determined to ensure that South African security began at Singapore rather than Cape Town – the guns would only generate a false isolationist confidence. Thus, when *Die Burger* lambasted Pirow for complicity in a 'British Imperial Rearmament Scheme', Antrobus wryly commented,

> It is rather amusing that he [Pirow] should be bombarded by the Malanites for taking the advice of the Committee of Imperial Defence in a matter in which he is having the greatest difficulty in persuading the Committee of Imperial Defence to follow his own wishes.[118]

British officials could therefore allow themselves the luxury of smug amusement when Pirow opened the Imperial Press Conference in Cape Town during February 1936 with a rousing declaration that he would have no truck with British rearmament.[119] Whilst the London press representatives (not privy to the real position) reacted with 'astonishment and indignation', the staff of the UK commission sat back and let Pirow indulge in harmless platform rhetoric.[120] But if Pirow's willingness to help the UK was to go beyond a few concessions such as Naval Control, the UK had to pay the price of South African participation in colonial security further north in the continent. Judging by mid-1936 that Whitehall was in a sufficiently shocked state to give this away, Pirow announced his intention of visiting London. The Dominions Office welcomed this as a sure sign that the Defence Minister had decided 'to burn his boats as far as the Malanite Opposition . . . is concerned';[121] and the permanent officials in the Colonial Office were now prepared to add their voice to Hankey's in recommending a 'swap'. Sir John Maffey[122] contended that

> When we have South Africa, with its difficult and sensitive political moods, seeking cooperation of this kind it would be unwise of us not to show every readiness to meet them. . . . We at least have learnt this much from Mr Pirow – that if we are to advance towards Imperial understanding we shall be wise to move down the paths he indicates. He knows what a Dutch stomach can digest in South Africa and what it cannot. It is a long and difficult process in which we shall have to show great patience and goodwill and some readiness to take a risk.[123]

Despite this shift in UK attitudes, however, Pirow's visit proved far from harmonious. Although greatly impressed with the multiple pom-pom exhibited at Portsmouth and the Blenheim Bomber displayed at Croydon, the South African Minister refused to attend most of the agenda which had been designed to emphasise the scale of British rearmament;[124] and he was bitterly annoyed when it emerged that his aviation requirements could still not be met.[125] Nonetheless, Pirow did agree to make provisional plans on his return to South Africa for the diversion of British shipping to the Cape in a future emergency whilst firmly stating that further cooperation would hinge on British concessions in the field of Union participation in African defence planning.[126] By the end of 1937, in fact, such concessions were fast approaching. In December 1937 Batterbee explained to Clark (who had long been urging Pirow's case[127]) that an expansion of the King's African Rifles was scheduled for the near future and authorised him to discuss in Pretoria plans for South African involvement.[128] Whilst the pressures of European diplomacy were cracking the structure of 'Empire

Foreign Policy', therefore, they were also creating a narrower framework within which the UK and the Dominions could define the practical interests they held in common.

The degree to which new priorities were asserting themselves in both the UK and the Dominions by 1937 is shown by the fact that Commonwealth cooperation had now penetrated not only problems of supply (aircraft being the main issue here) but had also begun to touch on the larger issue of the distribution of military–industrial plant. As early as 1935, indeed, the New Zealand leader, Coates, had sought to divert New Zealand orders from the UK factories to the Melbourne arsenal. He did so on the grounds that 'Imperial Security' necessitated a 'British' steel and armaments industry in the Southern Seas.[129] But from the British view the dispersal of munitions production (like Smuts's fifteen-inch guns at Cape Town) might only fuel Dominion isolationism and ultimately cut them loose from the British connection. Again, separatist tactics were suspected to lie beneath the guise of imperial rhetoric. This situation was altered, however, by American neutrality legislation which passed through Congress in January 1936 making trade between future belligerents and US manufacturers illegal. This had tremendous implications because the allied victory in the World War I was, by the 1930s, clearly seen to have been the product of interaction between British sea power and US industrial production. Hankey was quick to point out

> President Roosevelt's neutrality policy results in our having to assume that we cannot repeat this. To that extent we lose the immeasurable benefit of sea-power in enabling us to draw supplies from the whole world. The U.S. policy . . . places a premium on the aggressor who, particularly in the case of a totalitarian state, can prepare for war by a certain date, devoting his whole resources to building up a vast war machine with unlimited reserves and manufacturing capacity – as is happening in Germany and Italy today. . . . The Dominions, including Canada especially . . . can render immense assistance in supplementing our own hard-pressed and harassed resources.[130]

Hankey's meaning was plain. Either imperial resources had to be more effectively orchestrated or the UK too had to face up to a complete reorganisation of its economic and political structure. He therefore prevailed on Baldwin to put a scheme of industrial cooperation to Mackenzie King at their Chequers discussions in November 1936.[131] The Canadian Prime Minister, predictably, was not to be drawn into such long-term and publicly transparent commitments. But meanwhile, at the purely industrial level, Canadian manufacturing interests were clamouring in a haphazard but urgent manner to cater for the British rearmament programme. Ironically the restraint on the extension of such 'farming out' came from within the UK because both the domestic munitions interests and the War Office wished to see British production expanding under the pressure of surplus demand. Thus, by March 1937, La Flèche, the Canadian Deputy Minister of National Defence, was bitterly complaining that the UK War Office had sabotaged the establishment of a Bren gun factory in Toronto, whilst both Vickers and Dunlop had obstructed the use of their patents by Canadian competitors.[132] Floud warned Harding from Ottawa that satisfying the Canadian manufacturers' demands for a slice of the rearmament cake was

> the one real opportunity we have a) of giving the Dominions . . . sufficient work . . . to get their own industries going locally b) of thus creating a war potential in the Dominions c) of ensuring that the Dominions do not drift off to foreign markets of supply d) of preserving the principle of homogeneity of armaments within the Empire.[133]

The War Office, however, would go no further than to syphon off sufficient orders for the Dominions to establish small-scale plant adequate for their own 'probable future needs' but not for a complete shadow industry such as Hankey envisaged.[134] Even the Cabinet Secretariat had to admit that the threat of war needed to become much clearer before the UK could contemplate the huge financial subsidies which such a transference of productive capacity would entail.[135] Broadly, then, by early 1937 it was as much a case of Dominions trying to break into the British rearmament programme as of the UK luring them into imperial commitments.

Finance, too, was a major stumbling block to any precipitate expansion of defence cooperation. The Treasury, for example, had opposed Bruce's application, made in late 1936, to raise a London loan in concert with the British government for military spending. Bruce had cogently argued that, because Australia had to fund her defence budget at higher rates of interest than did the UK, and because Australian personnel and equipment bought with this money would probably be utilised defending British interests such as Singapore or Flanders, she should be allowed to 'come in on' British rearmament financing.[136] The Treasury, however, had stated categorically that the other Dominions would then immediately file requests for British money, and that it would be impossible to confine such joint financing to defence matters so that 'in the end we would find ourselves committed to a policy of guaranteeing the entire loan expenditure of the Dominions'.[137] The Dominions Office supported the Treasury in its opposition. Harding explained

I did not think that the readiness of any Dominion to spend additional money on defence would really be increased by any such artificial inducement as Mr Casey [Bruce's colleague in London] had suggested. I felt myself that the real inducement to the Dominions to take a greater share in imperial defence was appreciation of the increasing danger to which they felt themselves subject. I thought the only reason for Australia's recent increased expenditure was because she felt herself threatened by Japan.[138]

This response was dictated by the department's apprehension that joint financing programmes could end up generating inter-governmental differences. Reliance on the market forces of fear and insecurity to push the Australians into higher military expenditure might in the long term involve considerable risks, but in the short term it avoided the complex burdens of determining who should pay what.

British confidence in handling the Dominion governments was by late 1936 being reinforced by informal political understandings as to the *kind* of war likely to elicit 'imperial' responses. This boiled down to a Dominion commitment to participate in the defence of western Europe and, in return, a British determination to avoid any military role in Eastern Europe. This process of mutual adjustment predated Neville Chamberlain's premiership and his policy of appeasement. One example of this understanding taking shape was a prolonged exchange between Malcolm MacDonald and Dr Gie, South Africa's League representative, which took place in Geneva during October 1936. Gie had begun this conversation with the Dominions Secretary with a description of the essentially spiritual qualities, as he saw them, of Hitler's regime. 'His social reforms', Gie asserted, 'are the expression of the truest Hitler,'[139] and he went on to defend German aspirations in East and South–East Europe. MacDonald did not contest these statements. He merely emphasised in reply that Britain no longer sought to involve any of her Commonwealth partners in security obligations and that each Dominion was free to 'choose its own path'.[140] But he made full use of Gie's previous admission that South Africa was 'irretrievably' part of Europe, and he pressed home the implications of this.

I said I wondered whether the people of South Africa, for example, would feel that the independence of the Low Countries was not only a matter of vital concern to Great Britain, but to the people of South Africa as citizens of the British Commonwealth also. A threat to Great Britain was a threat to the whole Commonwealth. If the threat materialised and the independence of Great Britain destroyed, the position of the Dominions would become extremely weak. The political influence of the Nations of the Commonwealth would depend largely for a long time to come on the power of Great Britain.[141]

When Gie's response proved evasive, the Dominions Secretary repeatedly urged him to specify what the South African attitude would be to a 'British war' resulting from her obligations west of the Rhine. Finally Gie answered that

> he would give a frank reply to that question. Germany was the enemy whom we all had in mind. He thought that if we had not put obstacles in the way of Germany regaining control of the Germans in East and South-East Europe, if it could be shown that we wished to treat Germany fairly and that it was not our fault that she was not satisfied, then South Africa would be with us.[142]

If in the 1920s the League had functioned as a focal point for Commonwealth consensus, it was around this delimitation of British obligations within Europe that Anglo–Dominion understanding revolved in the late 1930s. The *modus vivendi* outlined by MacDonald and Gie was implicit in, if less overtly, the foreign policy debates of the Imperial Conference in May 1937. Before the Conference opened Eden, the Foreign Secretary, gave two major speeches at Leamington and Bradford; the first pointedly omitted any reference to Central Europe in a list of UK priorities, whilst the second offset this by stressing that security could not be attained within 'a Western European glass-house'.[143] He was disappointed if he hoped that these easy ambiguities were sufficient to soothe Dominion anxieties. Once the Conference opened Hertzog attacked Britain's appeasement of France, and especially Britain's failure to criticise the Franco–Soviet Pact

> As regards British policy with regard to Western Europe as outlined . . . at Leamington, he considered it sound and reasonable, and it would receive South Africa's approval as it had in the past. But for Great Britain to extend that policy to the East or Central Europe; or to associate herself with interference in matters pertaining to Eastern or Central Europe . . . would be to stultify peace and court war.[144]

It was the Anschluss question which divided delegates most acutely. The British might agree with Dominion personnel that Danzig or Memel or even Prague were distant and ultimately irrelevant aspects of West European security; but for them Austria remained the key to South-East Europe, and Vienna was indisputably a European, nor merely regional, capital. Eden was willing to concede that the UK had no precise or pre-ordained role to play in the Austrian question, but he was scathing towards Hertzog's contention that Austrians 'wanted' to join the Reich: no Socialist, Liberal, Catholic or Jew wished for any such thing.[145] But Eden's most critical point was that under current conditions it simply was not possible to disengage from the Central European jigsaw and leave the other pieces undisturbed; a statement of British 'disinterest' in the area, for example, would be interpreted by Hitler as an invitation to take it over by force.[146] As the Foreign Secretary and the South African leader harried each other on these lines it seemed that Commonwealth members had finally arrived at a point of fundamental divergence. It was Neville Chamberlain (having succeeded to the premiership midway through the Conference) who averted confrontation.

> Mr Chamberlain said that he himself to a large extent sympathised with the desire for the 'Anschluss'. Proposals of this kind, however, had to be thought of in the light of their probable reactions on the remainder of Europe. Our constant objective should be the re-storation of confidence.[147]

This clearly shifted the balance of argument towards the Hertzog position, and Chamberlain's interventions at the Conference were a stage in his struggle with Eden for the direction of foreign policy and for control of the Conservative party. More immediately, Chamberlain now emerged as a British Prime Minister with a unique influence with other Commonwealth leaders: here at last, it seemed, was a British leader prepared to confront the warmongers in the Foreign Office and to re-think diplomatic priorities. But, although Chamberlain had, by ap-parently accepting the likelihood of Anschluss, widened the area of consensus, there were still too many substantive differences for any rousing statement on Empire unity to be made.

Nor did the defence discussions of the Conference lead in any positive direction. Beforehand Malcolm MacDonald had outlined to the UK Cabinet a 'strategy of fear' for pushing the Dominions into concrete military commitments,[148] an indication of the psychological metamor-phosis the Dominions Office had undergone since the early 1930s. Sir Thomas Inskip[149] adopted this approach to the extent of using sarcasm and threats. After New Zealand had criticised the weakness of British policy in the face of aggression, he scoffed at the 'relative immunity' of such an isolated place as New Zealand whose usual practice was to encourage others to heroic sacrifices.[150] He warned South Africa that both Italy and Germany were determined to extend their influence throughout Africa.[151] He pointed out that Roosevelt's neutrality legislation and the political systems of the Fascist alliance gave the latter a very clear industrial lead. Inskip concluded that it had now gone beyond Britain's capacity 'to act as the guardian of universal security, whenever and wherever threatened by an agressor'.[152] The thrust of this was obvious – cooperate or lose the protective shield that the Commonwealth had always provided. Above all, Inskip attempted to promote a broad agreement on war industry. If the Dominions could, as a minimum contribution, develop the capacity to satisfy their own potential war needs, UK resources could be released to supply neutral countries whom it was vital to keep outside the enemy orbit; it would also provide reserve industries outside German bombing range. But Inskip stated, too, that all this new plant would have to be paid for by Dominion subsidies and not from the British order-book, for the pace of the UK's rearmament could not be held back whilst the Dominions gradually equipped themselves as industrial arsenals. The Dominion response to these suggestions was poor. Australia tried hard to cajole the others into at least a comprehensive discussion of likely needs, and Sir Archdale Parker, the Australian Defence Minister, stressed the importance of the main theatres of war rather than the irrelevancies of local defence.[153] But none of the other Dominions followed, and Mackenzie King made sure that the final defence communique was emasculated.[154]

But if no concrete defence commitments had emerged, the Conference had pointed towards a stabilisation in Empire relations, albeit of a makeshift kind. The raw facts and style of Inskip's presentation showed that the negotiating balance had shifted. At the same time there were signs that British policy was moving towards an accommodation with Germany which Dominion statesmen had long advocated. Above all, a British Prime Minister had emerged who seemed able to articulate political emotions shared throughout the Commonwealth countries. Mackenzie King left London with an intense admiration for Neville Chamberlain only to be exceeded by a fascination with Hitler acquired on his ensuing trip to Berlin.[155] In fact a South African official fresh from the Nuremberg rally soon reported that the cohesion of the Imperial Conference had had a 'sobering effect' on the Nazi leadership.[156] This cohesion sprang not, as yet, from the precise shape of Chamberlain's views, but from the impression he created of a man ready to look at any solution capable of preserving a peace which was vital to all Commonwealth governments.

In the two years between the 1937 Imperial Conference and the eventual outbreak of war Chamberlain's progressive definition of a policy of appeasement did provide the Commonwealth with a tense but (given the madness around it) relatively stable equilibrium. This period will not be looked at here in detail, partly because the qualitative changes in the Commonwealth structure had already taken place by 1937 and partly because an analysis of Commonwealth and appeasement is already available.[157] The events of 1938–39, nonetheless, did have important effects on the Anglo–Dominion relationship. Before noting these, however, it is important to stress one exception to the appeasement consensus. Just when everybody else was moving towards the idea of political settlement, New Zealand swung in the opposite direction and became loudly sanctionist. There had been indications of this at the Imperial Conference, and at one point Savage had almost accused Britain of hovering uncertainly between the fascist and democratic camps.[158] Subsequently on two issues – Spain and the Sino–Japanese War which erupted in mid-1937 – New Zealand's position caused the UK considerable embarrassment in Geneva. Both of these episodes convey something of the contemporary Geneva atmosphere. Once an attempt got under way to bury the Spanish issue in the Non-Intervention Committee, key powers, not only the British, began to suspect that the New Zealanders would break ranks. Cockram, the Dominions Office observer, checked the room of the main New Zealand delegate, Jordan, before the Assembly debate and was pleased to find that he was not even aware that Spain was on the agenda.[159] But all did not go smoothly. After the Spanish spokesman had sat down in the debate, Jordan jumped to his feet without notes and delivered

> an unstudied impromptu in which he referred, fortunately by hearsay, to Italian destroyers machine-gunning victims from a ship they had sunk, went on to appeal to 'peoples' against their 'governments', and finally suggested a Class A Mandate for Spain, to get rid of corrupt elections and murder of civilians. By the end the Spanish Prime Minister must have been longing to be saved from his friends.[160]

If New Zealanders felt deeply involved in the Spanish tragedy, their representatives were even more agitated by Japan's renewed movements on the Asian mainland. When Stanley Bruce put it to an Empire delegates meeting in September that the impossibility of intervening in the Sino–Japanese dispute should be admitted, Jordan let off further steam

> At an earlier period in his [Jordan's] life he had been connected with Scotland Yard, and he was familiar with the attitude of the Police towards a gunman. What the League was being asked to do was to approve the policy, not of trying to stop the gunman's activities, but of deciding to give medical assistance to his victims. It did seem to him that to confine the League's action to such a proposal was to confess that the League, as an institution, was bankrupt. Surely the question had passed from the sphere of political theories to one where every dictate of humanity demanded action.[161]

Cockram felt that Jordan's refusal to 'toe the line' reflected on the reputation of all the Dominions and threatened their continued representation on the Council; above all, such heroics brought war nearer and worsened the predicament of Spanish villagers and Chinese peasants whose interest lay in as undramatic a handling of the political situation as possible.[162] At first, because Britain and Australia already had seats, it seemed that New Zealand could be kept off the Far East Advisory Committee. The Russians, however, were not slow to see the possibilities, and Litvinoff seconded New Zealand representation. Jordan and Lord Cranborne subsequently sat next to each other at these meetings, and, although the New Zealander softened his words, his presence was a disquieting factor.[163] Not surprisingly, New Zealand's sympathies for Spain and China were later widened to embrace Austria and Czechoslovakia. What explains this course of events? The answer lies in New Zealand's identity as a small and vulnerable state. All the other Dominions had larger resources or enjoyed particular advantages which gave them a much greater chance of responding effectively to attack. Thus, as the growing likelihood of war made other nations resentful and evasive towards League obligations, New Zealand clung more desperately to collective security as an assurance that 'democratic forces', which meant the Royal Navy, would come to her aid in a crisis. Jordan's anguish over Guernica was thus in large part a premonition of General Tojo riding into Wellington.

If Japanese troops in New Zealand were a nightmare vision of the future, on 12 March 1938 German troops in Vienna became an immediate reality. One ripple effect of this was to move the British and Dominion positions still closer, since, by taking the Anschluss off the agenda, Hitler had removed the largest emotional obstacle to British adoption of an appeasement programme. On 24 March Chamberlain staked out his position in the House of Commons.[164] He listed the situations in which the UK would go to war (giving primacy to the Empire, but also specifying France, Belgium, Portugal, Iraq and Egypt) and making it clear that Britain's only eastward connection lay through the very attenuated link of the Covenant. The Dominion governments sensed that a decisive shift had taken place and they rallied around Chamberlain's text. Australia asserted that she would not participate in any commitments to Czechoslovakia, whilst Mackenzie King assured MacDonald that he now agreed with the main lines of British policy and thought it the only way to save the Empire.[165] From this point on the argument that a European settlement was essential to the very preservation of Commonwealth became a central theme of events. It was used recurrently by Dominion leaders attempting to push the UK further towards appeasement, by Chamberlain attempting to persuade a doubting Cabinet that pacific methods were an effective way of dealing with Hitler, and by British diplomats trying to find excuses when their French counterparts called on them to face the German challenge.

One question which inevitably derives from this is whether Commonwealth pressures can be considered a 'cause' of appeasement.

Was it not a policy which arose from an authentic sense of a Commonwealth likely to be pulled apart by its regionalism if war were to take place? In retrospect certain of the participants did see things in this light,[166] not least because it was a useful argument for ruined politicians subsequently seeking to escape conviction as the 'guilty men' of appeasement; whilst some historians have credited the stance of the Dominions between 1937 and 1939 as a causal factor.[167] What is certainly true is that Commonwealth-wide support for a peaceful settlement became part of those driving forces which made appeasement such a rare policy, one which generated tremendous powers of community solidarity. It is, however, much less likely that the formulation of Chamberlain's strategy had any very direct connection with Dominion pressures. Any conclusion on this naturally hinges on interpretations of the Munich crisis in September 1938. Meetings between the Dominion High Commissioners and relevant British Ministers went on in tandem with the Anglo–German discussions, but, apart from a slightly more strident hysteria, the declarations by Massey, te Water, Dulanty and Bruce differed little from those they made in 1935 during the Rhineland affair: the right of all Germans to live together, the selfishness of the French and the need to maintain Commonwealth unity. The fact that Dominion views, unlike events, showed few signs of development in the meantime suggests that they were not a dynamic element in the situation. The High Commissioner meetings, moreover, were not in any significant way plugged into London's decision-making procedures; they were useful reflectors of Dominion attitudes as events ran increasingly out of control, but not a medium through which the British Cabinet could be pressurised. The fact that they concentrated, not on the broad lines of policy, but rather on the wide range of possible scenarios which the Czech crisis presented, indicates that a more fruitful approach is to see them as an attempt to define what outbreak 'sequence' was best calculated to duplicate the imperial responses of 1914. Much of the Commonwealth consultation between Munich and September 1939, in fact, concerned this calculation of varying circumstances, so that when Hitler finally exceeded the limits of what Governments found acceptable, it would be possible to convince the various public opinions of the Commonwealth that their fundamental interests were indeed at stake. As for the general question of Commonwealth and appeasement, Ovendale's simple answer is appropriate to what is basically a non-question: that although Chamberlain was sensitive to Dominion opinion and incorporated it into his basis for policy-making, he was motivated by other financial, political and diplomatic considerations.

Appeasement and the drama of Chamberlain's September travels had one critical effect on Commonwealth: it consummated Chamberlain's stature as a man of peace who could be trusted to run foreign policy. Almost all the Dominion leaders had supported the Prime Minister, either publicly or privately, to an extent that implicated them in his policy. Mackenzie King, for example, had encouraged the original British move of sending Runciman to Prague as a mediator,[168] and as the crisis had mounted he concluded that it was 'Canada's self-evident national duty' to fight if Britain thought war necessary.[169] Mackenzie King, two Canadian historians have argued, had by this point ceased to be the ideological exponent of an American alignment and had become a pragmatic supporter of Empire cooperation.[170] Even de Valera assured Chamberlain on 15 September, shortly before the latter left for Berchtesgaden, that he had the full support of the Dublin regime.[171] After Munich had catalysed a deeply emotional sense of a common determination among Commonwealth partners to preserve peace, statements in Dominion Parliaments reserving their own powers of decision carried much less significance.

To this pattern of constrained consensus at the time of Munich there appeared to be one exception – South Africa. Although te Water was party to all the tactical discussions of the High Commissioners, Hertzog remained ominously silent in Pretoria, and on 2 September he had forced Smuts and the Cabinet to accept an unpublished statement of neutrality. This fact might be taken to contradict the general picture of South Africa being coerced by external events into Empire cooperation from the mid-1930s onwards; and it leads to the belief that only Smuts's prompt actions in September 1939 finally brought South Africa into line with the rest of the Commonwealth. Whitehall officials were especially nervous throughout the Munich period as to South African responses, but these anxieties really concerned the time lag between war breaking out and South Africa's eventual entry.[172] Hertzog's neutrality 'decision' on 2 September was more of a ploy in the domestic factional struggle than a genuine declaration of intent. The fact that Smuts accepted it so easily suggests this. It was framed only at a moment when Hertzog had convinced himself that Chamberlain would not allow war to take place anyway. Hertzog's neutrality, too, referred only to the immediate circumstances of Czechoslovakia; once military operations had spread westwards the British were sure that the South Africans would come in, and there is nothing to suggest that this reading was any less accurate in September 1938 than it proved in September 1939. Certainly Pirow's visit to London after the end of the Czechoslovak affair to discuss an extension of military cooperation indicates that South Africa, like the other Dominions, had been unceremoniously bundled into an imperial alliance.

The accelerated absorption of the Dominions into the British rearmament programme, indeed, was one of the major consequences of Munich. The Anglo–South African 'swap' initially broached in 1936, with South African involvement north of the Limpopo and naval cooperation off the Cape, now matured. A Chiefs-of-Staff sub-committee spoke of using South African manpower 'as far north as the shores of the Mediterranean'.[173] Meanwhile the Australian and Canadian governments gave way to British and domestic pressures for industrial agreements. From October 1938 the UK Cabinet authorised the placing of 'educational' aircraft orders with Canadian plant, and by August the following year British and Canadian officials were at work establishing a framework for purchasing policy not only for war materials but also for food and raw materials.[174] As for Pacific planning, defence experts from Britain, Australia and New Zealand met in Wellington in April 1939 to discuss both industrial and naval matters.

Given these developments, it is not surprising that the UK policy-makers gave much less attention to the Dominions after Munich than before. David Carlton explains this by the fact that British opinion hardened against Germany more rapidly compared with the Dominions from late 1938 onwards, making consultation potentially more combustible.[175] Probably more important, however, was the British awareness that the Dominions were now in no position to act independently, and with this consultation ceased to have any real value. Finally, after Hitler's take-over in Prague in March 1939, the whole Dominion case for distancing themselves from Britain – that German aspirations in Europe were just, peaceful and limited – fell irreversibly to the ground. Subsequently they had no real arguments to combat the British Cabinet's counter-strategy of guarantees to Yugoslavia, Greece, Turkey, Rumania and Poland. These guarantees aroused painful emotions in some Dominions whose leaderships had spent years denouncing such military alliances (Mackenzie King ranted to the British High Commissioner about Balkan entanglements[176]), but these sentiments did not amount to viable alternatives. When te Water, Savage and Bruce attempted to soften the British position on Danzig, they did so because they thought it the least likely flashpoint in Central Europe to activate Commonwealth opinion as a whole. From a Commonwealth viewpoint it was, perhaps, fortunate that Hitler chose to initiate proceedings by invading Poland since on this issue the fundamental choices were relatively clear. New Zealand and Australia immediately announced that they were automatically bound by the British decision to go to war once the ultimatum had expired at 11 a.m. on 3 September. Mackenzie King reserved the power of declaration to the Canadian Parliament, but his broadcast address concentrated clearly on the hegemonic conflict between democratic good and fascist evil, and when Parliament urgently reassembled not even the Quebec representatives demanded neutrality. In South Africa for a while the matter seemed to hinge on the balance of forces in the Assembly, and entry to war only followed the Governor-General's refusal of a dissolution to Hertzog and his replacement by Smuts; and there is some evidence that the British High Commissioner intervened, against all convention, in these caucus-antics.[177] Even so, Hertzog does not appear to have made a serious effort to keep South Africa neutral. In the end the only Dominion who stayed out of war was the Irish Free State. This was no surprise and no disappointment since de Valera was clearly willing to cooperate on the questions that counted, such as the use of Irish ports, alien control and the denial of all facilities to the enemy. Admittedly, the atmosphere of 1939 was not that of 1914. The Kitchener enthusiasms, the overwhelming sense of the political and cultural reintegration of the British diaspora, that marked the hot August of twenty-five years before was not reflected in the Commonwealth psychology prevailing after Chamberlain's decision to confront Hitler. Instead there was a deep suspicion of the objectives prevailing amongst the alliance partners and a jockeying for position as the competition to grab the benefits, and avoid the burdens, of war began. This reflected new structures of power which cut across Commonwealth lines, and no amount of skilful management by British officials and politicians could have made it otherwise. But in the crude world of bureaucratic objectives, Whitehall had succeeded in its chief imperial task: the British nations were once again at war *en famille*.

11 Conclusion

This study began by relating ideas of imperial development in the early 1900s to the chief preoccupations of Britain's political leaders. Those preoccupations were the same as bedevilled the governing classes throughout Europe: the search for methods to make democratic systems compatible with state interests, for ways to sustain external trade when economic nationalism was beginning to reassert itself and for continued means of access to raw materials when industrial demand was straining supply. The construction of a world-wide British alliance appeared to many as an appropriate response to these issues because it would permit a gradual integration of the financial, military, manpower and trading needs of its constituent parts. World War I gave some credence to these aspirations, partly through the concrete economic cooperation between the UK and the Dominions which it entailed, but also through the propaganda machine which sought to project the image of the great British diaspora finally unified under the stress of conflict. The post-war years only served to intensify the pressures which had created this imperial ideology. Britain, like all the other industrial nations, found itself in a crisis of urban unemployment, under-utilised capacity and a level of production costs which outstripped profits. If the causes of this crisis were economic, the results were social and political decay. Although instability found its quickest and most dramatic expressions in Germany, signs were not lacking that consensus politics was being undermined in Britain as well. The Governments of each industrial block had rapidly to improvise means of limiting this process. Markets had to be found, adequate supplies of raw materials located and currencies protected. In the late 1920s and early 1930s there was a concerted attempt to find common approaches through the League of Nations. This broke down, and each country tried to work out its own economic salvation: the US through its New Deal, France through the gold bloc, Germany through the establishment of a new economic system in Central and South-East Europe, and Britain through a strategy of Empire trade. All of these arrangements proved capable of halting the deflationary tide, but none of them were able to provide a broad enough basis for resumed growth. By the end of the 1930s most organised economic interests were attempting to diversify out of the commercial strait-jackets they had clamped around themselves at the height of the crisis. In particular the British and German industrialists were showing signs of moving towards a West European front. But it was too late. The economic nationalism of the early part of the decade had spawned a politics possessing its own internal conflicts. In the end Britain had a war imposed on her and her Commonwealth just when the latter relationship was ceasing to have any fundamental relevance to the UK's long-term interests.

It is when set against this background that the Commonwealth developments after 1918 can be seen to have historical substance. The imperial economic model espoused by Leopold Amery and which permeated Conservative ranks then emerges as a significant response to the problems of modernity. Given relatively stable conditions, this model may have had some chances of success. British industry could have moved away from certain basic sectors to provide elbow-room for Dominion manufacturers, whilst Dominion agriculture could have escaped the dangers of depending on a few inelastic commodities by developing those animal products for which a large market existed in the UK. But any hope of this was vitiated by the fault-line which separated industrial and rural nations once the agricultural crisis deepened after 1928. This dislocated exchanges within the Commonwealth, hastening industrialisation in the Dominions and promoting agricultural protectionism in Britain. Talks on Anglo–Dominion industrial cartels, the Ottawa tariffs and subsequent commodity quotas patched up this disequilibrium, but the inevitable long-term effect was to destroy the logic of economic cooperation in the Empire. The productive alliance of World War II was lubricated by American, not British, initiatives.

The Commonwealth story between 1918 and 1939, however, was not simply economic. It has traditionally been told in constitutional terms. The conventional portrait is of a neat linear transition from an imperial authority in the early twentieth century to the devolved sovereignties described by the 1926 Balfour Declaration. This does not conform very well with the pattern of economic events which alternated between bouts of independent management and cooperation, becoming increasingly bilateral and disjointed. These constitutional events are best appreciated, not as an exercise in legal change, but as a process in which the British authorities and 'nationalist' regimes in the Dominions thrashed out a deal in which both preserved their essential interests. Once anti-imperialism ceased to be a dominant theme in Dominion politics (i.e. after 1929) this vocabulary of inter-imperial competition disappeared. It continued, it is true, in the course of the Anglo–Irish confrontation after de Valera's election in March 1932, and it was de Valera's republicanism which finally manoeuvred Whitehall into a new and looser rationale of Commonwealth. This redefinition is of interest in that it shows the genesis of those tactics of disembodiment which, after 1947, allowed the Commonwealth to become an acceptable form for regimes with totally different constitutions, ideologies and alignments. But for the Commonwealth as a group, the constitutional problem can be said to have dissolved as soon as the slump made politicians scamper after a new set of slogans.

The constitutional emphases of the 1920s were also a function of cultural change. The repetitive theme of 'British evolutionism' in these debates was just one part of a general tendency after 1918 to stress the immutability of British society. Although the work of the Empire Marketing Board, the Overseas Settlement Committee and the Empire Exhibitions all had obvious economic objectives, their organisational records also convey a pervasive sense of cultural purpose. This purpose partly arose from the fact that British officialdom had itself been effectively conditioned by the Lloyd George–Beaverbrook propaganda machine between 1914 and 1918 and continued to act under its influence even when it had been disbanded. It was also in part a conscious manipulation of cultural arguments by the bureaucracy to buttress the Commonwealth alliance in peacetime when other unifying factors were absent. But by the 1920s it was increasingly an instinctive response to external threats, and in particular to the challenge of American power. Anti-Americanism remained an important ingredient of Commonwealth thinking right through the inter-war years, reaching a peak in 1933–4; after that the even greater obsession with Germany revived the aspirations to Anglo–Saxonism. The sources of this antagonism towards the transatlantic cousinship were many and disparate. The UK entertainment industry, for example, was predictably resentful of being displaced in the mass affection by the Hollywood star system. But it was most acutely felt and expressed among the UK political–administrative classes whose self-image was based on their capacity to act unilaterally in world affairs. The emergence of an American veto on UK action instilled among the Whitehall cadres a determination to restore at least some measure of unilateralism by pooling the resources of the British nations. Cultural identity and political motives thus reinforced each other.

In this way the Commonwealth idea was closely linked to the foreign policy debate between the wars. The heart of that debate was precisely this question of Britain's ability to act independently of other considerations, American or European. The consultative network instituted in the Commonwealth during the 1920s was designed to increase the Empire's resistance to external influences. But, although there was a UK consensus along these lines, in fact politicians and civil servants were deeply divided over the long-term significance of Commonwealth. Austen Chamberlain, most of the foreign policy establishment and the centre-left groups in British politics saw it only as an association which gave the UK a strong bargaining power within the international arena, and they always conceived the main thrust of British diplomacy to be the maintenance of stability through international cooperation. Leopold

Amery and the Tory Right thought of the Commonwealth association as an alternative strategy altogether. These divisions were blurred, and amidst the crisis of 1931–2 the imperial thesis coloured attitudes from Oswald Mosely's British Union of Fascists, with their cry of 'Greater Britain', to the National Labourites who followed Ramsay MacDonald into the Coalition. The Commonwealth, then, became a component of the party political scene and was inflated by the struggle for power within the bureaucracy.

Finally, the period covered in this volume witnessed the decline of naval power as a strategic determinant. It was not entirely eclipsed, and it was only during World War II that the secondary role of warships became incontestable; the *amour propre* of naval bureaucracies was among the minor victims of Hiroshima. But it was during the 1930s that the blue-water school was definitely forced on the defensive, and for an alliance whose historical shape reflected the sufficiency of naval protection this was a sapping experience. The Singapore base had as much a psychological as a military role in cushioning the early blows, but by the outbreak of war the Empire governments involved knew very well that no comprehensive security cover existed. Ironically, the British Services had fudged any military commitments to Europe on the grounds that their chief priority was defence of the Empire, whereas in fact the gap between the resources required for imperial defence and those actually available had widened as the crisis deepened. The truth, of course, was that the democratic logic which had finally taken hold of British politics did not permit the financing of an adequate strategic response.

The inter-war Commonwealth was thus not merely the legacy of a freebooting past. It was a coalition of economic interests which had increasingly interlocked after the 1890s. It was an alliance in that its intended function was the mobilisation of resources. It was Britannic in that its membership was limited to the British nations, and cultural homogeneity was part of its rationale. It was just one of a number of associations (the League of Nations, the Pan-American Union, the other colonial empires, and the more informal operation of German hegemony in Central Europe) whose task was to protect their respective adherents against the instability sweeping world politics. That instability, however, was too complex, and its social and economic roots too diverse, for any of these groups to successfully insulate themselves. They each lacked (except in the German case after 1933) the existence of an effective central authority to make their group aims realisable. It was the absence of centralising institutions which prevented the Commonwealth from adopting reconstructive policies capable of averting the crisis of modernity between 1918 and 1939; but at the same time the devolutionary qualities of that association reconciled its constituent leaderships, cushioned the imperial system against radical political change and made military alliance possible.

Notes

CHAPTER 1

1. Lord Milner to Lady Edward Cecil 25 March 1903. Quoted in C. Headlam (ed.), *The Milner Papers (South Africa) 1899–1905* (London, 1933) p. 446.
2. F. A. Johnson, *Defence by Committee* (London, 1960) pp. 48–81.
3. W. K. Hancock, *Survey of British Commonwealth Affairs: Problems of Nationality 1918–36* (Oxford, 1937) pp. 49–50.
4. For a treatment of the 1911 Conference see J. Kendle, *The Colonial and Imperial Conferences 1887–1911* (London, 1967) pp. 169–84.
5. P. Wigley, *Canada and the Transition to Commonwealth 1917–26* (Cambridge, 1977) p. 28.
6. See W. R. Louis, *Great Britain and Germany's Lost Colonies 1914–19* (Oxford, 1967).
7. For the Empire and the Peace Conference see M. Beloff, *Imperial Sunset: Britain's Liberal Empire 1897–1921* (London, 1969) pp. 279–91.
8. Quoted in Lord Hankey, *The Supreme Control at the Paris Peace Conference* (London, 1963) p. 26.
9. R. C. Snelling, 'Peacemaking, 1919: Australia, New Zealand and the British Empire Delegation at Versailles', *Journal of Imperial and Commonwealth History*, vol. IV, October 1975.
10. Lambert minute, 29 January 1919, CO532/135.
11. Wigley, op. cit., p. 84.
12. R. Davenport, *A Modern History of South Africa* (London, 1977) p. 191.
13. Wigley, op. cit., pp. 98–104.
14. Minutes of Group Council 'D', 22 March 1921, CO532/193.
15. Foreign Office Memorandum, 'Treaty-Signing Powers of the Dominions', September 1923, CO532/251.
16. Colonial Office Memorandum on Treaty-Signing Powers of Dominions, September 1923, CO532/251.
17. Davis Minute, 6 February 1925, CO532/278.
18. Trant to Geddes, 23 January 1923, CO532/247.
19. Arthur to Devonshire, 9 February 1923, CO532/247.
20. Wellesley to Amery, 7 September 1921, CO532/185.
21. J. Eayrs, *In Defence of Canada: From the Great War to the Great Depression* (Toronto, 1964) pp. 149–55.
22. Colonial Office Minute, 29 March 1923, CO532/265.
23. Geddes to Curzon, 3 June 1921, CO532/183.
24. Ibid.
25. Beloff, op. cit., pp. 336–43.
26. Harding Minute, 4 April 1921, CO532/183.

27. S. Roskill, *Hankey: Man of Secrets,* vol. II (London, 1973) pp. 238–77.
28. J. McCarthy, *Australia and Imperial Defence 1918–39* (Queensland, 1976) p. 47.
29. This account of the Chanak episode is drawn from D. Walder, *The Chanak Affair* (London, 1969).
30. Drummond, *Imperial Economic Policy 1917–1939* (London, 1974) p. 52.
31. Barstow to Amery, 13 February 1923, CO532/264.
32. McNaughten Minute, 20 April 1922, CO532/221.
33. Ibid.
34. Minutes of Group Council 'C', 3 January 1923, CO532/222.
35. Treasury Memorandum, 'Currency Cooperation in the British Empire', 2 May 1923, CO532/264.
36. Reardon to Stephenson, 22 February 1923, CO532/259.
37. Floud to Amery, 28 March 1923, CO532/265.
38. Harding Minute, 3 July 1923, CO532/261.
39. Drummond, op. cit., pp. 90–9.
40. H. Blair Neatby, *William Lyon Mackenzie King: 1923–32. The Lonely Heights* vol. II (Toronto, 1963) p. 161.
41. See Davenport, op. cit., pp. 192–8.
42. Athlone to Thomas, 11 April 1924, CO532/276.
43. Ibid.
44. Athlone to Thomas, 2 July 1924, CO532/276.
45. Ibid.
46. See Sir Frank Pakenham, *Peace by Ordeal: the Negotiation and Signature of the Anglo-Irish Treaty, 1921* (Oxford, 1934).

CHAPTER 2

1. J. Ellis Barker, *Economic Statesmanship* (London, 1918) p. 58.
2. Minutes of Overseas Committee, 27 November 1930; FBI Committees, June–December 1930.
3. Notes of First Plenary Meeting of the Montreal Steel Conference, 5 July 1932, BT11/58.
4. See below, p. 103
5. Memorandum on Inter-Imperial Trade, 12 February 1936, FBI/c/2/1936.
6. Minutes of the Empire Committee, 4 May 1938, FBI/c/2/1938.
7. See below, p. 148
8. M. Ruth Megaw, 'Australia and the Anglo–American Trade Agreement, 1938', *Journal of Imperial and Commonwealth History*, January 1975.
9. See the Joint Declaration of the Reichsgruppe Industrie and the FBI at the Dusseldorf Industrial Conference, 15/16 March 1939, FBI/c/1/1939.
10. Bertrand Russell to Clifford Allen, 18 December 1917. Quoted in Martin Gilbert, *Plough My Own Furrow: The Story of Lord Allen of Hurtwood* (London, 1972) p. 103.
11. Fleetwood Chiddell, *Australia–White or Yellow?* (London, 1926) p. xl.
12. Michael Howard, *The Continental Commitment: The Dilemma of British Defence Policy in the Era of Two World Wars* (London, 1972) pp. 79–80.

13. R. Meyer, 'Britain, Europe and the Dominions in the 1930s', *Australian Journal of Politics and History*, vol. XXII, 1976.
14. Amery to Baldwin, 17 November 1928, DO35/56.
15. Parliamentary Debates (Commons) *Hansard*, 16 November 1925, vol. 188, cols. 419–534.
16. Howard, op. cit., p. 95.
17. T. H. Stoddard, *The Rising Tide of Colour* (London, 1920).
18. H. Tinker, *Race, Conflict and the International Order: From Empire to United Nations* (London, 1977) p. 29.
19. Macmillan to Curtis, 16 May 1935, MSS. Curtis 91, General Correspondence and Papers, Bodleian Library, Oxford.
20. W. K. Hancock, *Survey of British Commonwealth Affairs: Problems of Nationality 1918–36* (Oxford, 1937) p. 204.
21. Dawson, Geoffrey (1874–1944). Private Secretary to Lord Milner in South Africa 1901–5; editor of *The Johannesburg Star* 1905–10; editor of *The Times* 1912–19 and 1923–41.
22. Amery to Dawson, 12 June 1925, DO121/1.
23. Garvin, James (1877–1945). Editor of *Pall Mall Gazette* 1912–15; editor of *The Observer* 1908–42.
24. Amery to Garvin, 12 June 1925, DO121/1.
25. Harcourt-Smith minute, 9 December 1929, N5758 FO371/14035.
26. Basu, Bijay Kumer (1880–1937). Mayor of Calcutta 1928–9; Government of India Delegate to the League of Nations 1935.
27. Harding to Floud, 23 July 1935, DO35/167.
28. Ibid.
29. Ibid.
30. See below, p. 161
31. S. Tallents to Whiskard, 8 July 1929, DO35/74.
32. Amery minute, 6 June 1929, DO35/79.
33. Furse minute, 6 June 1929, DO35/79.
34. Beckett-Platt minute, 1 October 1929, DO35/80.
35. Beckett-Platt Memorandum, 15 November 1929, DO35/76.
36. Ibid.
37. Dixon minute, 19 November 1929, DO35/76.
38. Beckett-Platt Memorandum, 15 November 1929, DO35/76.
39. Tallents, Sir Stephen (1884–1958). Imperial Secretary, Northern Ireland 1922–6; Secretary to the Empire Marketing Board 1926–33; Principal Secretary, Ministry of Town and Country Planning 1943–6.
40. Tallents to Whiskard, 8 July 1929, DO35/74.
41. Minutes of Geddes, Londonderry and Thomas meeting, 25 May 1932, DO35/191.
42. Wiseman minute, 12 October 1929, DO35/83.
43. Report of Evidence of Sir Eric Geddes to the Cabinet Committee on Commercial Air Transport, 16 February 1934, C.A.T. (33) 2nd Meeting CAB 27/558.
44. Bullock to Edgecumbe, 19 February 1929, DO35/72.
45. Minutes of McNaughten, Batterbee and Holmes meeting, 9 March 1932, DO35/191.
46. Geddes to Beatty, 6 February 1933, DO35/191.

47. C. B. Schedvin, *Australia and the Great Depression* (Sydney, 1970) p. 30.
48. Montgomery-Massingberd, Sir Archibald (1871–1947). Chief of the Imperial General Staff 1933–6.
49. Admiral Massingberd to Hankey, 15 August 1933, CAB 21/369.
50. E. T. Miller to H. S. Martin, 24 August 1926, DO35/14.
51. Sir Francis Newdegate to Baldwin, 30 July 1926, DO35/14.
52. Clive Lord to Sir Francis Newdegate, 30 July 1926, DO35/14.
53. Note on the UK Film Industry, CP 201 (33) CAB 24/197.
54. Trappes-Lomax, Thomas (1895–1962). Promoted Brigade-Major 1927; Chief Instructor, Royal Military College, Sandhurst 1939–40; Brigadier, Southern Army, India 1942–5.
55. 'Report by Captain T. B. Trappes-Lomax on his trip to Canada, October–November 1925' enclosed in Director of Military Operations to the DO, 23 February 1926, DO35/17.
56. Ibid.
57. Ibid.
58. Amery to Worth, 15 March 1926, DO35/17.

CHAPTER 3

1. This description of the early Dominions Department is largely drawn from J. A. Cross, *Whitehall and the Commonwealth: British Departmental Organisation for Commonwealth Relations 1900–66* (London, 1967).
2. Cross, op. cit., p. 9.
3. Cross, op. cit., p. 38.
4. Wigley, op. cit., pp. 98–104.
5. L. Amery, *My Political Life*, vol. 2 (London, 1955) p. 241.
6. Amery, op. cit., pp. 240–1.
7. Churchill to Amery, 7 December 1924, DO121/1.
8. Ibid.
9. Amery Memorandum, 'The Dominions and the Colonial Office: Proposals for Reorganisation', February 1925, DO121/1.
10. Report of the Scott Committee, 20 February 1925, DO121/1.
11. Amery to Baldwin, 26 February 1925, DO121/1.
12. Cross, op. cit., p. 47.
13. See above, p. 32.
14. Amery to Baldwin, 26 February 1925, DO121/1.
15. F. A. Johnson, *Defence by Committee* (London, 1960) pp. 192–3.
16. The 'dual Secretaryship' was restored for brief periods in 1931 and 1938–9, but this only reflected passing difficulties in the distribution of offices.
17. Cross, op. cit., p. 52.
18. Ibid.
19. Parliamentary Debates (Commons) *Hansard*, 27 July 1925, vol. 187 (Fifth series) col. 93.
20. Austen Chamberlain to Robert Cecil, 28 September 1925, FO800/258.
21. Austen Chamberlain to Leopold Amery, 19 June 1925, FO800/258.
22. DO Memorandum, 1 June 1926, DO35/15.
23. Wigley, op. cit., p. 241.

24. Foreign Office Memorandum, 10 September 1925, DO35/12.
25. Ibid.
26. 'The Security Pact', *The Round Table*, September 1925; see also 'The Locarno Treaties', *The Round Table*, December 1925.
27. Parliamentary Debates (Commons) *Hansard*, 18 November 1925, vol. 188 (Fifth Series) cols. 419–535.
28. Bruce to Amery, 6 May 1925, FO800/258.
29. Ibid.
30. Smuts to Austen Chamberlain, 21 October 1925, FO800/258.
31. Amery to Austen Chamberlain, 15 June 1925, FO800/258.
32. Cecil, Robert (1864–1958). Assistant Secretary of State for Foreign Affairs 1918; Minister for Blockade 1916–18; Lord Privy Seal 1923–4; Chancellor of the Duchy of Lancaster 1924–7.
33. Amery to Austen Chamberlain, 8 August 1925, FO800/258.
34. Howard-Smith to Harding, 10 March 1926, DO35/12.
35. Hertzog to Austen Chamberlain, 3 January 1926, FO800/259.
36. See below, p. 69.
37. Amery to Austen Chamberlain, 18 December 1925, FO800/258.
38. Parliamentary Debates (Commons) *Hansard*, 18 November 1925, vol. 188 (Fifth Series) col. 432.
39. Bruce to Amery, 24 December 1925, FO800/259.
40. DO Memorandum, 1 February 1926, FO800/259.

CHAPTER 4

1. Balfour, Arthur (1848–1930). Leader of the House of Commons 1891–2; Prime Minister 1902–5; Foreign Secretary 1916–19; President of the Council 1925–9.
2. For an appreciative version of Hertzog's role at the Conference see O. Pirow, *J.B.M. Hertzog* (London, 1958) pp. 102–18; also see C. M. van den Heever, *General J.B.M. Hertzog* (Johannesburg, 1936) pp. 208–11. For Mackenzie King see H. Blair Neatby, *William Lyon Mackenzie King*, vol. 2 (London, 1963) pp. 176–96. For Balfour see Blanche Dugdale, *Arthur James Balfour* (London, 1936) pp. 374–88.
3. O'Higgins, Kevin (1892–1927). Vice-President of the Executive Council and Minister of Justice, Irish Free State 1923–7.
4. D. Harkness, *Restless Dominion* (London, 1969) pp. 80–134.
5. Duncan Hall, 'The Genesis of the Balfour Declaration', *Journal of Commonwealth Political Studies*, vol. 1 1961–3 (Leicester, 1963).
6. Selborne, William (1859–1942). Under-Secretary of State for the Colonies 1895–1900; First Lord of the Admiralty 1900–5; High Commissioner in South Africa 1905–10.
7. Selborne to Amery, 10 July 1926, DO35/20.
8. Wigley, op. cit., p. 268.
9. See above, p. 20.
10. Davenport, op. cit., pp. 200–1.
11. Hertzog to Amery, 26 July 1926, DO117/32.

12. Austen Chamberlain to Amery, 8 October 1926, FO800/259.
13. T. de Vere White, *Kevin O'Higgins*. (London, 1948) p. 221.
14. Amery to Austen Chamberlain, 15 October 1926, FO800/259.
15. Austen Chamberlain to Amery, 16 October 1926, FO800/259.
16. Ibid.
17. Amery to Austen Chamberlain, 15 October 1926, FO800/259.
18. Austen Chamberlain to Amery, 21 December 1926, FO800/259.
19. Ibid.
20. Austen Chamberlain to Hankey, 21 November 1926, FO800/259.
21. Harkness, op. cit., p. 93.
22. Harding minute, 29 August 1933, DO35/396.
23. Satge minute 'Imperial Conference 1926: Social Engagements', 26 November 1926, DO35/11.
24. Amery (1955), op. cit., p. 395.
25. Amery to Hertzog, 1 April 1926, DO35/10.
26. Ibid.
27. See M. Gilbert, *The Roots of Appeasement* (London, 1966).
28. Amery (1955), op. cit., p. 385.
29. Hankey to Balfour, 1 November 1926. Quoted in S. Roskill, *Hankey: Man of Secrets*, vol. 2 (London, 1972) p. 429.
30. 'The Imperial Conference', *The Round Table*, March 1927, p. 227.
31. Lord Athlone to Amery, 22 December 1926, DO35/25.
32. Bede Clifford to Under-Secretary of State DO, 30 March 1928, DO35/49.
33. Clifford, Sir Bede (1890–1969). Secretary to the Governor-General of South Africa 1921–4; United Kingdom High Commissioner in South Africa 1928–32; Governor of the Bahamas 1932–7; Governor of Mauritius 1937–42.
34. Clifford to Amery, 13 January 1928, DO35/49.
35. Bennett, Richard (1870–1947). Minister of Justice in Canada 1921; Prime Minister 1930–5.
36. Clark to Amery, 31 October 1928, DO35/49.
37. Ibid.
38. *The Sunday Times*, 28 November 1926.
39. Low, Sir Sydney (1879–1932). Lecturer on Constitutional History, University of London.
40. Amery to Low, 29 November 1926, DO35/20.
41. Low to Amery, 17 December 1926, DO35/20.
42. Amery to Davis, 6 July 1926, DO35/12.
43. See L. S. Amery, *The Forward View* (London, 1935) pp. 182–6.
44. 'The Imperial Conference 1930', Sankey Papers c. 507, Bodleian Library, Oxford.
45. See above, p. 157.
46. Risley, Sir John (1867–1957). Principal Legal Advisor to the Colonial Office 1911–31.
47. Risley minute, 12 October 1929, DO35/76.
48. 'Note on Merchant Shipping Legislation', 13 September 1929, DO35/75.
49. Lang, John (1876–1975). Colonial Treasurer in New South Wales Government 1920–22; Treasurer and Premier 1925–7 and 1930–2.
50. Schedvin, op. cit., pp. 97–8.

51. War Office Memorandum, 14 November 1929, CAB 27/399.
52. *Report of the Conference on the Operation of Dominion Legislation*, Cmd 3479 (HMSO, 1930) p. 12, paragraph 24.
53. Amery minute, 21 September 1929, DO35/55.
54. Cosgrave, William (1880–1965). President of the Executive Council, Irish Free State 1922–32.
55. Ramsay MacDonald to King George V, 28 November 1929, PREM 1/68.
56. King George V to Ramsay MacDonald, 30 November 1929, PREM 1/68.
57. Houston-Boswall to Under-Secretary of State DO, 23 May 1930, DO35/92.
58. Ibid.
59. Houston-Boswall, Sir William (1892–1955). Entered Foreign Office 1921; seconded to the DO for service in South Africa 1929–32; British Minister in Beirut 1947–51.
60. Houston-Boswall to Harding, 30 May 1930, DO35/92.
61. Duncan, Sir Patrick (1870–1943). Colonial Secretary in the Transvaal 1903–6; Minister of Interior 1921–4; Minister of Mines 1933–6.
62. Houston-Boswall to Harding, 30 May 1930, DO35/92.
63. Ibid.
64. See above, p. 116.
65. Bodenstein, Helgard (1881–1959). Assistant Chief Editor of *Die Burger*1919–21; Professor of Roman Dutch Law, University of Stellenbosch 1922; Secretary, Department of External Affairs 1927–41.
66. Houston-Boswall to Under-Secretary of State DO, 2 July 1929, DO35/92.
67. Peters, Sir William (1889–1964). Commercial Secretary to the British Mission in Russia 1924–7; Trade Commissioner in the Irish Free State 1929–35; Senior Trade Commissioner in South Africa 1936–45.
68. Peters to Batterbee, 24 September 1930, DO35/90.
69. Hadow, Sir Robert (1895–1963). Entered Diplomatic Service 1919 and served in Washington, Tehran and Ankara; Seconded to Dominions Office and attached to British High Commission to Canada 1928–31.
70. Hadow to Passfield, 31 May 1930, DO35/92.
71. Hadow to Passfield, 29 May 1930, DO35/92.
72. Clark, Sir William (1876–1952). Member for Commerce and Industry, Council of Viceroy of India 1910–16; Comptroller-General, Board of Trade 1917–28; United Kingdom High Commissioner in Canada 1928–34; United Kingdom High Commissioner in South Africa 1934–9.
73. Clark to Passfield, 23 January 1930, FO426/1.
74. Batterbee minute, 2 July 1930, DO35/92.
75. Keith, Arthur Berriedale (1879–1944). Lecturer on the Constitution of the British Empire, University of Edinburgh 1927–1944.

CHAPTER 5

1. Amery (1955), op. cit., p. 377.
2. Casey, Richard (1890–1976). Australian Government liaison officer in London 1924–31; Federal Treasurer 1935–9; Member of the UK War

Cabinet 1942–3; Governor of Bengal 1944–6; Australian Minister for External Affairs 1951–60.

3. Lord Casey, *Friends and Neighbours* (Melbourne, 1954) pp. 30–1.
4. Stonehaven, Lord John (1874–1941). Parliamentary Under-Secretary for Royal Air Force 1918; Parliamentary Under-Secretary, Home Office 1919–22; Minister for Transport 1922–4; Governor-General of Australia 1925–30; Chairman of Conservative Party 1931–6.
5. Austen Chamberlain to Lord Stonehaven, 12 May 1926, FO800/259.
6. Amery to Austen Chamberlain, 23 December 1926, FO800/259.
7. Austen Chamberlain to Amery, 28 December 1926, FO800/259.
8. See below, p. 56.
9. Amery to Austen Chamberlain, 23 December 1926, FO800/259.
10. Austen Chamberlain to Amery, 26 December 1926, FO800/259.
11. Amery to Austen Chamberlain, 23 December 1926, FO800/259.
12. Coates, Joseph (1866–1943). Minister of Public Works, New Zealand 1920–6; Prime Minister 1925–8; Minister of Public Works in Coalition ministry 1931–3; Minister for Finance 1933–5.
13. Coates Memorandum, 1 May 1927, DO35/487.
14. Bell, Sir Francis (1851–1936). Minister of External Affairs, New Zealand 1923–6; Prime Minister 1925; Minister of Marine 1928.
15. Note of Amery's meeting with New Zealand Ministers, 27 May 1927, DO35/52.
16. Ibid.
17. Ibid.
18. Joint Memorandum by the Secretary of State for Foreign Affairs and the Secretary of State for Dominion Affairs on Representation of the UK Government in the Dominions, 3 May 1927, CP 140 (27) CAB 24/191.
19. Minutes of Cabinet Committee on Representation in the Dominions of the UK Government, 22 June 1929, BRD (27)1st meeting CAB 27/347.
20. Ibid.
21. Ibid.
22. Willingdon, Lord (1866–1941). Governor of Bombay 1913–19; Governor of Madras 1919–24; Governor-General of Canada 1926–31; Viceroy of India 1931–6.
23. Lord Willingdon to George V, 13 February 1928, PREM 1/65.
24. Lord Willingdon to Baldwin, 9 August 1928, PREM 1/65.
25. Vansittart, Robert (1881–1957). Entered Foreign Office 1903; Assistant Secretary 1920; Private Secretary to Secretary of State 1920–4; Private Secretary to Prime Minister 1928–30; Permanent Under-Secretary of State, Foreign Office 1930–8; Diplomatic Advisor to Government 1938.
26. Vansittart to Stamfordham, 22 March 1928, PREM 1/65.
27. Cabinet Conclusion 41 (27) 6 CAB 23/56.
28. Minutes of Cabinet Committee on Representation in the Dominions of the UK Government, 27 June 1929, BRD (27) 2nd meeting CAB 27/347.
29. Ibid.
30. Clifford, Sir Bede (1890–1969). Secretary to Governor-General of South Africa 1921–4; United Kingdom High Commissioner in South Africa 1928–32; Governor of the Bahamas 1932–7; Governor of Mauritius 1937–42.

31. Crutcheley, Earnest (1878–1940). Appointed British Migration Commissioner in Australia in 1928; British Government Representative in Australia 1931–5.
32. Nicholls, Sir Philip (1894–1962). Entered Foreign Service 1920; United Kingdom liaison officer to New Zealand Government 1928–30; First Secretary, Rome Embassy 1933–7.
33. See above, p. 34.
34. Note of Conversation between Amery and Mackenzie King, 15 October 1928, DO35/56.
35. Smit, Jacobus (1878–1960). South African High Commissioner to the UK 1925–9; Administrator of the Transvaal 1929–34; South African Delegate to the League 1925–7.
36. Under-Secretary of State, Dominions Office, to Bede Clifford, 12 November 1928, DO114/22.
37. Clark Memorandum, 15 November 1928, DO114/22.
38. Ibid.
39. Circular to His Majesty's Ambassadors at Posts Affected by Dominion Appointments, 25 July 1929, DO35/77.
40. Smiddy, Timothy (1875–1962). Envoy of Dail Eirann to the US 1922–4; Free State Minister to the US 1924–9; Free State High Commissioner to the UK 1929–30.
41. Howard, Esme (1863–1939). Ambassador to Spain 1919–24 and to USA 1924–30.
42. Howard Memorandum, 'The Free State Legation in Washington', March 1929, DO35/77.
43. O'Kelly, Sean (1882–1966). Irish Republican Envoy to Paris and Rome 1919–22; Free State Commissioner in Belgium 1925–8; Vice-President of the Executive Council and Minister for Local Government 1939–45; President of Ireland 1945–59.
44. Wingfield Memorandum, 4 January 1926, DO35/12.
45. Grahame to Villiers, 5 January 1926, DO35/12.
46. Grahame, Sir George (1873–1940). Minister in Paris 1918–1920; Ambassador to Belgium 1920–8; Ambassador to Spain 1928–35.
47. Grahame to Villiers, 5 January 1926, DO35/12.
48. Ibid.
49. Villiers to Whiskard, 11 January 1926, DO35/12.
50. Stephenson minute, 12 January 1926, DO35/12.
51. Amery minute, 31 January 1926, DO35/12.
52. Crowe to Selby, 4 October 1928, DO35/60.
53. Fallon, Rt Revd Michael (1867–1931). Bishop of London, Ontario 1910–31.
54. 'Relations between Canada and Mexico: An Aide Memoire', 27 February 1928, DO35/58.
55. Canadian Government to UK Government (Telegram), 26 January 1928, DO114/22.
56. UK Government to Canadian Government (Telegram), 13 February 1928, DO114/22.
57. Ibid.

58. Canadian Government to UK Government (Telegram), 19 February 1928, DO114/22.
59. 'Memorandum on Diplomatic Rupture between a Dominion and a Foreign Country', 12 March 1926, FO426/1.
60. Foreign Office Memorandum, 'Function of the Proposed Canadian Minister in Paris', 25 August 1928, DO114/22.
61. Stamfordham, Arthur (1849–1931). Private Secretary to Queen Victoria 1895–1901; Private Secretary to King George V 1910–31.
62. Stamfordham to Amery, 5 October 1928, DO35/51.
63. Cushendun, Baron (1861–1934). Parliamentary Under-Secretary for Foreign Affairs 1922–5; Financial Secretary to the Treasury 1925; Chancellor of the Duchy of Lancaster 1927–9.
64. Cushendun to Amery, 29 September 1928, DO35/51.
65. Ibid.
66. Amery to Davis, 12 February 1928, DO35/58.
67. Harding Paper 'Equality of Status between Great Britain and the Dominions' delivered to the Institute of Public Administration, 29 January 1929, DO35/73.
68. Dominions Office Memorandum, 15 February 1929, DO35/77.
69. Lindsay, Sir Ronald (1877–1945). Under-Secretary at the Foreign Office 1921–4; British Representative at Constantinople 1924–6; British Ambassador to Germany 1926–8; Permanent Under-Secretary of State at the Foreign Office 1928–30; British Ambassador to the United States 1930–9.
70. Amery to Lindsay, 24 September 1928, DO35/51.
71. Cushendun to Wellesley, 29 August 1928, DO114/22.
72. Price minute, 28 September 1928, DO35/55.
73. Price, Sir Charles (1893–1963). Entered Colonial Office in 1921 and transferred to the Dominions Office in 1925; made an Assistant Secretary in 1932 and attached to the British Delegation at the League 1928, 1932–4 and 1939.
74. Price to Batterbee, 22 September 1928, DO35/55.
75. Murphy to Harding, 17 September 1928, DO114/22.
76. Hertzog to Amery, 7 November 1928, DO35/50.
77. Liesching, Sir Percival (1895–1973). Served on the UK High Commission in Canada 1928–32; attached to UK High Commission in South Africa 1933–5; Secretary to UK High Commission in Australia 1936–8.
78. Liesching Memorandum, 30 August 1928, DO114/22.
79. Imperial Secretary, South Africa, to Amery, 21 July 1928, DO114/22.
80. Ibid.
81. Imperial Secretary, South Africa, to Harding, 16 August 1928, DO114/22.
82. Ibid.
83. Clifford to Amery, 26 September 1928, DO114/22.
84. Clifford to Batterbee, 24 October 1928, DO114/22.
85. Clifford to Batterbee, 10 December 1928, DO114/22.
86. Ibid.
87. Ibid.
88. Marler, Sir Herbert (1876–1940). Quebec businessman; Canadian Minister to Japan 1929–36.

89. Hadow to Koppell, 1 February 1929, DO35/77.
90. Harding to Clark, 18 June 1929, DO35/76.
91. Tilley to Foreign Office (Telegram), 19 January 1929, DO35/76.
92. Tilley, Sir John (1867–1952). British Ambassador in Brazil 1921–5; British Ambassador in Japan 1926–31
93. Tilley to Austen Chamberlain, 28 January 1929, DO35/58.
94. Tilley to Austen Chamberlain, 31 January 1929, DO35/58.
95. Harding minute, 19 June 1929, DO35/59.
96. Skelton to Harding, 3 July 1929, DO35/76.
97. Stephenson, Sir John (1893–1967). Assistant Private Secretary to Secretary of State for Colonies 1920–3; Appointed Assistant Secretary, Dominions Office 1930.
98. Stephenson minute, 10 November 1929, DO35/160.
99. Ingram to Lampson, 21 March 1930, DO35/165.
100. Ibid.
101. Ingram to Lampson, 22 March 1930, DO35/165.
102. Lampson, Sir Miles (1880–1964). British Minister to China 1926–33; UK High Commissioner in Egypt and the Sudan 1934–6; British Ambassador to Egypt 1936–46.
103. Ingram to Lampson, 22 March 1930, DO35/165.
104. Ibid.
105. Lampson to Orde, 7 April 1930, DO35/165.
106. Price minute, 7 July 1930, DO35/165.
107. Clutterbuck minute, 29 May 1931, DO35/165.
108. Clark to Thomas, 11 June 1931, DO35/165.
109. Clutterbuck, Sir Alexander (1897–1976). Private Secretary to Under-Secretary of State, Dominions Office 1928–9; Appointed Principal 1929; Assistant Under-Secretary 1942–6; Permanent Under-Secretary of State, Commonwealth Relations Office 1959–61.
110. Clutterbuck minute, 25 June 1931, DO35/165.
111. Clark to Passfield (Telegram), 7 July 1931, DO35/165.
112. Mounsey to Clive, 5 March 1934, DO35/160.

CHAPTER 6

1. Ponsonby, Arthur (1871–1946). Under-Secretary of State for Foreign Affairs 1924; Parliamentary Under-Secretary for Dominion Affairs June–December 1929.
2. 'The Dominions and Foreign Affairs', Ponsonby Papers, Mss. Eng. Hist. C. 671, Bodleian Library, Oxford.
3. Clark to Amery, 6 December 1928, DO35/47.
4. Lampson to Henderson, 17 September 1929, DO35/81.
5. Dixon Memorandum, 30 December 1929, DO35/81.
6. 'The Dominions and Foreign Affairs', Ponsonby Papers, Mss. Eng. Hist. C. 671, Bodleian Library, Oxford.
7. Liesching Memorandum, 15 May 1927, DO35/47.
8. Reynardson, Lieutenant-Colonel Birch (1892–1959). Secretary to the

Governor-General of South Africa 1927–33.
9. Birch Reynardson to Harding, 27 June 1927, DO35/25.
10. Ibid.
11. See below, p. 110.
12. For a more dispassionate consideration of Skelton's influence on Canadian foreign policy see R. Veatch, *Canada and the League of Nations* (Toronto, 1975) pp. 115–24.
13. Dominions Office Memorandum, 2 April 1928, DO35/46.
14. Harding minute, 30 April 1928, DO35/46.
15. Koppell minute, 4 May 1928, DO35/46.
16. Koppell, Percy (1876–1932). Principal in News Department, Foreign Office 1917; Transferred to Political Intelligence Department 1918–20; Appointed Counsellor 1925.
17. Koppell to Dixon, 9 March 1928, DO35/58.
18. Clifford to Amery, 14 December 1927, DO35/47.
19. Ibid.
20. Wiseman Memorandum, 27 June 1929, DO35/79.
21. Amery to Austen Chamberlain, 15 August 1927, FO800/261.
22. Chamberlain to Balfour, 7 November 1927, FO800/261.
23. Chamberlain to Hertzog, 24 November 1927, FO800/261.
24. Ibid.
25. Ibid.
26. Clifford to Davis, 3 February 1928, DO35/49.
27. Clifford to Amery, 9 March 1928, DO35/49.
28. Ibid.
29. Secretary of State for Dominions to the South African Department of External Affairs, 7 June 1928, CAB 21/311.
30. MacReady, Lieutenant-General Sir Gordon (1891–1956). Assistant Secretary to the Committee of Imperial Defence 1926–32; Assistant to the Chief of the Imperial General Staff 1940–2.
31. MacReady to Hankey, 11 June 1928, CAB 21/311.
32. Madden Memorandum on 'Dominion Neutrality', June 1928, CAB 21/311.
33. Ibid.
34. Hankey to Harding, 12 June 1928, CAB 21/311.
35. Ibid.
36. Ibid.
37. Harding to Hankey, 18 June 1928, CAB 21/311.
38. Ibid.
39. Baldwin to Hankey, 23 November 1928, CAB 21/311.
40. Ibid.
41. 'The Dominions and Foreign Affairs', Ponsonby Papers, mss. Eng. Hist. C. 671, Bodleian Library, Oxford.
42. Secretary of State for Foreign Affairs Memorandum to Cabinet Committee on Compulsory Arbitration, 27 July 1926, CAB 27/330.
43. Attorney-General's Statement at the Cabinet Committee on Compulsory Arbitration, 27 July 1926, CAB 27/330.
44. Australian Government to Canadian Government (Telegram), 22 February 1929, DO35/77.

45. Canadian Government to UK Government (Telegram), 24 January 1929, DO35/77.
46. Lindsay to Vansittart, 2 March 1929, DO35/77.
47. Batterbee minute, 1 February 1929, DO35/77.
48. Price minute, 8 February 1929, DO35/77.
49. DO Memorandum, March 1929, DO35/74.
50. Leeper to Farrer, 17 April 1929, W3555 FO371/14103.
51. Parliamentary Debates (Lords) *Hansard*, 1 May 1929, vol. 74 (Fifth Series), col. 289.
52. Parmoor, Lord (1852–1941). Lord President of the Council 1924 and 1929–31.
53. Parliamentary Debates (Lords) *Hansard*, 1 May 1929, vol. 74 (Fifth Series), col. 318.
54. Inter-Departmental Meeting on the Optional Clause, 20 June 1929, DO35/79.
55. Ibid.
56. Batterbee minute, 9 July 1929, DO35/79.
57. Berendsen, Carl (b. 1895). Head of Prime Minister's Office, New Zealand 1932–43; Secretary of External Affairs 1928–43; New Zealand Ambassador to the United States 1944–8.
58. Nicholls to Koppell, 26 August 1929, W9505 FO371/14106.
59. Kirkpatrick minute, 22 July 1929, W8125 FO371/14105.
60. Lindsay to MacDonald, 17 August 1929, W8136 FO371/14105.
61. MacDonald Memorandum to Cabinet Committee on the Optional Clause, 18 August 1929, CAB 27/392.
62. Cecil Memorandum, 19 August 1929, W8095 F0371/14104.
63. Cecil/Minute, 20 August 1929, W8568 FO371/14105.
64. Cecil to Ramsay MacDonald, 21 August 1929, W8259 FO371/14105.
65. Ibid.
66. MacDonald to Bruce, 23 August 1929, DO114/27.
67. Irish Free State Government to UK Government (Telegram), 24 August 1929, DO114/27.
68. Canadian Government to UK Government (Telegram), 23 August 1929, DO114/27.
69. Australian Government to Secretary of State for Dominion Affairs, 24 August 1929, DO114/27.
70. Passfield, Lord (1859–1947). President of the Board of Trade in Labour administration 1924; Secretary of State for Dominions 1929–30; Secretary of State for the Colonies 1929–31.
71. Meeting of the Cabinet Committee on the Optional Clause, 27 August 1929, CAB 27/392.
72. Ibid.
73. Coates to MacDonald, 31 August 1929, DO114/27.
74. Hurst Memorandum, September 1929, DO114/27.
75. See C. D. W. Goodwin, *The Image of Australia* (Durham, 1974).
76. Harding Minute, 15 December 1926, DO35/20.
77. C. B. Schedvin, *Australia in the Great Depression* (Sydney, 1970).
78. Ibid., p. 50.
79. Ibid., p. 62.

80. Hore-Ruthven, Brigadier-General Alexandra (1872–1955).Governor of South Australia 1928–34; Governor of New South Wales 1935; Governor-General of Australia 1936–44.

81. Hore-Ruthven to Amery, 6 August 1928, DO35/45.

82. Governor of Queensland to Amery, 8 December 1927, DO35/45.

83. Schedvin, op. cit., p. 97.

84. See R. C. Mills, 'Australia's Loan Policy' in P. Campbell (ed.), *Studies in Australian Affairs* (Melbourne, 1928); also Sir Hal Colebatch, 'Australian Credit as Viewed from London', *Economic Record*, November 1927.

85. Nicholls to Koppell, 5 October 1929, DO35/81.

86. Archer, Norman (1892–1970). Transferred from the Colonial Office to the Dominions Office 1925; Secretary to the UK High Commissioner in Canada 1932–36.

87. Archer Memorandum 'Notes on Unemployment and Immigration in New Zealand', May 1929, DO35/73.

88. Skevington Memorandum on Economic Conditions in Canada, September 1929, DO35/73.

89. Ibid.

90. See above, p. 17.

91. Drummond, op. cit., p. 127.

92. Niemeyer, Otto (1887–1962). Controller of Finance in the Treasury 1924–7; Director of the Bank of England 1938–52.

93. Drummond, op. cit., p. 128.

94. Ibid., p. 99.

95. Memorandum on the Settlement of ex-Indian Army Officers in Victoria, 7 June 1928, DO35/52.

96. Drummond, op. cit., p. 93.

97. Archer Memorandum 'Notes on Unemployment and Immigration in New Zealand', May 1929, DO35/73.

98. Drummond, op. cit., pp. 132–44.

99. 'British Miners and the Canadian Harvest', *The Round Table*, December 1929, pp. 174–85.

100. Amery to Clark, 5 December 1928, DO35/47.

101. Hancock, W. K., *Survey of British Commonwealth Affairs. Problems of Economic Policy*, part I (Oxford, 1940) p. 187.

102. I. Drummond, *British Economic Policy and the Empire 1919–39* (London, 1972) p. 29.

103. Schedvin, op. cit., p. 96.

104. Drummond (1974), op. cit., p. 131.

105. Fountain to Whiskard, 7 January 1926, DO35/15.

106. Cunliffe-Lister, Philip (1884–1968). President of the Board of Trade 1922–3, 1924–9 and 1931; Secretary of State for the Colonies 1931–5.

107. Cunliffe-Lister to Amery, 10 February 1926, DO35/15.

108. Clifford to Harding, 4 September 1928, DO35/50.

109. Ibid.

110. Clifford to Harding, 5 December 1928, DO35/50.

111. Bruwer, Andries. Chairman, South African Board of Trade and Industries.

112. Clifford to Harding, 14 December 1928, DO35/50.

113. Hoad Minute, 16 October 1926, DO35/14.
114. Stephenson Minute, 18 June 1929, DO35/50.
115. See above, p. 18–19.
116. Thomas, J. H. (1874–1949). Secretary of State for the Colonies 1924, 1931 and 1935–6; Secretary of State for the Dominions 1930–5.
117. Batterbee to Thomas, 28 March 1930, DO35/194.
118. Clark to Passfield, 28 March 1930, DO35/194.
119. DO Memorandum, January 1930, DO35/194.
120. Wiseman Minute, 29 June 1930, DO35/194.
121. Hadow to Thomas, 6 September 1930, DO35/90.
122. Ibid.
123. Clark to Thomas, 20 November 1930, DO35/195.

CHAPTER 7

1. Snowden, Philip (1864–1937). Chancellor of the Exchequer in Labour administrations 1924 and 1929–31; Lord Privy Seal in National Government 1931–2.
2. S. Roskill, *Hankey: Man of Secrets*, vol. 2 (London, 1972) p. 485.
3. Ramsay MacDonald to Hankey, 15 August 1929. Quoted in Roskill, op. cit., p. 488.
4. Sankey, Lord (1855–1948). Chairman of Royal Commission on the Coal Industry 1919; Lord Chancellor in Labour and National Governments 1929–35.
5. 'The Imperial Conference 1930', Sankey Papers C. 507, Bodleian Library, Oxford.
6. See above p. 53.
7. Amery to Jowitt, 8 August 1930, Ramsay MacDonald Papers, PRO 30/69/1/347, Public Record Office.
8. Hankey to Ramsay MacDonald, 10 August 1930, Ramsay MacDonald Papers, PRO 30/69/1/347, Public Record Office.
9. Holmes, Sir Stephen (b. 1896). Principal in the Dominions Office 1928–36; Senior Secretary to the UK High Commissioner in Canada 1936–9; Deputy Under-Secretary of State, Commonwealth Relations Office 1951–2.
10. Holmes to Ramsay MacDonald, 11 August 1930, Ramsay MacDonald Papers, PRO 30/69/1/357, Public Record Office.
11. Ibid.
12. Ibid.
13. Ramsay MacDonald minute, 11 August 1930, Ramsay MacDonald Papers, PRO 30/69/1/347, Public Record Office.
14. Corelli Barnett, *The Collapse of British Power* (London, 1972) pp. 24–8.
15. For a full treatment of the Flag Controversy see H. Saker, 'The Flag Controversy in South Africa', unpublished doctoral thesis, University of Cape Town (1977).
16. Clifford to Harding, 5 December 1928, DO35/50.
17. Houston–Boswall to Under-Secretary of State, Dominions Office, 30 July

1930, Ramsay MacDonald Papers, PRO 39/69/1/357, Public Record Office.

18. Hankey to Duff, 10 September 1930, Ramsay MacDonald Papers, PRO 30/69/1/357, Public Record Office.
19. Waterfield to Harding, 2 May 1930, DO35/90.
20. Ibid.
21. Batterbee minute, 29 May 1930, DO35/90.
22. Ibid.
23. Milne, Field Marshal Sir George (1866–1948). G. O. C., Eastern Command 1923–6; Chief of the Imperial General Staff 1926–33.
24. Sir George Milne to Ramsay MacDonald, 29 October 1930, 'Imperial Conference 1930: Foreign Policy and Defence', C/I.C. (1930)/1, CAB 21/336.
25. Hankey to Sir George Milne, 14 November 1930, 'Imperial Conference 1930: Foreign Policy and Defence', C/I.C. (1930)/1, CAB 21/336.
26. Ibid.
27. For a fuller discussion of the economic aspects of the 1930 Imperial Conference see Drummond (1974), op. cit.
28. First Report of the Inter-Departmental Committee on the Imperial Conference, 12 February 1930, DO35/90.
29. Scullin, James (1876–1953). Leader of the Federal Party in Australia 1928–35; Prime Minister 1931–2.
30. Drummond (1974), op. cit.
31. Amery to Jowitt, 8 August 1930, Ramsay MacDonald Papers, PRO 30/69/1/347, Public Record Office.
32. Cabinet Conclusion 52(30) 18, 17 September 1930, CAB 23/65.
33. Fitzgerald, James (1878–1969). Minister of Justice, Irish Free State 1927–32.
34. J. Fitzgerald to Mrs Fitzgerald, 20 October 1930. Quoted in Harkness, op. cit., p. 206.
35. Risley minute, 23 July 1929, DO35/72.
36. Dominions Office Memorandum 'Inter Se Applicability' December 1929 DO35/76.
37. For Sankey's obsession with his mother see his Diary, Mss. Eng. Hist. E.242–E.299, Sankey Papers, Bodleian Library, Oxford.
38. 'Imperial Conference 1930', Sankey Papers C.507, Bodleian Library, Oxford.
39. 'Imperial Conference 1926', Stenographic Notes of Meetings CAB 32/46.
40. Sankey note, 9 July 1930, MacDonald Papers, PRO 30/69/1/347, Public Record Office.
41. Ibid.
42. 'Imperial Conference 1930', Sankey Papers C.507, Bodlein Library Oxford.
43. MacGilligan, Patrick (1889–1967). Secretary to the Free State High Commissioner to the UK 1923; Minister for External Affairs 1927–32; Minister for Industry and Commerce 1924–32.
44. 'Imperial Conference 1930', Sankey Papers C.507, Bodleian Library, Oxford.

45. J. Fitzgerald to Mrs Fitzgerald, 13 October 1930. Quoted in Harkness, op. cit., p. 197.
46. 'Imperial Conference 1930', Sankey Papers C.507, Bodleian Library, Oxford.
47. See L.F. Crisp, 'The Appointment of Sir Isaac Isaacs as Governor-General of Australia: J. H. Scullin's Account of the Buckingham Palace Interviews', *Historical Studies, Australia and New Zealand*, XI, No. 42 (Melbourne, 1964).
48. Guthrie, Hugh (1886–1952). Minister of Defence, Canada 1920–1; Minister of Justice 1930–5.
49. Harkness, op. cit., p. 206.
50. Forbes, George (1869–1947). Appointed leader of the United Party, New Zealand 1928; Prime Minister in 1930–1 (United Government) and 1931–5 (Reform–Coalition Government).
51. 'Imperial Conference 1930', Sankey Papers C.507, Bodleian Library, Oxford.
52. Mounsey to Sankey, 13 November 1930, Sankey Papers c. 507, Bodleian Library, Oxford.

CHAPTER 8

1. Robert Vansittart, 'An Aspect of International Relations in 1931', CP 125 (311) CAB 24/221.
2. Ibid.
3. Vansittart Memorandum, 'The British Position in relation to European Policy', 11 January 1932, CP 4 (32) CAB 24/227.
4. Simon, John (1873–1954). Secretary of State for Home Affairs in Liberal Government 1915–6; Secretary of State for Foreign Affairs in National Government 1931–5; Chancellor of the Exchequer 1937–40; Lord Chancellor in the Coalition Government 1940–5.
5. Simon Memorandum, 'Changing Conditions in British Foreign Policy', 26 November 1931. CP 310 (31) CAB 24/225.
6. Wilford, Sir Thomas (1870–1939). Leader of the Liberal Party of New Zealand 1919–25; New Zealand High Commissioner in London 1930–4; London Director, National Bank of New Zealand 1934–7.
7. Collins, James (1869–1934). Australian Financial Advisor in London 1926–33; Leader of Australian Delegation to the League of Nations 1931.
8. Clutterbuck to Tait, 21 September 1931, DO35/183.
9. Peters to Department of Trade, 30 September 1931, DO35/252.
10. Clark to Passfield, 12 December 1930, DO35/195.
11. *The Financial Post Business Year Book for 1931* (Toronto, 1932) p. 23.
12. Whiskard, Sir Geoffrey (1886–1957). Transferred from the Colonial to the Dominions Office 1925; Assistant Under-Secretary of State, Dominions Office 1930–5; UK High Commissioner in Australia 1936–41; Permanent Secretary, Ministry of Works and Buildings 1941–3; Permanent Secretary, Ministry of Town and Country Planning 1943–6.
13. Whiskard minute, 10 October 1931, DO35/252.
14. Vanier, General George (1888–1967). ADC to Governor-General of

Canada 1926–8; Canadian Representative on Preparatory Disarmament Commission at the League 1928–31; Secretary, Canadian High Commissioner to the UK 1931–8; Canadian Ambassador to France 1944–53.
15. Harding minute, 19 October 1931, DO35/252.
16. Havenga, Nicolaas (1882–1957). Minister of Finance in Nationalist–Labour Pact 1924–9; Leader of Afrikaner Party 1939–48; Finance Minister in Nationalist Government 1948–53.
17. Stanley to Thomas, 26 November 1931, DO35/251.
18. Campbell minute, 19 October 1931, DO35/251.
19. Stanley to Harding, 7 October 1931, DO35/251.
20. Ibid.
21. Stanley to Thomas, 14 October 1931, DO35/251.
22. Leith-Ross to Batterbee, 9 November 1931, DO35/251.
23. Dominions Office Memorandum, 30 September 1931, DO35/251.
24. te Water, Charles (1887–1964). South African High Commissioner to the UK 1929–39; President of the Assembly of the League of Nations 1933.
25. Thomas to te Water, 10 December 1931, DO35/251.
26. Leith-Ross to Batterbee, 9 November 1931, DO35/251.
27. Stanley, Sir Herbert (1872–1955). Private Secretary to the Governor-General of South Africa 1910–15; Resident Commissioner, Southern and Northern Rhodesia 1915–18; Governor of Northern Rhodesia 1924–7; Governor of Ceylon 1927–31; UK High Commissioner in South Africa 1931–5; Governor of Southern Rhodesia 1935–42.
28. Louw, Eric (1890–1968). South African High Commissioner to the UK 1929; South African Minister to the United States 1929; South African Delegate to the League of Nations 1929, 1934 and 1935; Minister of Foreign Affairs 1956–63.
29. Stanley to Harding, 8 December 1931, DO35/251.
30. Ibid.
31. Stanley to Thomas, 30 December 1932, DO35/252.
32. FBI Memorandum, 27 November 1930, 'Finance and Industry: Effects of Monetary Deflation on Prices', FBI/c/2/1930, FBI Papers.
33. Minutes of the Grand Council, 1 October 1930, FBI Committees 1930, FBI Papers.
34. Minutes of President's Advisory Committee on Fiscal Policy, 16 September 1931, FBI/c/2/1931B, FBI Papers.
35. David Marquand, *Ramsay MacDonald* (London, 1977) pp. 671–701.
36. Drummond (1974), op. cit., pp. 212–13.
37. Schedvin, op. cit., pp. 169–283.
38. Secretary of State for Dominions Memorandum to Cabinet, 13 November 1931, CP 288(31) CAB 24/224.
39. Whiskard to Harding, 22 August 1932, DO121/61.
40. Ibid.
41. 'Ottawa Diary', 7 August 1932, Neville Chamberlain Papers, NC2/17, University of Birmingham.
42. Whiskard to Harding, 3 August 1932, DO121/61.
43. I. Drummond (1974) op. cit., p. 276.
44. A. Nove, *An Economic History of the U.S.S.R.* (London, 1969) p. 211.

45. 'Ottawa Diary', 24 July 1932, Neville Chamberlain Papers, NC2/17, University of Birmingham.
46. Ashton-Gwatkin, Frank (1889–1957). Appointed First Secretary, Foreign Office 1930; UK delegation to the Ottawa Conference 1932; UK delegation at the World Economic Conference 1933; Appointed Assistant Under-Secretary of State 1947.
47. Ashton-Gwatkin to Vansittart, 27 July 1932, FO426/3.
48. *Imperial Economic Conference at Ottawa: Appendices to the Summary of Proceedings*, Cmd 4175 (1932) pp. 859–927.
49. Whiskard to Harding, 19 August 1932, DO121/61.
50. Runciman, Walter (1870–1939). President, Board of Education in Liberal Government 1908–11; President, Board of Agriculture 1911–14; President, Board of Trade 1914–16 and 1931–7; Lord President of the Council 1938–9.
51. Whiskard to Harding, 19 August 1932, DO121/61.
52. 'The Australia and New Zealand Negotiations and a duty on meat', August 1932, PREM 1/112.
53. Ibid.
54. 'Ottawa Diary', 9 August 1932, Neville Chamberlain Papers, NC2/17, University of Birmingham.
55. Drummond (1974), op. cit., p. 237.
56. Drummond (1974), op. cit., pp. 240–1.
57. O (U.K.) (32) 27th meeting, 3 August 1932, CAB 32/101.
58. Drummond (1974), op. cit., p. 252.
59. 'Ottawa Diary', 9 August 1932, Neville Chamberlain Papers, NC2/17, University of Birmingham.
60. Whiskard to Harding, 22 August 1929, DO121/61.
61. Ibid.
62. Drummond (1974), op. cit., p. 285.
63. Sir Ralph Glyn to Ramsay MacDonald, 22 September 1932, MacDonald Papers, PRO 30/69/5/191, Public Record Office, London.
64. Samuel, Herbert (1870–1963). President of Local Government Board in Liberal administration 1914–15; High Commissioner in Palestine 1920–5; Minister for Home Affairs in National Government 1931–2.
65. Herbert Samuel to Ramsay MacDonald, 28 September 1931, MacDonald Papers, PRO 39/69/5/191, Public Record Office, London.
66. Snowden to Ramsay MacDonald 28 September 1932, MacDonald Papers, PRO 39/69/5/191, Public Record Office, London.
67. Drummond.(1974), op. cit., p. 286.
68. G. Locock to O. MacDonald, 9 April 1934, FBI/S/Walker/4, FBI Papers.
69. Hancock (1940), op. cit., p. 245.
70. Ibid., pp. 245–6.
71. Crutchely to Whiskard, 30 May 1934, DO35/283.
72. Memorandum by the Australian Association of British Manufacturers, 26 January 1938, FBI/c/2/1938, FBI Papers.
73. J. McCarthy, *Australia and Imperial Defence 1918–39* (Queensland, 1976) p. 115.
74. Clark to Thomas, 2 March 1933, BT11/175.
75. Ibid.

76. Clark to Thomas, 16 November 1933, BT11/175.
77. Fountain to Whiskard, 8 March 1933, BT11/175.
78. Griffiths to Wiseman, 18 April 1935, BT11/175.
79. Lindsay to Foreign Office (Telegram), 17 November 1935, BT11/395.
80. W. Brown minute, 18 September 1935, BT11/335.
81. Dunning, Charles (1885–1958). Premier of Saskatchewan 1922–6; Minister of Finance in Liberal administrations 1929 and 1935–9.
82. Floud to Malcolm MacDonald, 27 February 1936, DO35/271.
83. P. S. Gupta, *Imperialism and the British Labour Movement, 1914–64* (London, 1975) p. 234.
84. Economic Advisory Council Report, May 1935, CP 157 (35) CAB 24/255.
85. Hancock (1940), op. cit., pp. 186–190.
86. Ibid.
87. Inter-Departmental Report on Migration Policy, August 1934, CP 62(35) CAB 24/254.
88. Ibid.
89. Economic Advisory Council (E1) 74, 9 June 1934, CAB 58/19.
90. Meeting of British and Dominion Delegates on Meat Problems, 22 January 1935, CP 18 (35) CAB 24/253.
91. The Economic Situation and Inter-Imperial Relations, 20 July 1934, CP 197 (34) CAB 24/252.
92. Secretary of State for Dominions Memorandum, 10 April 1934, CP 105 (34) CAB 24/248.
93. Ibid.
94. See Megaw, op. cit.

CHAPTER 9

1. For a detailed treatment of the Statute of Westminster see Sir Kenneth Wheare, *The Statute of Westminster and Dominion Status* (Oxford, 1938).
2. Attorney-General Memorandum, 23 September 1930, CP 312 (30) CAB 24/215.
3. Shaw to Thomas, 3 November 1930, DO35/92.
4. Sir Ralph Glyn to Ramsay MacDonald, 21 November 1931, PREM 1/91.
5. Sankey Diary, 3 November 1931, Mss. Eng. Hist. E. 284, Bodleian Library, Oxford.
6. Casey Memorandum on Constitutional Development, September 1936, DO35/108.
7. W. K. Hancock, *Survey of British Commonwealth Affairs. Problems of Nationality 1918–1936* (Oxford, 1937) pp. 92–146, 320–69.
8. P. N. S. Mansergh, *The Irish Free State; its Government and Politics* (London, 1934); also see *Survey of British Commonwealth Affairs. Problems of External Policy 1931–9* (Oxford, 1952) pp. 270–328.
9. D. W. Harkness, *The Restless Dominion* (London, 1969); also see D. Harkness, 'Mr de Valera's Dominion', *Journal of Commonwealth Political Studies*, vol. viii (Leicester, 1970).
10. The Earl of Longford and Thomas O'Neill, *Eamonn de Valera* (London, 1970).

11. Harkness, op. cit., p. 256.
12. Hancock (1937), op. cit., pp. 322–4.
13. Lionel Curtis to Winston Churchill, 17 December 1928, Mss Curtis 90, General Correspondence and Papers, Bodleian Library, Oxford.
14. Dominions Office Memorandum, 10 April 1929, DO35/74.
15. Peters to Batterbee, 25 September 1930, DO35/90.
16. Ibid.
17. Malcolm MacDonald minute, 6 October 1931, DO35/251.
18. De Valera to Hertzog, 7 April 1932, DO35/397.
19. Sankey Diaries, 15 July 1932, Mss. Eng. Hist. E. 286, Bodleian Library, Oxford.
20. Curtis to Thomas, 14 April 1932, Mss. Curtis 6, General Correspondence and Papers, Bodleian Library, Oxford.
21. Ibid.
22. Hailsham, Lord (1872–1950). Lord Chancellor 1928–9; Minister of War 1931–5; Lord Chancellor 1935–8.
23. Note on the Ministerial Visit to Dublin, 8 June 1932, CP 198 (32) 8 CAB 24/236.
24. Parliamentary Debates (Commons) *Hansard*, 4 July 1932, vol. 268 (Fifth Series), col. 122.
25. Harding minute, 17 August 1932, DO35/397.
26. Dominions Office minute, 8 August 1932, DO35/397.
27. Ibid.
28. Ibid.
29. Harding minute, 2 August 1932, DO35/397.
30. Hankey to Ramsay MacDonald, 10 August 1932, DO35/397.
31. Harding minute, 17 August 1932, DO35/397.
32. Sankey to Ramsay MacDonald, 15 August 1932, Ramsay MacDonald Papers, PRO 30/69/2/35, Public Record Office, London.
33. Whiskard to Harding, 22 July 1932, DO121/61.
34. Sankey Diary, 15 July 1932, mss. Eng. Hist. E. 286, Bodleian Library, Oxford.
35. Ramsay MacDonald to Thomas, 18 August 1932, DO35/397.
36. Ramsay MacDonald to the Archbishop of York, 13 September 1932, Ramsay MacDonald Papers, PRO 30/69/2/36, Public Record Office, London.
37. Ibid.
38. Curtis to Thomas, 5 January 1933, Mss. Curtis 90, General Correspondence and Papers, Bodleian Library, Oxford.
39. Batterbee minute, 10 September 1932, DO35/398.
40. Coupland, Sir Reginald (1884–1952). Editor of *The Round Table* 1917–19; Beit Professor of Colonial History, University of Oxford 1920–48.
41. 'The Situation in the Irish Free State' by Reginald Coupland, June 1933, DO35/398.
42. Ibid.
43. Harding minute, 29 August 1933, DO35/398.
44. Harding minute, 28 June 1933, DO35/398.
45. Secret meeting between Batterbee and a Free State delegate, 10 September 1934, DO35/399 part 1.

46. Peters to Batterbee, 25 September 1934, DO35/399 part 1.
47. Lemass, Thomas. Minister for Industry 1932–47.
48. Ryan, Joseph. Minister for Agriculture 1932–47.
49. Derrig, Thomas. Minister for Education 1932–39.
50. Peters to Batterbee, 30 May 1934, DO35/399 part 1.
51. Malcolm MacDonald minute, 18 July 1933, DO35/397.
52. Price to Wiseman, 21 September 1934, DO35/186.
53. Eden, Anthony (1897–1977). Parliamentary Under-Secretary of State, Foreign Office 1931–3; Lord Privy Seal 1934–5; Minister for League Affairs 1935; Foreign Secretary 1935–8; Secretary of State for Dominions 1939–4; Foreign Secretary 1940–5; Deputy Prime Minister 1951–5; Prime Minister 1955–7.
54. Note of meeting between Batterbee and Walsh, 2 October 1935, DO35/156.
55. Ibid.
56. Eden memorandum, 15 October 1935, DO35/399 part 2.
57. Ibid.
58. Batterbee to Malcolm MacDonald, 20 October 1935, DO35/158.
59. Dulanty, John (1884–1950). Free State Trade Commissioner to the UK 1926–30; Free State High Commissioner to the UK 1930–50.
60. MacDonald minute, 26 February 1936, DO35/399 part 2.
61. Hacking, Douglas (1884–1950). Parliamentary Under-Secretary, Home Office 1933–4; Parliamentary Under-Secretary, Dominions Office 1935–6; Chairman of Conservative Party Organisation 1936–42.
62. Note of meeting between Hacking and de Valera, February 1936, DO35/399 part 2.
63. Ibid.
64. Ibid.
65. Note of meeting between de Valera and Malcolm MacDonald, 10 April 1936, DO35/399 part 2.
66. Longford and O'Neill, op. cit., p. 290.
67. Dominions Office Memorandum on the Free State Situation, 17 December 1936, DO35/399 part 2.
68. Ibid.
69. Ibid.
70. Longford and O'Neill, op.cit., pp. 312–26.
71. Wigram, Clive (1873–1960). Assistant Private Secretary to King George V 1910–31; Private Secretary 1931–5.

CHAPTER 10

1. C. Thorne, *The Limits of Foreign Policy* (London, 1972) p. 141.
2. Ritchie Ovendale, *Appeasement and the English-Speaking World, 1937–9* (Cardiff, 1975).
3. Birdwood, Field Marshal William (1865–1951). General Officer Commanding, Australian and New Zealand Army Corps 1914–18; Commander-in-Chief, Army of India 1925–30.
4. Birdwood to Simon, 6 November 1931. Quoted in Thorne, *Limits of Foreign Policy*, p. 177.

5. Lytton, Lord (1876–1947). Government of India Delegate to the League 1927–8; UK Delegate to the League 1931; Chairman of 1931 League Commission to investigate the Manchurian incident.
6. Price to Dixon, 23 November 1932, DO35/100.
7. Memorandum by the President of the Board of Trade, 20 March 1934, CP 81(34) CAB 24/248.
8. Latham, Sir John (1877–1964). Australian Minister of External Affairs and Deputy Premier 1932–4.
9. Crutchely to Under-Secretary of State, Dominions Office, 20 June 1935, DO35/181.
10. Clive to Simon, 7 January 1935, CP 80(35) CAB 24/254.
11. Memorandum by the Secretary of State for Dominion Affairs, 15 March 1934, CP 78(34) CAB 24/248.
12. Memorandum by the Secretary of State for Foreign Affairs, 16 March 1934, CP 77(34) CAB 24/248.
13. Menzies, Sir Robert (1894–1978). Attorney-General, Australia 1934–9. Commonwealth Treasurer 1939–40; Prime Minister 1939–41 and 1949–66.
14. Second Meeting of the Commonwealth Prime Ministers, 7 May 1935, P.M.(35) CAB 32/125.
15. Meeting of Commonwealth Delegates to the London Naval Conference, 13 November 1934, DO121/3.
16. Dixon Memorandum, February 1930, DO35/88.
17. Riddell, Walter (1881–1963). Canadian Delegate to the League of Nations 1933–6.
18. Desy, Pierre. Canadian Delegate to the League of Nations 1932–3.
19. Price to Cadogan, 27 March 1933, DO35/100.
20. Harding minute, 2 May 1935, DO35/100.
21. Hankey Memorandum to Cabinet, 14 February 1935, CP 38(35) CAB 24/253.
22. Sankey Diaries, 18 December 1932, Mss. Eng. Hist. E.286, Bodleian Library, Oxford.
23. Batterbee Memorandum on Sanctions, September 1931, DO35/100.
24. Harding minute, 2 May 1933, DO35/100.
25. Dominions Office Memorandum, 24 June 1932, DO35/100.
26. Crutchely to Batterbee, 12 December 1933, DO35/183.
27. Dominions Office Memorandum, 19 January 1933, DO35/100.
28. Stanley to Harding, 9 June 1933, DO35/395.
29. Geddes, Sir Eric (1875–1937). Member of Imperial War Cabinet 1919; Minister of Transport 1919–21; Chairman of Imperial Airways Limited 1930–7.
30. Note of Meeting between Geddes and Batterbee, 21 March 1933, DO35/195.
31. Hankey to Harding, 23 April 1934, DO35/186.
32. Naval Intelligence Memorandum on South African Defence Situation, 17 April 1934, DO35/186.
33. Stanley to Batterbee, 5 May 1934, DO35/200.
34. Pirow, Oswald (1890–1959). Minister of Justice in Nationalist Government 1929–33; Minister of Defence, Railways and Harbours in

Coalition Government 1933–9.

35. Minutes of Committee of Imperial Defence Meeting, 24 July 1933, enclosed in DO35/186.
36. Floud minute, 12 April 1933, DO35/186.
37. Cunliffe-Lister minute, 18 June 1934, PREM 1/174.
38. Hankey to Londonderry, 18 June 1934, PREM 1/174.
39. Cunliffe-Lister minute, 18 June 1934, PREM 1/174.
40. Chancery, Berlin Embassy to Foreign Office, 12 February 1935, DO35/160.
41. *Die Vaderland*, 15 January 1935, DO35/160.
42. Stanley to Thomas, 22 August 1934, DO35/160.
43. Press Attache, Berlin Embassy to Willert, 11 April 1934, DO35/160.
44. Stanley to Harding, 12 November 1934, DO35/160.
45. Stanley to Thomas, 4 February 1935, DO35/160.
46. Ibid.
47. Cunliffe-Lister minute, 12 March 1935, DO35/160.
48. Stanley to Thomas, 30 October 1934, DO35/186.
49. Dixon minute, 16 May 1935, DO35/108.
50. Andrews to Thomas, 7 March 1934, DO35/405
51. te Water to Thomas, 23 May 1934, DO35/405.
52. Foreign Office minute, 8 May 1934, DO35/405.
53. Stanley to Batterbee, 29 March 1934, DO35/200.
54. Liesching to Harding, 18 July 1934, DO35/186.
55. Hankey to Ramsay MacDonald, 15 November 1934, PREM 1/174.
56. Hankey to Sir George Milne, 31 January 1935, PREM 1/174.
57. Hankey to Ramsay MacDonald, 7 September 1934, PREM 1/174.
58. Ibid.
59. S. Roskill, *Man of Secrets*, vol. III, p. 126.
60. First Plenary Meeting of Commonwealth Prime Ministers, 30 April 1935, P.M. (35) CAB 32/125.
61. Ibid.
62. Third Plenary Meeting of Commonwealth Prime Ministers, 9 May 1935, P.M. (35) CAB 32/125.
63. Ibid.
64. Dixon minute, 4 September 1935, DO35/108.
65. Cockram, Ben (b. 1903) Private Secretary to Parliamentary and Permanent Under-Secretaries of State, Dominions Office 1929–34.
66. Hoare, Samuel (1880–1939). Secretary of State for India 1931–5; Foreign Secretary 1935–6; Minister for Home Affairs 1937–9; Lord Privy Seal 1939–40.
67. Cockram to Wiseman, 11 September 1935, DO35/186.
68. Ibid.
69. Quoted in K. Middlemas and J. Barnes, *Baldwin*, pp. 856–7.
70. Hankey to Batterbee, 21 September 1935, DO35/156.
71. Parr, Sir John (1869–1941). Minister of Education, New Zealand 1920–6; New Zealand High Commissioner in the UK 1926–9 and 1934–6; New Zealand representative at the League 1926, 1927, 1929 and 1934.
72. Batterbee-Walsh meeting, 21 September 1935, DO35/156.
73. Ibid.

74. Note of conversation between Mr Brooks and Mr Wiseman, 4 March 1935, DO35/157.
75. The Italian–Abyssinian Dispute and its Effects on British Foreign Policy, December 1936, DO114/66.
76. Wallinger, Sir Geoffrey (b. 1903). Political Secretary to UK High Commissioner in South Africa 1931–5; Counsellor in Foreign Office 1947–9; Ambassador to Brazil 1954–8.
77. Wallinger to Wiseman, 15 October 1935, DO35/157.
78. Archer to Syers, 11 October 1935, DO35/192.
79. Ibid.
80. Floud to Malcolm MacDonald, 5 December 1935, DO35/156.
81. Note of Meeting of Commonwealth Delegates at the League, 5 December 1935, DO114/66.
82. Floud to Malcolm MacDonald, 5 December 1935, DO35/156.
83. Hankinson to Under-Secretary of State, Dominions Office, 11 November 1935, DO35/157.
84. Hankinson to Harding, 22 October 1935, DO35/157.
85. Ibid.
86. te Water to Secretary of State, Dominions Office, 16 December 1935, DO35/157.
87. Cockram minute, 26 August 1936, DO35/165.
88. Archer to Batterbee, 9 January 1936, DO35/156.
89. Massey, Vincent (1887–1967). Canadian Minister to the United States 1926–30; Canadian High Commissioner to the UK 1935–46; Canadian Delegate to the League 1936; Governor-General of Canada 1952–9.
90. Minutes of High Commissioners' Meetings with the Dominions Secretary, 9 March 1936, DO35/185.
91. South African Government to the UK Government, 12 March 1936, DO35/185.
92. Minutes of High Commissioners Meetings with the Dominions Secretary, 13 March 1936, DO35/185.
93. Minutes of the High Commissioners Meetings with the Dominions Secretary, 2 April 1936, DO35/185.
94. Ibid.
95. Antrobus to Malcolm MacDonald, 11 May 1935, DO35/157.
96. Ibid.
97. Ibid.
98. Wiseman minute, 24 May 1936, DO35/157.
99. K. Middlemas and J. Barnes, *Baldwin* (London, 1969) p. 939.
100. *Die Burger*, 13 June 1936, enclosed in DO35/157.
101. *Natal Mercury*, 13 June 1936, enclosed in DO35/157.
102. The Italo–Abyssinian Dispute CP159 (36) 18 June 1936 CAB 24/266.
103. Harding minute, 16 June 1936, DO35/158.
104. Cabinet Conclusion 42 (36) 13, 17 June 1936, CAB 23/84.
105. Ibid.
106. Ibid.
107. Garner to Cockram, 30 September 1936, DO35/165.
108. Garner, Sir Saville (b. 1908). Appointed Principal in the Dominions Office 1930; Attached to the UK delegation at the League 1936; Deputy Under-

Secretary, Commonwealth Relations Office 1948–51; UK High
Commissioner in Canada 1956–61; Permanent Under-Secretary of State,
Commonwealth Relations Office 1962–5.
109. Garner to Cockram, 30 September 1936, DO35/165.
110. Note by the Dominions Secretary of a conversation at Geneva with
Mackenzie King, 20 September 1936, DO35/165.
111. Hankey to Harding, 8 October 1937, DO35/546.
112. Mackenzie King to Floud, 26 February 1937, DO35/534.
113. Crutchely to Under-Secretary of State, Dominions Office, 3 September
1935, DO35/182.
114. Wallinger to Batterbee, 3 October 1935, DO35/186.
115. Ibid.
116. Ibid.
117. Antrobus to Batterbee, 21 January 1936, DO35/187.
118. Antrobus to Batterbee, 19 March 1936, DO35/186.
119. UK High Commissioner, South Africa to Malcolm MacDonald, 6
February 1936, DO35/186.
120. Ibid.
121. Dominions Office Memorandum, May 1936, DO35/186.
122. Maffey, Sir John (1877–1968). Permanent Under-Secretary for the
Colonies 1933–7.
123. Maffey minute, 23 June 1936, DO35/186.
124. Wiseman to Antrobus, 9 July 1936, DO35/186.
125. Malcolm MacDonald minute, 1 July 1936, DO35/186.
126. Ibid.
127. Clark to Stanley, 22 April 1936, CAB 21/642.
128. Batterbee to Clark, 19 November 1936, DO35/187.
129. Hankey to Henderson, 24 May 1935, CAB 21/401.
130. Hankey to Robinson, 22 October 1936, CAB 21/440.
131. Pritchard to Burgis, 22 October 1936, CAB 21/440.
132. Floud to Harding, 15 March 1937, CAB 21/668.
133. Ibid.
134. Brown to Robinson, 13 April 1937, CAB 21/668.
135. Robinson to Brown, 21 April 1937, CAB 21/668.
136. Fraser to Harding, 13 February 1937, DO35/547.
137. Ibid.
138. Harding to MacDonald, 6 May 1937, DO35/547.
139. Note of a conversation between Mr MacDonald and Dr Gie in Geneva, 6
October 1936, DO35/185.
140. Ibid.
141. Ibid.
142. Ibid.
143. Lord Avon, *Memoirs: Facing the Dictators* (London, 1962) p. 477.
144. 'Imperial Conference 1937', 2nd Meeting, 21 May 1937, CAB 32/128.
145. Ibid.
146. Ibid.
147. Ibid.
148. 'Imperial Conference 1937: General Policy', 2 April 1937, CAB 32/127, E
(B) (37) 1.

149. Inskip, Sir Thomas (1876–1947). Attorney-General in Conservative Government 1928–9; Minister for the Coordination of Defence 1936–9; Secretary of State for Dominions, in National Government 1940.
150. 'Imperial Conference 1937', Fifth Meeting, 24 May 1937, CAB 32/128.
151. Ibid.
152. Ibid.
153. Ibid.
154. Ovendale, op. cit., pp. 49–50.
155. Mackenzie King Note on his Meeting with Hitler, 29 September 1937, FO371/20750 C 5187/5187/18.
156. DO minute, 18 September 1937, DO35/560.
157. Ovendale, op. cit.
158. 'Imperial Conference 1937', Fifth Meeting, 24 May 1937, CAB 32/128.
159. Cockram to Wiseman, 16 September 1937, DO35/560.
160. Ibid.
161. DO minute on Empire Delegates Meeting, 27 September 1937, DO35/560.
162. Cockram to Wiseman, 28 September 1937, DO35/560.
163. 'Note on Far Eastern Advisory Committee', October 1937, DO35/560.
164. Parliamentary Debates (Commons) *Hansard*, (Fifth Series), vol. 333, 24 March 1938, cols. 1399–1413.
165. Ovendale, op. cit., pp. 216–27.
166. Earl of Halifax, *Fullness of Days* (London, 1957) p. 198.
167. D. C. Watt, 'Appeasement. The Rise of a Revisionist School?', *Political Quarterly*, xxxvi (1965) pp. 191–213.
168. Mackenzie King to Runciman, 29 July 1938, Mackenzie King Papers, quoted in J. Eayrs, *In Defence of Canada* (Toronto, 1965) p. 63.
169. Mackenzie King Diary 13 September 1938, quoted in J. L. Granatstein and R. Bothwell, 'A Self-Evident National Duty: Canadian Foreign Policy 1935–9', *Journal of Imperial and Commonwealth History*, Vol. 111, January 1975, No. 2.
170. Ibid.
171. De Valera to Neville Chamberlain, 15 September 1938. Quoted in K. Feiling, *The Life of Neville Chamberlain* (London, 1946) p. 364.
172. Speaight minute, 19 September 1938, FO371/21738 C 10023/1941/18.
173. Davenport, op. cit., p. 191.
174. Ovendale, op. cit., p. 311.
175. D. Carlton, 'The Dominions and the Gathering Storm', *Journal of Imperial and Commonwealth History*, January 1978.
176. Granatstein and Bothwell, op. cit., p. 228.
177. Ovendale, op. cit., p. 305.

Bibliography

(A) GOVERNMENT RECORDS

(i) *Unpublished*

The materials of this study are mostly drawn from the administrative records of government departments available in the Public Record Office. The most useful source in this respect was the Dominions Office since that department was most consistently involved in Commonwealth affairs. Relevant series are as follows:

Dominions Office	DO35	Original Correspondence
	DO114	Confidential Print
	DO121	Private Office Papers
Colonial Office	CO352	Dominions File
Foreign Office	FO371	Political Correspondence
	FO426	Correspondence on Inter-Imperial Relations
	FO800	Private Collections (Austen Chamberlain Papers)
Board of Trade	BT11	Commercial Department: Correspondence and Papers
Prime Minister's Office	PREM 1	Correspondence and Papers to 1940
Cabinet	CAB 21	Registered Files
	CAB 23	Cabinet Minutes to 1939
	CAB 24	Cabinet Memoranda to 1939
	CAB 27	Cabinet Committees to 1939
	CAB 32	Imperial Conferences to 1939

(ii) *Published*

Imperial Conference, 1926: Summary of Proceedings, Cmd. 2768 (HMSO, 1926).

Report of the Conference on the Operation of Dominion Legislation, 1929, Cmd. 3479 (HMSO, 1930).

Imperial Conference, 1930: Summary of Proceedings, Cmd. 3717 (HMSO, 1930).

Economic Advisory Council Committee on Empire Migration: Report, Cmd. 4075 (HMSO, 1932).

Imperial Economic Conference at Ottawa, 1932: Summary of Proceedings and Copies of Trade Agreements, Cmd. 4714 (HMSO, 1932).

Imperial Committee on Economic Consultation, 1933: Report, Cmd. 4335 (HMSO, 1933).

Imperial Conference, 1937: Summary of Proceedings, Cmd. 5482 (HMSO, 1937).

(iii) *'Hansard' parliamentary debates*

(B) PRIVATE PAPERS

Neville Chamberlain	(University of Birmingham)
Ramsay MacDonald	(Public Record Office)
Lord Ponsonby	(Bodleian Library, Oxford)
Lord Sankey	(Bodleian Library, Oxford)
Lionel Curtis	(Bodleian Library, Oxford)

(C) OTHER COLLECTIONS

The Federation of British Industries

(D) SELECT BOOKS

Aikin, J., *Economic Power for Canada* (Toronto, 1930).

Amery, L. S., *The Empire in the New Era* (London, 1927).

——, *A Plan of Action* (London, 1932).

——, *My Political Life*, 3 vols (London, 1953).

——, *The Forward View* (London, 1935).

Barker, J., *Economic Statesmanship* (London, 1918).

Barnett, C., *The Collapse of British Power* (London, 1972).

Batterbee, H. F., *The Idea of Commonwealth* (London, 1960).

Baxendale, A., *Empire and World Currency* (London, 1932).

Bean, C., *Official History of Australia in the War* (Sydney, 1921).

Behrens, E., *A Practical Monetary Policy for the Ottawa Conference* (London, 1932).

Beloff, M., *Imperial Sunset* (London, 1969).

Brooks, C., *This Tariff Question* (London, 1931).

Bruce, S., *The Imperial Economic Situation* (London, 1931).

Chiddell, F., *Australia– White or Yellow?* (London, 1926).

Clifford, Sir Bede, *Proconsul* (London, 1964).

Colvin, I., *Vansittart in Office* (London, 1965).

Cook, R., *The Politics of John W. Dafoe and The Free Press* (Toronto, 1963).

Copland, D. B., *Australia in the World Crisis 1929–33* (Cambridge, 1934).

Coupland, R., *The Empire in these Days* (London, 1935).

Cox, Sir Frank, *The Mastery of the Pacific: Can the British Empire and the United States Agree?* (London, 1928).

Cross, J., *Whitehall and the Commonwealth* (London, 1967).

Curtis, L., *Civitas Dei*, vols 1–3 (London, 1934–7).

Darling, J. F., *Economic Unity of the Empire: Gold and Credit* (London, 1926).

Davenport, R., *A Modern History of South Africa* (London, 1977).

Dawson, R. M., *The Development of Dominion Status 1900–36* (Oxford, 1937).

——, *William Lyon Mackenzie King*, vol. 1 (London, 1958).

Drummond, I. M., *British Economic Policy and the Empire 1919–39* (London, 1972).

——, *Imperial Economic Policy 1917–39* (London, 1974).

Dugdale, B., *Arthur James Balfour* (London, 1936).

Eayrs, J., *In Defence of Canada: From the Great War to the Great Depression* (Toronto, 1964).

——, *In Defence of Canada: Appeasement and Rearmament* (Toronto, 1964).

Feiling, K., *A Life of Neville Chamberlain* (London, 1946).

Fiddes, G. V., *The Dominions and Colonial Offices* (London, 1926).

Findlay, R. M., *Britain Under Protection* (London, 1934).

Fraser, L., *Protection and Free Trade* (London, 1931).

Fuller, J. F. C., *Empire Unity and Defence* (London, 1934).

Garner, J., *The Commonwealth Office 1925–68* (London, 1978).

Ghosh, D., *The Ottawa Agreements–A Study in Imperial Preference* (Bombay, 1932).

Gibbs, N., *Grand Strategy: Rearmament Policy* (London, 1976).

Hancock, W. K., *Survey of British Commonwealth Affairs*, vol. 1, *Problems of Nationality 1918–36* (London, 1937); vol. 2, *Problems of Economic Policy* (Oxford, 1940).

——, *Smuts*, vol. 1, *The Sanguine Years 1870–1919* (Oxford, 1962); vol. 2, *The Fields of Force 1919–50* (Oxford, 1968).

Harkness, D. W., *The Restless Dominion: The Irish Free State and the British Commonwealth of Nations 1921–31* (London, 1969).

Harrison, H., *Ireland and the British Empire, 1937: Conflict or Collaboration?* (London, 1937).

Headlam, C., ed., *The Milner Papers (South Africa) 1889–1905*, vols 1–2 (London, 1933).

Heever, C. M. van den, *General J. B. M. Hertzog* (Johannesburg, 1946).

Hewins, W. A. S., *Apologia of an Imperialist*, vols 1–2 (London, 1929).

Hodson, H. V., ed., *The British Empire: A Report on its Structure and Problems by a Study Group of the Royal Institute of International Affairs* (Oxford, 1938).

Howard, M., *The Continental Commitment* (London, 1972).

Hughes, W. M., *The Splendid Adventure* (London, 1929).

Hurd, P. and Hurd, A., *The New Empire Partnership* (London, 1915).

Johnson, F. A., *Defence by Committee: The British Committee of Imperial Defence 1880–1959* (London, 1960).

Jones, A., *A Diary with Letters* (London, 1954).

——, *Whitehall Diary* (London, 1969).

Keenlayside, H., *The Growth of Canadian Policies* (Durham, N. C. 1960).

Keith, Sir Arthur Berriedale, *The Sovereignty of the British Dominions* (London, 1929).

——, *Speeches and Documents on the British Dominions 1918–31* (Oxford, 1932).

Kendle, J., *The Colonial and Imperial Conferences 1887–1911* (London, 1967).

——, *The Round Table Movement and Imperial Union* (Toronto, 1975).

Leacock, S., *Economic Prosperity in the British Empire* (MacGill, 1930).

Longford, Lord and O'Neill, T., *Eamonn de Valera* (London, 1970).

MacCarthy, J., *Australia and Imperial Defence: A Study in Air and Seapower* (Queensland, 1976).

MacDougall, R., *Sheltered Markets* (London, 1925).

Madden, A. F., *Imperial Constitutional Documents 1765–1965, A Supplement* (Oxford, 1966).

Manning, C. A. W., *Policies of the British Dominions in the League of Nations* (London, 1932).

Mansergh, P. N. S., *The Irish Free State: Its Government and Politics* (London, 1934).

——, *Survey of British Commonwealth Affairs. Problems of External Policy 1931–9* (Oxford, 1952).

——, *The Commonwealth Experience* (London, 1969).

Marquand, D., *Ramsay MacDonald* (London, 1977).

Massey, V., *What's Past is Prologue* (Toronto, 1963).

Meyer, F. V., *Britain's Colonies in World Trade* (London, 1948).

Middlemas, K. and Barnes, J., *Baldwin* (London, 1969).

Middlemas, K., *Diplomacy of Illusion: The British Government and Germany 1937–9* (London, 1972).

Miller, J. D. B., *Britain and the old Dominions* (London, 1966).

——, *The Commonwealth and the World* (London, 1965).

Mosely, Sir Oswald, *The Greater Britain* (London, 1932).

Neatby, H. B., *William Lyon Mackenzie King*, vol. 2 (London, 1958).

Schedvin, C. B., *Australia in the Great Depression* (Sydney, 1970).

Sinclair, K., *Walter Nash* (Oxford, 1977).

Taylor, A. J. P., *Beaverbrook* (London, 1972).

Thompson, L., *The Unification of South Africa* (London, 1964).

Thorne, C., *The Limits of Foreign Policy: The West, the League and the Far Eastern Crisis of 1931–3* (London, 1972).

Vansittart, Lord, *The Mist Procession* (London, 1958).
Veatch, R., *Canadian Foreign Policy and the League of Nations* (Toronto, 1975).
Walters, F. P., *A History of the League of Nations* (London, 1952).
Watt, D. C., *Personalities and Policies* (London, 1965).
Wheare, K. C., *The Statute of Westminster and Dominion Status* (Oxford, 1938).
——, *The Constitutional Structure of the Commonwealth* (Oxford, 1960).
White, T. de Vere, *Kevin O'Higgins* (London, 1948).
Whyte, W. F., *William Morris Hughes: His Life and Times* (Sydney, 1957).
Wigley, P. E., *Canada and the Transition to Commonwealth: British–Canadian Relations 1917–1926* (Cambridge, 1977).
Wiseman, H. V., *Britain and the Commonwealth* (London, 1965).
Young, K., *Arthur James Balfour* (London, 1963).
Zimmern, A. E., *The Third British Empire* (London, 1927).

(E) SELECT ARTICLES
Hall, H. D., 'The Genesis of the Balfour Declaration', *Journal of Commonwealth Political Studies*, vol. 1, no. 3, 1963.
Harkness, D., 'Mr de Valera's Dominion: Irish Relations with Britain and the Commonwealth 1932–8', *Journal of Commonwealth Political Studies*, vol. 8, no. 3, 1970.
Hillmer, N., 'A British High Commissioner for Canada, 1927–8', *Journal of Imperial and Commonwealth History*, vol. I, no. 3, 1973.
Lee, Michael, 'The dissolution of the Empire Marketing Board, 1933: Reflections on a Diary', *Journal of Imperial and Commonwealth History*, vol. I, 1972.
Megaw, Ruth, 'Australia and the Anglo-American Trade Agreement of 1938', *Journal of Imperial and Commonwealth History*, vol. III, January 1975.
Ross, A., 'Reluctant Daughter or Dutiful Dominion? New Zealand in the Inter-War Years', *Journal of Commonwealth Political Studies*, vol. X, no. 1, 1972.
Snelling, R. C., 'Peacemaking, 1919: Australia, New Zealand and the British Empire Delegates at Versailles', *Journal of Imperial and Commonwealth History*, vol. IV, October 1975.
Spence, J., 'Tradition and Change in South African Foreign Policy', *Journal of Commonwealth Political Studies*, vol. I, no. 2, 1963.
Trotter, A., 'The Dominions and Imperial Defence: Hankey's Tour in 1934', *Journal of Imperial and Commonwealth History*, vol. II, no. 3, October 1974.

(F) UNPUBLISHED DOCTORAL THESES
Constantine, S., 'The formulation of British policy on Colonial development 1914–29,' Oxford, 1975.

Cross, J. A., 'The Dominions Department of the Colonial Office: origins and early years 1905–14', University of London (external), 1965.

Cuneen, A., 'The Governor-General's Role in Australia 1901–27', Australia National University, 1976.

Henderson, M. D., 'The Dominions and British Foreign Policy 1919–23: A Case Study in Inter-Governmental Cooperation', University of London, 1970.

Hillmer, M., 'British Canadian Relations 1926–37', University of Cambridge, 1975.

Saker, H., 'The Flag Controversy in South Africa', University of Cape Town, 1977.

Index